The Best of Grant MacEwan

The Best of Grant MacEwan

Edited by R. H. Macdonald

Western Producer Prairie Books
Saskatoon, Saskatchewan

Cover design by Craig Romanyk

Printed and bound in Canada by Modern Press ⟶1
Saskatoon, Saskatchewan

Western Producer Prairie Books publications are produced and manufactured in the middle of western Canada by a unique publishing venture
owned by a group of prairie farmers who are members of Saskatchewan
Wheat Pool. From the first book in 1954, a reprint of a serial originally
carried in the weekly newspaper, *The Western Producer,* to the book
before you now, the tradition of providing enjoyable and informative
reading for all Canadians is continued.

Canadian Cataloguing in Publication Data

MacEwan, Grant, 1902-
    The best of Grant MacEwan

    Commemorates MacEwan's 80th birthday.
    ISBN 0-88833-091-x

    1. Northwest, Canadian - History - Addresses, essays,
lectures.   I. Macdonald, R. H., 1915-

    II. Title.
    FC3206.M32   971.2   C82-091207-7
    F1060.M32

Contents

Foreword   vii

Introduction   ix

Another Unknown   1
Sodbusters

Mother of Exhibitions   6
Agriculture on Parade

Chuck-Wagon Romance   12
Between the Red and the Rockies

Battle of the Booze   19
Eye Opener Bob

Gandhi of the Prairies   28
Fifty Mighty Men

The Winter of Hungry Cattle   34
John Ware's Cow Country

Adam and Eve of the Cattle Kingdom   43
Blazing the Old Cattle Trail

Pacers and Preachers   48
Hoofprints and Hitchingposts

Professor to Politician   53
Poking into Politics

Loaned for a Season   58
Entrusted to My Care

Gold in the Interior   63
A Short History of Western Canada

The West in Confederation Year   68
A Short History of Western Canada

The Dawn of a New Day   76
Harvest of Bread

Man with a Message   81
Tatanga Mani: Walking Buffalo of the Stonies

The Battle of the Breeds   86
Power for Prairie Plows

More Power, More Comfort, More Debt   91
Power for Prairie Plows

Crowfoot: Man of Wisdom   95
Portraits of the Plains

Bull Faces the Commission   105
Sitting Bull: The Years in Canada

The Diary of a 1932 Passenger   115
Battle for the Bay

A Name Is Chosen   123
Calgary Cavalcade

Caroline "Mother" Fulham: The Lady Kept Pigs   126
And Mighty Women Too

Old Bill, Faithful and True   132
Memory Meadows

The Founding Father   135
Cornerstone Colony

War Years and War Horses   142
The Rhyming Horseman of the Qu'Appelle

The Growing Grassland Empire   150
Pat Burns, Cattle King

The "Ugly Duckling"   156
Illustrated History of Western Canadian Agriculture

William Kennedy: History's Forgotten Hero   162
Métis Makers of History

Thumbnail Sketches   171
Alberta Landscapes

Appendix   181
Books by Grant MacEwan

Notes   183

Index   187

Foreword

The Best of Grant MacEwan was compiled to commemorate Grant MacEwan's eightieth birthday. For more than forty of his eighty years, Grant MacEwan has been ambitiously engaged in recording biographies of notable individuals and recounting the events that shaped western Canada.

With thirty-one published books to his credit, the task of identifying MacEwan's best work is formidable. No other individual has worked so diligently, or with such commitment, to bring the history of the West before a wide reading audience.

The excerpts which appear in this collection clearly represent the best of Grant MacEwan's writing, or perhaps more accurately, the selections present the "best exposure" of his work. In examining the imposing list of publications which carry the MacEwan name, it was necessary to bring another critical factor to the judgment regarding the suitability of material for inclusion. Major significance was placed on conveying to the reader the variety of subject matter and the wide geographic range which MacEwan has successfully explored over the years.

It should be noted that MacEwan's earliest works were of an academic nature and addressed topics related to the science of agriculture. Since these volumes depart from the popular history theme for which MacEwan is best known, selections from his first four books do not appear in this collection.

The Best of Grant MacEwan contains excerpts from all other MacEwan books up to and including 1982 with the exception of the promotional publication *This Is Calgary* (1973), the subject of which is dealt with more fully in *Calgary Cavalcade* (1959, revised edition 1975).

The selections appear in chronological order with some exceptions. The original plan was to publish one example of MacEwan's writing from each title, but this objective was waived in a few cases. Two selections were made from *A Short History of Western Canada* (1968): "Gold in the Interior" to extend the coverage of the collection to British Columbia and "The West in Confederation Year" to reveal MacEwan's interpretation of the background to a subject much in the minds of most Canadians in the 1980s. *Power for Prairie Plows* (1971) yielded two selections on problems old and new. His contributions to *Alberta Landscapes* (1982) made it possible to include enough brief sketches of Alberta cities and regions (prairie, foothills, and mountains, from north to south in the settled areas) to illustrate his knowledge and appreciation of his adopted province. It matters little, but will be detected here and there, that the sketches were designed to appear opposite landscape photographs which do not appear in this volume. Minor changes have been made in the text to allow for the absence of the landscapes.

It is hoped that the chronological arrangement of the excerpts will permit the reader to appreciate the evolution of MacEwan's writing and the sequence in which he developed various historical themes.

Most of the selections stand alone and appear exactly as they did when first published. However, as the books were printed by several publishers, minor alterations in house style were necessary for the sake of consistency and appear unmarked in this volume.

The editor is grateful to those who contribute so much to a work of this nature but who prefer to remain behind the customary veil of anonymity. The same is true of those who lent prized MacEwan works from their collections to fill gaps in the editor's collection. As usual, a debt is owed the staffs and collections of public libraries — Saskatoon, Calgary, Edmonton, and Winnipeg — and to university libraries in Saskatoon, Calgary, and Edmonton.

R. H. Macdonald

Introduction

He broke virgin sod with horse and plow, inspired a generation of agriculture students, produced four textbooks where none had existed before. He was a politician of sorts, a master livestock judge. He ran a city and represented Her Majesty the Queen in the province of Alberta.

The list of accomplishments is incomplete. There are many other achievements, many in the creative field as well, including at a conservative estimate more than 2,500 newspaper columns, 5,000 speeches, and 1,000 broadcasts, to say nothing of uncounted magazine articles and contributions to scholarly, technical, and popular publications.

Despite such an enormous and varied output, it is certain that John Walter Grant MacEwan will be remembered mainly for his works on the human history of western Canada. It is this achievement that *The Best of Grant MacEwan* celebrates in his eightieth year.

To date MacEwan has written thirty-one books. Of these the first four, appearing from 1936 to 1945, were agricultural textbooks, two of them written in collaboration with his friend and colleague the late A. H. Ewen. There are other collaborations: *A Short History of Western Canada* (original title *West to the Sea*) written with Maxwell Foran, MacEwan's son-in-law, and published in 1968; *This Is Calgary* produced with Toby Rankin, photographer; *Alberta Landscapes* with text by MacEwan and landscapes (photo) by the editor.

It was thirty-nine years ago that Grant MacEwan, an animal husbandry professor at the University of Saskatchewan, resolved to make western Canadian history one of his main avocations. The decision arose naturally from his early background as well as from more recent associations.

As a boy he had grown up on a farm north of Brandon, Manitoba, where he was surrounded by Grants — aunts and uncles on his mother's side — an active and vigorous lot who regaled him with stories of early Nova Scotian days; of adventure, endurance, accomplishment; of the highland Grant clan. Nearer to home he heard in graphic, often humorous, vein stories of pioneering days in Manitoba, some of the main characters being Grants and MacEwans. When he entered school and began studying history, he was shocked to discover that this thrilling oral history was obliterated by the necessity of committing to memory lists of kings, foreign wars, and distant places. Western Canadian history, if dealt with at all, received only cursory attention — and that obviously written by outsiders.

Later, as a professor in Saskatoon, he struck up a friendship with Arthur Silver Morton, venerable historian and tireless searcher for the locations of long lost fur trading posts that had studded the water courses of the West during the country's fur trade era. Once again history sprang to life in the hands of the old scholar through inspiration, by example and direct encouragement. From that time onward, MacEwan resolved to spend as much time and travel as he could in order to ferret out and record the feats of early western pioneers.

It mattered little to the two friends that Morton was a pure historian who produced scholarly works whereas MacEwan's interests were concentrated on human history designed to entertain, amuse, and inform the average reader who would shy away at the sight of a footnote. They traveled and searched together, each extracting information for his own purposes. Dr. Morton read MacEwan's early efforts, advising and encouraging him in full knowledge that though they were writing for different audiences, they held a common objective: the recording and preservation of a fast dwindling commodity — western Canadian history.

Morton set the boundaries for MacEwan. His was the mid-west, the three prairie provinces which MacEwan adopted — although Mac-Ewan's works were to include stories about British Columbia.

Dr. Morton also suggested areas for further study, one of them being the Selkirk settlement, the importance of which, he maintained, had not yet been fully recognized. MacEwan's mentor began feeding him material on the Red River settlement, and although it took more than thirty years to do so, the old historian's hopes were fulfilled with the publication of MacEwan's *Cornerstone Colony* (1977) long after Morton's death.

To the Canadian Broadcasting Corporation goes the credit for first "discovering" MacEwan and giving him the audience his fledgling efforts deserved. In 1942 they suggested he do a series of four broadcasts on a subject of his own choosing under his own title. The result was a quartet of short biographies of western pioneer personalities. The programs were well received by his listening audience and were renewed the following two years. In 1948, they were published (with some additions) by Thomas Nelson and Sons, Toronto, as a book under the same title — *Sodbusters*.

When asked to send his broadcast notes to be made into a book, he did just that and was dismayed to see the results of placing in type without rewriting or strict editing what had been written for the spoken word. He was never happy with it. Afterwards he learned much from Toronto book editor Jessie McEwen, who worked on a number of his books and demonstrated the merits of revision and tight editing.

Sodbusters was his first human history book for a popular audience. There were to be many more. After dashing off a history of fairs for the Western Canada Fairs Association, *Agriculture on Parade* (1950), he produced what could be taken as the master plan for his work extending over the next thirty or forty years. This was the book *Between the Red and the Rockies* (1952) in which, with broad sweeping strokes, he sketched the story of the development of the region that was to become his literary territory and his major interest, in particular agriculture and the people who developed half a continent of nearly empty grassland into a bread basket for the world within one generation.

It was a miracle, he told his readers, and he wrote about it with such verve that it confused some scholars but captivated the public. The reaction of reviewers to *Between the Red and the Rockies* established the shape and tone of receptions of most of MacEwan's subsequent works. The *Globe and Mail* (December 20, 1952) was cool, saying MacEwan had attempted too much for a short book; the Montreal *Star* (December 13, 1952) found the story and characters "fascinating"; the Toronto *Star* (October 11, 1952) termed it "a highly informative and interesting addition to Canadiana"; on "Critically Speaking," CBC (November 30, 1952), Norman Ward, who had been lecturing at the University of Saskatchewan when MacEwan was there, said it was no literary masterwork and MacEwan no historian but he did find it an "amiable discourse, sometimes amusing, frequently interesting, and occasionally fascinating," its strong points being MacEwan's familiarity with pioneer farming in the first quarter of the century. The broadcaster ended by saying that the author had attempted to be so comprehensive in the space available that towards the end the book fell apart. *Canadian Historical Review* (June, 1953) wondered if the book was indeed history and found parts that could be questioned by specialist historians, but the review found much that brought "the early west to life in a wholly admirable fashion."

The above may seem a lengthy review of reviews for a book published thirty years ago. There were others; newspapers in the West, with some exceptions, welcomed the book with open-handed enthusiasm.[1] But it is of importance because his future books would be greeted by reviewers in much the same manner. Academics would experience difficulty placing MacEwan as a writer for the simple reason that he refused to fit into well established categories in use at the time; he was no ordinary writer. After first expressing puzzlement, they usually admitted, some grudgingly, that his work carried with it the unmistakable enthusiasm of one who had actually been there — an eyewitness of and participant in the agricultural revolution and feats of endurance about which he wrote.

Although he spoke mainly of novelists when he addressed the first Western Canadian Studies Conference in Calgary[2] in February of 1969, George F. G. Stanley[3] might well have been referring to Grant MacEwan when, in his paper entitled "The Western Canadian Mystique," he pointed out that literature on western Canada had first been written by visitors, one could call them tourists, who swept through the countryside and described what they saw for the people back home. The next wave of writers were those whose upbringing had been in other regions, other countries, and who arrived with previously formed sets of cultural assumptions based on experience foreign to the West. Excellent though many of their books were, and indispensable though they undoubtedly are for those who would study the early West, they nevertheless suffered in that they did not, could not, spring from the grass roots of the country about which they were written.

Professor Stanley said we had to await the works of writers such as W. O. Mitchell (*Who has Seen the Wind,* 1947) and Edward McCourt, (*Music at the Close*, 1947) to enjoy the undoubted integrity of works written about western Canada by writers born in western Canada whose early impressions and outlook were formed and set in western Canada.[4]

Grant MacEwan is found in the right company and the proper context in *Prairie Pespective 2,* edited by Anthony W. Rasporich and Henry C. Klassen. The editors rightly say that "until recently, Western Canada's cultural heritage has been the dearly bought harvest of a few determined scholars and writers. A handful of them have ploughed furrows across the prairie west, sometimes singly as with G. F. G. Stanley, Edward McCourt, and Grant MacEwan and sometimes in matched teams with identical surnames, like the Mortons, the Thomases and the Grays. Without their persistent efforts against a highly resistant and unliterary landscape, as W. L. Morton has put it elsewhere, the intellectual traditions of Western Canada would still be as dark as Sinclair Ross's bleak tale of the 'dirty thirties' — *The Lamp at Noon.* Sometimes the direct victims of the 'dirty thirties' or its lesser victims in the poor universities of the West, these men established a sense of the West where there was little or none. And by the nineteen fifties they had succeeded in producing a durable strain of western culture as tough as its northern wheat, calculated to grow and mature in a few short summer months, with a minimum of watering from granting agencies."[5]

When asked to assess MacEwan's contribution as a writer, John P. Gillese — film and literary arts director, Alberta government, Edmonton — told the editor: "His role in the development of regional writing is not only oustanding, it is probably impossible to assess ... he writes with stark simplicity, usually in between a maximum of other labours, and with undiminished stamina.

"When we finally got a Literary Arts branch operating within Alberta Culture, and held our first Honors Night for a trio of Alberta novelists, Grant MacEwan not only honored us with his presence as lieutenant-governor, he took time to reminisce on how far literary arts had come in the West. 'I never thought,' he said, 'I'd see this day.'

"It might surprise him to learn how much his example made possible that day — the first of many a day of triumph for a growing band of new western authors. Admiration for him has grown with the years — a remarkable thing in our burgeoning literary landscape. He has broken through while still remaining in Western Canada, and that is no mean feat for one living in a community so long dominated by other cultures. His example is a living inspiration to all Western writers," John Gillese said.

Kenneth Glazier, chief librarian, University of Calgary, said of MacEwan: "He writes about Western Canada out of his own experience, what he has learned through the soles of his shoes."[6]

Dr. Glazier was right. Grant MacEwan strode about the western provinces tirelessly searching until he knew every acre intimately, finding interest wherever he looked. He is a truly western Canadian writer. When he writes, he does not look over his shoulder toward eastern Canadian publishers, critics, reviewers. Nor does he look toward New York and Hollywood or seek to impress colleagues as many other "western" writers do.

There is one person he never forgets — the reader — and it shows in his work when he describes in his own readable way western characters and feats of courage and endurance as he sees them. Until MacEwan came along, many westerners tended toward the view that nothing of interest could occur in their own midst, nothing worth writing about let alone reading about; all the great feats, all the heroes were either British, European, or American.[7] In his first sketches he attacked this colonial view, and in *Eye Opener Bob* (1957) and *Fifty Mighty Men* (1958) he disproved it to a growing and appreciative following. *Eye Opener Bob* became an instant best seller and *Fifty Mighty Men,* one of the all-time western best sellers, having sold more than 25,000 copies to date. At last, here were genuine characters well worth reading about, and they were to be found in western Canada's past. Western readers rewarded MacEwan as they have no other author, having bought, at an educated guess, about 150,000 copies of his books.

As MacEwan began producing manuscripts at an accelerating rate, the ground was being prepared for the production of his books at home.

In 1944 William Clarence Richards brought out the first of many books to be published by his newly formed Institute of Applied Art, Edmonton. *The Western Producer,* Saskatoon, which had been concentrating on serials written by western writers since 1950, turned one into a book in 1954. That debut proved to be the start of the publishing enterprise now called Western Producer Prairie Books. In 1958 it published MacEwan's *Fifty Mighty Men* — the first full fledged hard cover book with dust jacket, illustrations, and all the trimmings. In 1967 book dealer turned publisher Mel Hurtig, Edmonton, brought out his first book as did Mary Scorer with her newly formed Peguis Press in Winnipeg.

Thus MacEwan was relieved of the necessity of searching eastern Canada for publishers in sympathy with manuscripts which they often termed as being "too regional" to be sold to their national audiences. And so as MacEwan approached his cruising speed, the institutions capable of handling his works were springing up around him. Regrettably, Mr. Richards' enterprise died with him — but not before he had published four MacEwan books: *Eye Opener Bob* (1957), *Calgary Cavalcade* (1959), *John Ware's Cow Country* (1960), and *Poking Into Politics* (1966), among twenty books all told.

Two of MacEwan's books on Indians were brought out by Hurtig Publishers Ltd.: *Tatanga Mani* (1969) and *Sitting Bull* (1972). However, Western Producer Prairie Books and MacEwan grew closer as time went on. Following the death of Richards, it bought the rights to the Institute's list and thus fell heir to the four MacEwan books, which were reprinted and kept alive. So far, counting Institute reprints, Prairie Books has published nineteen of his books and, it appears, will continue to be his sole publisher for the foreseeable future.

In assembling the first biographical sketches, MacEwan was well aware that they would form a rich source of material for larger works produced either by himself or by writers who would follow his lead. To date he has worked six of them into full scale book-length biographies: *Eye Opener Bob; John Ware's Cow Country; Tatanga Mani: Walking Buffalo of the Stonies; Sitting Bull: The Years in Canada; The Rhyming Horseman of the Qu'Appelle;* and *Pat Burns, Cattle King.*

During the late 1950s when he served as member of the Legislative Assembly in Edmonton and as alderman in Calgary, he began earning the reputation of a book-a-year writer. Later MacEwan revealed his method: "When you get inspiration, open a file; when the file's thick enough, write a book." He adheres to no rigid plan save the resolve to write every possible moment of the day and night. He works on his own account and resources and has never applied for a Canada Council or any other grant.

He appears to be in harmony with the timeless rhythm of nature, moving with it where it takes him: "I've started a good many books that have never seen the light of day. Often in researching one book I run into a new train of thought — or something near it — that is much more interesting than what sent me to the research material in the first place. I drop the original one, finish the new."

He learns as he goes on and changes technique or treatment as it seems wise to do so. While there is no apparent order to *Fifty Mighty Men*, in a similar but much later book, *Métis Makers of History* (1981), a series of sketches is arranged in chronological order. Says MacEwan: "*Fifty Mighty Men* was a series of blocks, standing by themselves. In *Métis Makers of History* the individuals tell the whole story themselves — they're in chronological order."

The latter sketches bear out MacEwan's preference "to teach history around personalities." In his university lectures he approaches history as "something more than just an academic plaything." He urges his students to "listen to history" to permit the story to teach, the personalities to send their voices from the past into the present to reveal how it really was. Those who speak from the past are not always human as in *Memory Meadows* (1976), where "biographical sketches of horses bring the equine view to the fore." The chatty style of *Memory Meadows* and the scholarly treatments adopted in *Cornerstone Colony* — as if the old long dead master, Morton, had been peering over his shoulder when he wrote — also are a clear demonstration of MacEwan's flexibility, varying his writing to suit the subject.

MacEwan departed from his by then well established human history theme when, after stepping down as mayor of Calgary, he neared his appointment as lieutenant-governor of Alberta. The year was 1966 and not only did it signal a brief alteration in the course of his books, but it marked the first time he would come out with two books in the same year. This would happen two or three times — indeed, in 1975 he produced three: two new, *Battle for the Bay* and *And Mighty Women Too,* and one revised with a chapter added, *Calgary Cavalcade.*

The 1966 departure saw him writing more about himself than he would probably ever permit himself to do in future. *Poking Into Politics* discusses his experiences as an alderman, federal candidate, member of the Legislative Assembly, party leader, and mayor. It also presents a rare display of MacEwan writing at white heat, barely able to restrain unaccustomed anger — which shows through as never before when he deals with his treatment at the hands of the University of Manitoba after he, the dean of agriculture, agreed to run as a candidate in a federal by-election.

The other departure was a book before its time. When he came out with *Entrusted to My Care* (1966), Grant MacEwan dealt with the principle that had guided him all his life — the principle of conservation. He wrote that we are placed on this earth to live in harmony with our fellow earth creatures, to till the soil and produce food, but that we are also charged by a Higher Power to leave the land behind us better than it was when we found it. *Entrusted to My Care* was unusual for a MacEwan book; it sold slowly and was allowed to go out of print. Perhaps his growing following among western Canadian readers were confused by this change of pace.

A Short History of Western Canada was MacEwan's first collaboration. MacEwan did most of the writing, but he persuaded Maxwell Foran to join in, more to introduce him to the field of book writing than anything else.

Battle for the Bay (1975) reveals to us the immense amount of detail MacEwan extracts from his experiences. In reading excerpts from his diary on the Hudson Bay route voyage to the port of Churchill from England, we may be amazed at his ceaseless curiosity and its rewards, but we become less so when contemplating his long list of books. One who devours facts and information as MacEwan obviously did during the voyage is bound to publish at a record pace.

His most recent collaboration, *Alberta Landscapes,* written in 1981, shows clearly that at seventy-nine years of age the man has lost none of his verve and love of the land. It also shows the writer at the top of his form using his wide knowledge of history — both natural and human — to add interest to the accompanying landscape photographs.

Many of MacEwan's followers would agree that western Canadians owe a debt of gratitude to the fact that he was born, and born curious, with the stamina to bring the results of such curiosity to fruition on a high frequency basis. We have come to know ourselves and our country the better because of the works of the able and energetic man whose eightieth birthday is marked by this publication. And so thousands will join (with future books in mind, no doubt) in saying in the language of his forebears — "Lang may your lum reek Grant MacEwan!"

Another Unknown

Seldom has MacEwan allowed his personal life to intrude into his writing. When he does, it is an event worthy of note. Hence appears this excerpt. The clue to the identity of the subject comes at the very end of the chapter leaving no doubt in the reader's mind as to the unknown sodbuster's relationship with the writer. (From Sodbusters, *Toronto: Thomas Nelson and Sons, 1948.)*

It would be quite wrong to give the impression that only men of distinction deserved a place among the Sodbusters. Actually, the Sodbuster heroes were common men, for the most part quiet men. They were good at minding their own business. They constituted the backbone of a young nation; but they are too soon forgotten. For that reason it seems expedient to draw out an average or sample specimen from time to time, and thus do honour to that host of pioneers whose names as individuals will never appear on the pages of history. That's why I choose, "Another Unknown."

The editor of "Who's Who" never heard of this one. Here was a Sodbuster who never won a sweepstake for wheat. He never won a championship for bulls and he never won an election. He won a homestead and a lifetime sentence tending his soil and fighting weeds and growing food to nourish human bodies. About the only picture of him to survive is a tintype made at the local fair at least half a century ago. But he is typical of an army of brave men who congregated with him on the frontier in the '80's. And I choose him because, as it happens, I know his story particularly well.

He was eighteen years of age when he arrived in Manitoba (in 1889). He had no money but he had the confidence of youth. He would stop at Brandon and work long enough to let him complete his journey to the ranch country. The pot of gold at the end of his rainbow was one thousand dollars he was told he could earn herding cattle or sheep for three years. He took a job on a farm at Chater. He had testimonials from Ontario, good ones which said "this young man is not afraid of work," and he was hired at $20.00 a month. That was considered big pay and there were no Income Tax deductions. But half of the monthly pay went back east to help the folk there and what remained was his reward for 30 days of hard labour at fifteen hours a day. His boss at Chater was a bachelor and as a cook he was no better than the worst of them. He could make tea and an indigestible something that might have been a cross between a bannock and a bismark. The meat wasn't of the Grade A kind. It was salt pork and the longer it reposed in the barrel, the saltier it became. In maggot season our young Sodbuster concluded it better to close his eyes and produce a temporary dim-out until the meat was eaten. The hens it seems, found that same meat barrel situated in the shed, to be a fine place to roost. That was all right except that last thing at night somebody had to turn the hens, heads to the centre.

Next year he heard about a job selling trees and shrubs for Cavers Brothers of Galt, Ontario, on a 20% commission. It appealed to his Scotch nature and he bought a horse and cart and started. But selling trees to homesteaders who didn't mean to remain long in the country was like selling woollen underwear at Palm Beach. The real tragedy came when he was obliged to drive through a flooded creek. The harness broke and the turbulent water soaked his order books and floated some of them out of the cart and away in the direction of Hudson Bay. It looked like the time to quit the nursery business and he went back to a North Brandon farm at $20.00 per month.

The trouble was, it would take a long time to save the cost of a farm that way. But he got the farm, first a quarter section and then another. One of those quarters was all raw land when he got it in the spring but with two walking ploughs and a lot of energy, the 160 acres were all broken that summer and backset that fall. Those walking ploughs cut a furrow of only 12 inches, but a Scottish neighbour who was ready to share his experience, remarked hopefully, "The more seams, the more lice." If it were so that the more seams one had in his clothing, the more parasites could be accommodated, then it might follow that the more furrows there were in the field, the more wheat should result, or something like that.

Financing was always a problem in those years. Cash was a commodity homesteaders talked about but never saw in abundance. The plough-share became dull and it would cost two dollars to get it sharpened. The settler had a load of hay which he could spare so he took it to town, hoping to sell it for six dollars and thus pay for the sharpening and also pay for a pair of beef-skin moccasins which he needed. But it was an unlucky day. The cast iron share fell from the load of hay and broke. There was only one thing to do, have the share welded at additional cost of a dollar and some lost time which would mean a livery bill and a hotel bill. Then it rained and the hay got wet so Alex Trotter bought the wet load for five dollars. He went home with a sharp plough-share but with an over-all debt of $1.75 and no beef-skin moccasins.

After a couple of years on the new farm and the sale of some frozen wheat, this specimen pioneer paid a visit to his home back east. Proud he was of achievements on the homestead. Pals of his youth glanced in admiration of the boy who had won the first round in the struggle with pioneer Western hardships. Sure he had some of the bulldog breed in him, the kind of bulldog which wouldn't stop for 50 miles of unbroken snow. When he was returning to Manitoba in that spring (of 1894) his train became snowbound in a March blizzard. For two nights and two days it was completely stuck at Belmont, about 50 miles southeast of Brandon. The railway company was furnishing the passengers with two meals a day but the travellers were becoming tired of each other's company. When the homesteader from Brandon could stand the inactivity no longer, he consumed his noon meal, checked his grip and struck off through the storm, on foot. Leather boots without rubbers didn't make the walking over the unbroken trail any better. At first he walked on the railroad grade and then the country roads, and both were bad. He walked to Wawanesa the first night and after a brief rest, he was on the road again and was in Brandon at 12 o'clock noon. He completed a 50-mile walk through a March storm in exactly 24 hours. And he didn't ask the railway company for a refund on his ticket either.

Farming was proving profitable if one could just get the crops harvested before the frost, since the soil held the accumulated fertility of a thousand years. Our Sodbuster made some money and then came the machine age and he put all his savings into a threshing outfit of the newest and biggest design. Manufacturers were competing to see who could build the mightiest steam engine and the biggest separator. The newest gadgets on threshing machines that year were self-feeders and wind stackers. His outfit consisted of a Minneapolis engine and a separator with a 40-inch cylinder. It was the first west of Portage la Prairie having both self-feeder and blower. Homesteaders came for miles to see the monster in action, to see a separator building its own stack and eating up sheaves which didn't have to be forced into its throat. The only trouble was that the new feeder didn't work and had to be discarded. So instead of having four men pitching sheaves into the automatic feeder, they had to be satisfied with eight men at the feeder end, four pitching from the loads to the tables, two cutting bands and two forcing sheaves into the cylinder. When noon time came and the threshing crew descended upon the farmer's kitchen, 23 ravenous men sat down to test the food resources and the patience of the good wife. But when things were going well, that big outfit threshed a lot of wheat. It threshed 1000 bushels in three hours one time, to say nothing of the bushels which went into the straw pile. That record stood a while and when the big outfit had to move from one farm to the next, it broke another record, a record for slow motion. And it usually broke a few bridges, because bridge builders hadn't reckoned with any such mechanical monstrosity. Indeed the same outfit went through the 18th Street bridge at Brandon on one occasion and after that if the river was to be crossed, the outfit was placed on a flat car at Chater and sent across on the rails.

Strangely enough the big outfit didn't ruin the old timer and it didn't drive him crazy. Some who bought threshers weren't so lucky. Anyway by 1908, he had a nice bank-roll and because it was fashionable to retire when one could, he sold his farm, held a sale at which T. C. Norris was the auctioneer, and went to live in the city. There were business opportunities and there was every inducement to speculate in city property. It would be easy to make money that way. But was it? There is just one thing wrong with real estate booms, they don't wear well. When this one backfired, the retired farmer was holding too much property. He felt a new yearning for the land. He became homesick for the farm. He would go back to the land, for there he would find new confidence. He would start again, and he did. But by this time the frontier had receded 400 miles to the North West and there in what was called Northern Saskatchewan he began from scratch to do it all again. His lawyer said, "What! you going to township 44? Should be the best place in the world to grow icicles; but what else can you grow?"

Well, the retired Sodbuster was on his way back to the land. He had no cash but he managed to make up a car load of so-called "settlers effects," two old "fox-meat" horses, a Jersey which had been the family cow in the city, a box of hens, a lot of furniture, a lawn mower, and the elder son as a stow-away. Yes, they called it "settlers effects." The freight train stopped at Dauphin for a few hours and the settler seized the opportunity to replenish his supply of bread and cheese. But when he was absent, the car was supposed to be unattended, the train conductor entered the box car, removed two of the best hens from the box and left with his prize in a bran sack, while the stow-away son watched it all from his hiding place behind a crate of furniture and had the good sense not to make a protest which would have cost the family a train fare.

The new farm up there in township 44 had no cultivation, no fence, no house, no well and no lawn on which to use the mower. What the new farmstead had was good soil, a lot of trees and an opportunity for heavy work. The furniture was piled around a small clearing in a cosy bluff of poplars and within that enclosure, the newcomers set up two beds and called it home. Nobody could say the roof leaked because there was no roof. However, it wasn't a bad place to live, just as long as the weather was fine.

And so, for a second time the pioneer was developing a farm. He bought another horse, Old Bill, noted for great age and chronic indigestion. He dug a well. In fact he dug six wells and each time alkali water that would make a dose of Epsom salts taste like orangeade, bubbled in; and he built a stable and tied the Jersey cow inside. His first crop was fair; the second was frosted; the third was rusted; the fourth was hailed 100 percent. But he stuck and saw the frost hazard diminish and the rust demon licked. Soon he went in for cattle. He bought three purebred Aberdeen Angus cows and build a herd. Later he took some of the cattle to England and saw them sold at Smithfield. He exhibited at the local fair; was made a director and then president.

The Provincial Live Stock Board recognized the contribution he had made in breeding good cattle and presented him with a scroll and said, "Long Live the Pioneer." And he did live long because he belonged to a hardy breed. He was in a hospital bed just once, when he had his arm broken in a tussle with a bull. But when he had to be there for a few days, he told the doctor to make the best use of time and give him an overhauling. So they set his arm, did a minor operation and pulled all his teeth. He was the pioneer; rugged individualist; the kind that blazed trail. And after he had more than fifty years of service to Canadian agriculture behind him, he retired for the second time. He sold his machinery and equipment but not his horses. They were not for sale. His order was that they would never leave the farm on which they had served. And they didn't. They were superannuated right there on their home farm. But in retirement, the pioneer continued to get up at 4:30 in the morning and disturb the peace of the community. He had done it all his life and no one could stop him.

I said I wasn't going to identify this Sodbuster. I've almost changed my mind. I'll tell this much about him. He gave me my first spanking.

Mother of Exhibitions

One of MacEwan's first loves is the western Canadian exhibition in all its forms, large and small. In this excerpt he displays his wide knowledge of the subject and leaves little doubt in the mind of the reader that here is an institution that has made an important contribution not only to western entertainment over the years but also to the economy. (From Agriculture on Parade, *Toronto: Thomas Nelson and Sons, 1950.)*

These institutions would dignify rural affairs, would excite a principle of emulation, would draw attention to useful discoveries and would gradually introduce a more effective and enlightened mode of practice.

John Young, Provincial Board of Agriculture,

Nova Scotia, 1818.

For all practical purposes, Brandon's Exhibition is of the same age as Brandon. The fight for the townsite was settled in the spring of 1881, when river floods soaked Grand Valley, the landing place for steamboats and main contender for the favours of the Canadian Pacific Railway. After the flood, however, C.P.R. engineers lost no time in fixing upon the higher and drier location a short distance to the west, where homesteader Robert Adamson had a shanty, a well and a clothesline. It was the birth of the Wheat City and, later in the season, rails connected the site with Winnipeg.

The first passenger train arrived on October 11th of that year and exactly one year later, Brandon held a fair under the auspices of the Brandon Electoral Division Agricultural Society. John Grant, a settler of '79, drove to town with Henry Nichol, who was exhibiting a mare and a foal, and recalled that the show was held in an unfenced field about where the Winter Fair Buildings are located today. There were classes for cattle, horses, pigs, poultry and grains and $200 in prize money had been raised from donations. But the settlers were scarcely ready for such an event and most of the classes were not filled. Of the 15 or 20 head of livestock on the grounds, most of them were the horses that brought the homesteaders to town.

John Grant said it wasn't much of a fair and Beecham Trotter, ("A Horseman and The West"), whose firm of Trotter and Trotter brought three million dollars worth of horses to Western Canada, had some scornful comment about the grain classes. When it was realized that the cereal classes would be without competition, the officials, rather more resourceful than scrupulous, borrowed enough wheat and other grains from a local elevator, to allow several entries in each of the important classes. Judges tried to appear like jurists facing grave decisions and spectators criticized the decisions as much as though the competitions were genuine. What the critical spectator didn't know was the first and second prize samples of wheat, about which argument arose, came from the same bin at the elevator.

Perhaps it wasn't much of a fair but there wasn't much to work with and at least it was a beginning. The next fair would be better. The next fair was better. Thirty-five acres were bought up for a fair grounds, a board fence was built and the frame structure placed in the centre of the lot given the dignified name of "Crystal Palace." Then the upstart Agricultural Society with Charles Whitehead, (who founded the *Weekly Sun* in 1882), as President, and Thomas Lockhart as Secretary, had the commendable audacity to apply to the Manitoba Board of Agriculture for authorization to hold the Provincial Exhibition in the year of 1883. And strangely enough, Brandon almost got the Provincial Exhibition; it was only when the President of the Board of Agriculture cast a deciding vote to break a tie, that Portage la Prairie was awarded the honour.

But the Brandon Society was determined to have a big fair in spite of Portage la Prairie and the Board of Agriculture. The dates were October 9th and 10th, and a generous prize list was announced. Ten dollars was an attractive prize for a mature stallion and prizes for "Durham cattle," Herefords, "Polled Angus," Devons and Ayrshires were almost as good. Holstein cattle were as yet unknown at Brandon. Horse races fared particularly well by the standards of that time and offered $50, $25 and $10 for the 1st, 2nd and 3rd prizes in the trotting event, and the same for a running race. That made a total racing purse of $170 and some of the critics said it was a luxury.

Inside the "Palace" were poultry, dogs, handiwork, ladies' work, dairy and garden produce, and manufactures. The manufactured articles were not in competition but where judges recognized sufficient merit, diplomas were awarded.

Among the Special Prizes listed were a set of sleigh bells for the "best walking team"; a silver medal given by Brandon *Sun* for the "Best herd of not less than 10 cattle"; a set of ox harness for the "Best walking ox"; a caddy of tea for the "Best rag carpet"; and $5 worth of stock food for the "Best collection of sheep."

That second Fair at Brandon brought out a thousand entries and the Lieutenant-Governor of Manitoba opened the show. Grain classes attracted the most favourable comment, especially the entries of Red Fife wheat. Already Brandon was being seen as the "Wheat City"; partly because of high quality in wheat and partly because wheat was being hauled great distances, up to 100 miles, to be sold there.

Gayest thing at the fair was John Bradley's dray team, dressed and decorated; and competing for public admiration were Van Tassell's Durham cattle and Dan McCuaig's Percheron stallion, Black Duke. That pioneer Percheron, first of his breed for miles around, made such a good impression that two more Percheron stallions were brought to the district through the offices of the Agricultural Society, in 1884. These were obtained from the well known United States breeder and importer, M. W. Dunham of Illinois and total cost was reported to be $2600.

Directors concluded that prizes had been too generous and for the third annual Fair, (October 8, 9, 1884) there was a slight reduction. Special prizes, however, remained numerous and full of interest. Sometimes the "Specials" did not represent as much magnanimity as appeared outwardly. At the Fair of 1885 for example, what appeared as a handsome cash prize of $15 was offered for the best 50 pounds of butter and $8 for the best 25 pounds of butter. But in each case there was a foxy stipulation that the prize butter would become the property of donor McKinnon. It would seem that the giver of the prize didn't mind paying just the slightest premium in order to ensure good butter for his family table. Also in that year, there was a "special" of a granite tea set offered for the "Handsomest sofa pillow"; an award of $5 from the Queen's Hotel for the "Fattest baby, 5 to 7 months old, from the country of Brandon"; and one dozen plated spoons for the "Best half dozen spring pigs." The latter seemed to work out at two spoons per pig or something like that.

Thereafter, fair days were Brandon's busiest during the year. Beecham Trotter tells how the hotels were full and the rigs and wagons that carried visitors from Rosser Avenue to the Fair at 15 cents per passenger made a month's wages in two days.

Brandon led the way in departing from autumn dates and held its 1889 fair in the month of July. The directors reasoned that Fall Fairs were all right for Ontario, but this was Manitoba and farmers would have more time to exhibit in midsummer than in the harvest month of September.

From this date forward, Brandon could claim the biggest and best draft horse show in all of Western Canada. When Sir Charles Tupper paid a visit in that year, Brandon's special entertainment was not a brass band, nor a massed choir; it was a parade of draft stallions, 25 of them, every one tried and true. Whether the statesman was interested in horses was never considered, but in any case he must have been impressed by those symbols of power.

The city became the headquarters of many of the leading importers and breeders in the West and the Brandon of the nineties claimed more livery stables per city block than any place in the world. It was the centre from which stallions and mares, brought from Scotland, England, France, Belgium, United States and Ontario, were sold and reshipped to the new farming districts. It may have been the "horsiest" city in the world and nowhere were the tan-bark battles more deadly than those that gave character to the Brandon Exhibition and Brandon Winter Fair.

Every show brought new horses together, many of them champions in other lands. Manitoba farmers watched the outcome of the judging with as much eager tenseness as the Brandon people now watch a Junior Hockey final with the Wheat Kings one goal ahead. When the aged Clydesdale stallions were being judged at the 1892 exhibition, it was said that all the people on the fair grounds were crowding around the ring to see if Colquhoun's big Charming Charlie could beat the Harkness and Smith horse called Sir Arthur. Sir Arthur was a former winner, but Charming Charlie placed over him and repeated it in each of the next two years to become the favorite topic of conservation on Rosser Avenue and at the Weekly Stable League, meeting between the rows of horses at Humesville Church stable, during the Sunday School hour. Said the Brandon *Sun,* "Everyone is not interested in a fat animal whether it be cattle, sheep or swine; but a good horse affects everybody." That was typical of Brandon sentiment.

Winnipeg returned to participate in Exhibitions in 1891 and Brandon was uneasy for fear that its show might be drowned in the wash. But Brandon, with the strongest agricultural traditions had little to fear.

On the strength of the Fair of '92, the *Farmer's Advocate,* conscious of Brandon's fear, said,

> we feel confident this society will uphold the reputation they have already gained of having the best exhibition outside of Winnipeg. The Brandon district is especially strong in draft horses.

But after the next show, that of 1893, the same magazine (of August 20, 1893) was even more reassuring to Brandon, saying, that from an agricultural standpoint, the Brandon Fair was "more of a success than the Winnipeg Industrial." Brandon had the advantage of more breeders of pure bred livestock residing nearby. John E. Smith was winning the highest honours with his Shorthorns and Herefords and J. D. McGregor with Aberdeen Angus. And Brandon's grain exhibits were now proclaimed as the "Best in the West." A sample of wheat from the Brandon competition of that year won the gold medal at the International Millers' and Bakers' Exhibition in London. And so Brandon decided not to worry about Winnipeg competition.

But the struggling Exhibition had troubles of other kinds, among them financial. The annual meeting in February, 1894, heard grim news, a deficit of $400 on the year's operations. But the finance committee, in the best treasury style, had a double-barrelled alibi, the hard times and the necessity of fixing the fence. Other gloom reported at the meeting, likewise not unfamiliar to Exhibition Managers of later years, was that the race horses permitted to occupy the stables had disrespectfully kicked holes through the walls.

The Territorial Exhibition at Regina overshadowed everything else in 1895, but the C.P.R. permitted the livestock moving from Winnipeg Industrial and Portage la Prairie Fair to stop for the show at Brandon and about 30 carloads filled the stables, taxed the water supply, used all the available bedding and exhausted the supplies of feed. It was an Inter-Provincial livestock show, at Regina's expense. But the biggest news story, nevertheless, was that the local Clydesdale stallion, Sir Arthur, with a lot of admirers, had got his first revenge in four years, by beating Charming Charlie.

Back in 1892, the Brandon Agricultural Society applied for incorporation as the Western Agricultural and Arts Association of Manitoba, the new organization to take over the franchise, assets and liabilities of the older body. Capital stock would consist of 1000 shares at $10 each. The new charter was obtained but not until February, 1897, was the first annual meeting of shareholders held and directors appointed. S. A. Bedford, who was Superintendent of the Dominion Experimental Farm, became President and F. J. Clark, the manager. Except for a period when he was at the South African War, Colonel Clark was the Brandon Secretary until 1908.

By approval of the Legislature, the new board could call its fair the Provincial Exhibition. Forty-two acres of land were bought and added to the existing grounds to make a total of 75 acres and the Manitoba Government was asked for an annual grant of $5000. The Government pointed out, however, that it could not support two Exhibitions on a large scale and gave Brandon $2500.

Brandon had now reached a certain maturity in development and set about to improve its facilities. Directors authorized a board fence, extended the grandstand to seat 1200 people and dug wells and installed windmills to provide needed water, spending in all about $12,000.

Brandon Exhibition had been rejuvenated. For its first Provincial Show, (August 3-5, 1897), the Board offered $5000 in prizes and pledged its determination to make the Exhibition a great force in the agricultural life of the Province. On Wednesday, 12,000 people attended and the *Colonist* wrote that an "unbroken procession of smart buggies, drawn by handsome horses and filled in every case by gaily dressed men and women, spoke volumes as to the general progress of the farmers." And of the 12,000 present that day, most of them watched the renewal of the old stallion feud between Charming Charlie and Sir Arthur. They saw "Charlie" gain another victory but they also saw Sir Arthur win a brand new class, for "stallion and six of his get."

·... In 1919 the name was changed again. The cumbersome title, "Western Agricultural and Arts Association" was dropped and "Provincial Exhibition of Manitoba" adopted. Nobody challenged the new name.

Chuck-Wagon Romance

The cowboy's story has been well documented in American fiction and non-fiction but not so well told in Canada. Perhaps the dramatic and colorful Mountie has attracted the lion's share of attention in this country. MacEwan goes a long way to rectify this omission — most notably in this excerpt from one of his early books. (From Between the Red and the Rockies, *Toronto: University of Toronto Press, 1952. Reprinted by Western Producer Prairie Books, 1979.)*

If the red-coated Mounted Policeman has a rival for the admiration of hero-worshipping small boys, it is the western cowboy. And if anyone could better the Mountie's record in ruffling the hearts of not-so-small girls, it would be the hero of the range in his good cowboy clothes.

Not that the working cowboy ever resembled the decorated and dashing hero of the movies. He fancied a coloured shirt for Saturday night when he moved in on Fort Macleod or High River but otherwise his garb, including broad-brimmed hat,[1] snug-fitting jeans, and high-heeled boots, was designed for utility. Masculine qualities outshone finery. A cowboy was a two-fisted gentleman, a man of action rather than of words.

From the days of the mighty trail herds of Longhorns, the cattleman's work was hazardous but exciting. It was coloured by wild stampedes, fights over water rights, rustling, shooting, hard riding, and the bleaching bones that told of hard winters. These were not merely the dreams of poets and romancers. They were the grim realities of a frontier industry. The cowboy's range made a perfect setting for film and short story. But many of those who wrote the stories never saw a ranch, and it was small wonder that the cowboys found it difficult to recognize either their habits or themselves. As W. P. Webb says, in *The Great Plains:*

> The Easterner with his background of forest and farm, could not always understand the man of the cattle kingdom. One went on foot, the other on horseback; one carried his law in books, the

other carried it strapped round his waist. One represented tradition, the other represented innovation; one responded to convention, the other responded to necessity and evolved his own conventions.

Life in the saddle attracted young men from many parts of the world. Remittance men came from England, bad boys from Ontario, earnest young fellows from everywhere, and experienced cattlemen from the South. The newcomers underestimated the hardships and many acknowledged disillusionment and left. Others felt the fascination of the range country; they remained to acquire a few cattle and sometimes ultimately large ranch holdings.

The typical cowboy of the Canadian West was unpolished but he had to be good stuff. The law of the range, born of necessity, said that he had to fight to defend himself, his boss's property, and the honour of the ranch. Often in the early years he was armed, and he knew that carrying a gun was a huge folly unless he could shoot straight and shoot fast. He learned to do both.

But he didn't go about shooting holes in people and barroom chandeliers. Those who concocted the biggest lies about his shooting and courting evidently overlooked the fact that he was a working man. His devotion to duty and his skills in handling cattle would have made truer and better reading. Cowboys who remained with the herd through a bad blizzard knew the meaning of duty and service. In the March storm of 1938, when heavy losses were sustained across the cow-country, there were riders who did not leave the drifting herds. Complete control of such herds was impossible but some guidance could be given. For two days the riders on one Alberta ranch remained with the cattle, allowing them to drift, but guiding them away from fences and other pitfalls. For miles and miles the riders and their faithful mounts felt the sting of the icy blizzard and for two days had neither food nor rest. In that herd no cattle were lost, notwithstanding an average wind velocity of sixty and a half miles per hour for eighteen consecutive hours, as measured at Manyberries. The storm continued for sixty hours.

Cowboy traditions were made on the trails from Texas. In those trail years a herd of 2,500 head was considered most suitable for a long drive. Larger herds were cumbersome and had to be moved slowly. Dale refers, in *The Range Cattle Industry*, to a huge trail herd numbering 25,000 head, which was spread along the route for 20 miles. It was too big to be efficient and nobody tried to duplicate the record.

A trail outfit included a chuck wagon, a cook, about six riders for every thousand cattle, six to ten horses for every cowboy, a horse wrangler, and the boss or captain. Only the best cowboys were employed.

Trailing demanded top riders and the best brains. The captain and the "old hands" with the most pronounced bow in their legs rode in the lead positions, while newcomers or inexperienced helpers, who were doing their best to walk bowlegged, rode in the dust at the "drag" end.

Twelve to fifteen miles a day was considered a good average for a trailing herd and the trip from Texas to Kansas took two months or more. A representative day consisted of grazing in the proper direction for two hours in the morning, driving briskly until noon, a two-hour rest stop, several more hours of slow travel to allow grazing, and then settling for the night. With careful driving it was possible to make the trip without shrinkage.

Riders, usually two in number, were on "night herd." Competition wasn't heavy for that post, especially in Indian country and on rainy nights. While the night herder waited for morning, he usually wished that he had taken up blacksmithing instead of punching cows. It was doubtless during the long dark hours that he composed many of the mournful cowboy ditties whose soporific monotones are so popular on radio programmes, and must have made even the cattle drowsy. What the night riders feared most was a stampede. It called for skilful riding; the hope was to turn the leaders, and get the herd running in a circle.

The cowboys spent most of their working hours in the saddle. They became artists with the lariat and they demonstrated how versatile a tool that instrument could be. Work that could not be accomplished by means of saddle horse and rope was considered beneath the cowboy's dignity and was likely to suffer from lack of attention. When a police officer at Macleod was unable to hire a man to dig a well, he attributed his failure to the fact that "a man cannot dig a well from a horse's back."

Even the language of the cowboy was distinctive. There was a sagebrush tang about it. It had traces of Spanish and reminders of Texas, but was mainly the product of a rare but simple chuck-wagon philosophy. Rodeo, remuda, bronco, chapparejos, lasso, and many other terms, including "ranch" itself, were Spanish or Mexican in origin. Lasso comes from the Spanish for slip-knot, and pinto means paint. A remuda was the band of extra saddle horses carried with the roundup for use in some sort of rotation as required by the cowboys. Bronco, which is applied to range horses with ambition to be wild, came from the Spanish word meaning rough. And bronco-buster, bronco-twister, and bronco-peeler were synonymous terms for the skilled cowboy whose duty it was to convert the wild horses to domesticity.

Terms of semi-local origin became as numerous and as expressive. Bed-ground is a remnant of trail days and applied to the place chosen for the night camp. Bow-wows were thin cattle, and dogies were young stocker cattle, who developed a profound homesickness for the farm on which they were raised. When the bronco-buster grasps the horn of the saddle to increase his security, he pulls leather and is subject to disqualification if he is in a contest. And scratching has no connection with itch; rather it refers to the use of the spurs in a bronco-riding competition.

If Canada had its cowboy centre in the heyday of the range, the honour belonged to Fort Macleod. It was a community of rugged, bowlegged men, among whom the ability to stay on a bad horse carried more prestige than a trunkful of good clothes or a diploma from Eton. Fort Macleod could boast more hitching posts than any town of its size in the world. And no other town north of the boundary saw so much of the big bull-team units which hauled heavy freight wagons to and from Fort Benton.

But the sixteen-ox freight teams and the saddle horses and cowboys which lined the street were no more distinctive than the Macleod Hotel and its colourful proprietor, Harry Taylor, alias "Kamoose" Taylor, alias "Old Kamoose." Taylor would never consent to be separated from the Macleod cowboys. Story has it that he had been a missionary in the gold diggings of the Cariboo fields but had decided that trading whisky in the Territories would be more lucative. It did pay better, but the arrival of the Mounted Police converted the traders to other professions and Taylor erected a hotel. This was a cowboys' hotel and there wasn't another like it. It dispensed good cheer more than luxury. Its roof was guaranteed to keep the snow off the beds and the walls were expected to break most of the wind. When a frost-bitten morning visitor from the road stood beside the stove in the hope of thawing the icicles from his mustache, a paying guest looked at him and asked, "What room did you occupy last night?" The hotel could furnish almost everything that came in bottles, but the guests who wanted door keys, clean sheets, or hot water, heard Kamoose say "This is not London."

There were no dull moments at old Fort Macleod. One could count on something resembling a rodeo event every day. An episode which lingered in the memories of the early residents concerned a tough horse and an equally tough cowboy. Horses from the Winder Ranch were being held in a corral at the livery stable, pending sale. The corral was fenced on three sides and bounded on the fourth side by a thirty-foot cutbank which dropped to the river and should have been as effective as a good fence.

A police officer arrived to select some horses for remounts and all went well until Charlie Sharples mounted a horse that evidently did not fancy joining the North West Mounted Police. The horse behaved badly and, near the cutbank, it balked. Sharples drove his spurs deep into the horse's flanks and the animal went into an explosive whirl, rushed at the cutbank and leaped straight out into space. Onlookers dashed to the river's edge, expecting to see a mangled mass of horse and human remains. What they saw was the cowboy still in the saddle, and the horse swimming to the opposite shore, none the worse for its leap. But then, this was Fort Macleod, where anything could happen.

No phase of early cowboying possessed more glamour than the roundup. It was like the threshing season on a wheat farm or election day at Prince Albert. Its mother was necessity and its father was a chuck wagon. It became the leading social and economic institution on the American and Canadian range.

There might be three roundups each year. The general roundup starting at the beginning of June was the most important, but a midsummer roundup might be held for the purpose of branding late calves, and in the fall roundup the fat beef were sorted out for shipment.

The general roundup, in the course of which the riders fanned out to cover the face of the cattle country, was a grand affair. But the range was too big and district roundups began to take the place of the general effort. Between the Cypress Hills and the mountains and south of the Canadian Pacific Railway, were eighteen organized districts, each of which had an executive body. The executive set the date for the commencement of the roundup, appointed the roundup captain, and owned the equipment, including corrals, tents, and wagons. Costs were paid by the ranchers according to the size of their herds.

At either the general or the district roundup, ranchers were represented by their cowboys. Each rider had his string of six to ten saddle horses, which were used in rotation for gathering and working the cattle. The captain was usually elected from among the ranch foremen present, and he bristled with authority as he issued working orders to the forty or sixty obedient cowboys. His post, like that of the Minister of Finance, was inclined to bring prestige rather than popularity, however. The only person whom he could not boss was the cook.

Nobody crossed the indispensable autocrat who ruled over the chuck wagon. He wielded too much power. He could inflict anything from humiliation to starvation upon his enemies. The roundup captain knew that he could fire the cook but he couldn't boss him.

The cook's wagon, made popular in recent years by daring chuck-wagon races, carried a ton or two of utensils and provisions for the camp. Occasionally that pioneer wagon figured in a cross-country race, but usually it was hauled steadily and not very fast, with four horses drawing it and the cook driving. In rough country, the chuck-wagon outfit was accompanied by one or two outriders who used their lariats to render assistance on bad grades or to ensure against upsetting on the hillsides.

One or two horse wranglers constituted an important part of the roundup gang. Theirs was the duty of herding and caring for the horses not in use. When two were employed, the senior member took the day shift and the "green" hand did night duty. Breakfast was served at sunrise and the wrangler was expected to have the horses in the corral before that time so that the cowboys could select their horses and saddle up without delay. Those early morning hours were the best in the day for roundup purposes and the rising alarm might sound at any time after two a.m., with the work day ending before the heat of noon.

Green horses were used to gather and deliver cattle to the nearest corrals where the "educated" horses were employed for the more technical work of "cutting" and sorting. Cows with calves to be branded were cut out first. The "cutting" was performed by the most skilful cowboys so that each calf was removed with its dam and thus its identity established. When a calf broke away from its mother, both were left until they reunited. Cows of one brand were herded together until the calves could be branded and then the herd was worked in the direction of its home range.

The roundup meant hard riding, long hours, and great fatigue. The entire range had to be combed because a rancher's profit depended upon the recovery of all cattle belonging to him. Cattle might travel a hundred miles or more from home range and it was not uncommon for Pincher Creek cattle to be found at Medicine Hat. Cattle that strayed so far were passed from one roundup district to the next, through the help of visiting "representatives," until they arrived on home grass.

If the modest hunt for Sergeant Whitney's fourteen cows and a bull which had been released so daringly amid buffalo and Indian hazards could be called a roundup, it was the first on the prairies. But the first organized cattle gathering having undisputed claim to the title was centred at Fort Macleod in August, 1879. Sergeant Parker was captain. Sixteen cowboys and one wagon participated, and the riders were handicapped by having only one mount each. They covered a lot of territory but did not get as many cattle as expected, about six hundred head in all. . . .

The biggest roundup in the history of the Canadian West took place in 1885. The men for that gigantic undertaking gathered at Fort Macleod on May 25. There were over a hundred cowboys, sixteen chuck wagons, and 500 saddle horses. The roundup gang split, with Captain Jim Dunlop leading one party in the Pincher Creek country and George Lane and another group combing the Willow Creek area. Over 60,000 cattle were collected. Rev. John McDougall told of looking down upon the valley of the Sun River in Montana in 1875 and seeing 23,000 cattle gathered there in one herd in the annual roundup. After viewing this herd, the exact number of which was known, McDougall ventured the guess that he had many times seen herds of buffalo numbering more than half a million head. . . .

However unconventional and varied those pioneers of ranch country may have been, they had two or three admirable qualities in common. They could work overtime without complaint; they depended upon their vigour and resourcefulness, and they would share their blankets or last loaf of bread with one in need.

The latch-string of the ranch-house hung on the outside, even during the owner's absence, and it was considered quite proper for a traveller to provision himself from the larder of a temporarily unoccupied house. But it was contrary to range law to take all the food. Men who were habitually careless about cattle brands never dreamed of yielding to the temptation to take more than half of a piece of bacon or half of the flour found in a cabin. Something was always left for the next traveller or the owner when he returned.

And let there be no mistake about it, loyalty was a conspicuous characteristic in the unorganized fraternity of cowboys. Few could speak with more authority than Senator Dan Riley. This was his tribute, in *Canadian Cattlemen:*

> He might be working for some haywire outfit, poorly mounted, poorly equipped, poorly bossed, but his loyalty never wavered. Blizzards might rage, rains turn streams into torrents and the country into a quagmire. It only added zest to his work. . . . Beef herds sometimes stampeded at night. He rode with them in their blind run, well knowing that the next jump might mean death to him. I never knew a man to quit and when the herd was finally circled and stopped, every man was in his place. . . . To the memory of these men, with whom I rode, stirrup to stirrup, for hundreds, nay thousands of miles, my tribute is, that according to their lights, their environment and their limitations, they served well and filled well the place God gave them here.

It is the cowboys who have made the cattle kingdom one of the last frontiers of picturesque romance, with its magnificent setting, its heroic drama, and its own quaint chivalry.

Battle of the Booze

One might well expect a writer who is teetotal himself to be censorious when writing about alcoholism and all its pitfalls. This is not true in MacEwan's case. He never preaches at the reader. This excerpt shows the writer at his charitable best, dealing with a character he obviously loves and understands despite the fact that their ways of living were miles apart. (From Eye Opener Bob, *Edmonton: Institute of Applied Art, 1957. Reprinted by Western Producer Prairie Books, 1974.)*

Every man has his favorite bird; ours is the bat.(May 13, 1905)
Yes, we agree, whiskey floats more troubles than it drowns.
(September 11, 1920)
The water wagon is certainly a more dangerous vehicle than the automobile. At least more people fall off it. (August 25, 1906)
Booze acts on the human character as developer on a photographic negative. It brings out the lights and shadows. It shows up the black spots . . .   (March 9, 1916)

Whiskey was Bob Edwards' great weakness and periodically it was his master. It was one enemy he seemed totally unable to overcome. He knew what it was to regain semiconsciousness amid strange and filthy surroundings after heavy drinking, feeling as though there was lead in his head and rubber in his legs, hating himself and the thought of sobering up, and seeing another drink as the only possible remedy for his sufferings. He knew what it was to be beaten up while drunk and to have bouts with "snakes" and "pink elephants." "When a man is driven to drink," he said, "he usually has to walk back." (August 4, 1906)
Indeed, his experience surpassed the customary "snakes" and "pink elephants" which went with severe hangovers; he had encountered bears. It was during his years at Wetaskiwin when he was drinking heavily that Jerry Boyce and others wondered if a real scare might not inspire Bob to change his ways. It was worth a trial, and according to the plan, one of Jerry's half-tamed bears from behind the hotel was tied to the bed post in

Bob's room. Late at night Bob staggered in, struck a match to light the candle, and saw the outline of the bear. He stared, unconvinced, and muttered to himself that no pink elephant or black bear was going to fool him. He kicked at the indistinct form, believing it to be imaginary, and promptly bruin struck back, tearing Bob's trousers and scratching his flesh to make the blood flow. Bob took to flight — didn't stop until he reached Jerry's room.

"What's the matter?" Jerry inquired.

"You'll say it's hallucinations," Bob replied, puffing like a broken-winded horse, "but, honest, Jerry, the hangover beasts around here are getting damned rough — one bit me — look there — blood!"

Several times he submitted to "cures," and following one of the treatments he appeared to have overcome the craving. But after about a year the temptations in alcohol were too much for his resistance, and he went back to the hospital. Once, at least, he abstained for two years; but the Alberta Press Association held its annual meeting in Medicine Hat that fall of 1906 and the hospitality was so intense that "the writer, who has clung to the water cart for two long and weary years, was seized with a panic and ducked his nut." (October 6, 1906) It was that occasion which inspired the remark that: "The water wagon is certainly a more dangerous vehicle than the automobile. At least, more people fall off it."

Some of those who considered themselves as friends of the editor didn't help him:

> What a lot of booze is offered you when it becomes generally known that you are on the water wagon. During Christmas week the temptation to fall off was great indeed. One idiot who was lit up for a fair, entered the *Eye Opener* office waving a bottle of Scotch and blithering out, "Dewar unto others as you would others Dewar you." (January 6, 1917)

Bob Edwards was not a daily drinker, but periodically he took too much. After several days of intoxication he might be taken to Holy Cross or Western Hospital where he would remain until recovered. *Eye Opener* publication would be suspended during those spells; but on a few occasions when an issue was already well on its way his faithful secretary, Miss Bertha Hart, with help from friends like Arthur Halpen of the *Albertan*, managed to get it out.

Readers usually knew when the editor had been incapacitated by drink. Either the paper failed to appear when expected, or there was a full explanation in the columns. Perhaps he wrote about it too freely. Perhaps he was needlessly frank and honest about his own defects. Had he been less inclined to relate his alcoholic misadventures, the weakness would have been less conspicuous, and he would have escaped many noisy criticisms and insults from uncharitable tongues. But he was, as friends said again,"A man without secrets."

As it was, a reader might have been misled by the mirthful way in which the subject of "booze" was treated. What was a reader to take from the frivolous account of the *Eye Opener* Road Race of 1906, for example? Oldtimers who were around at that date appeared vague about whether or not the race was a reality. In any case, this was Bob's alcohol-reeking account of the epic:

> The *Eye Opener* Road Race of 1906 was in the nature of a novelty and afforded intense amusement to the populace. Contestants started from the corner of First Street and Eighth Avenue, underneath our office in the Cameron Block, to the shot from a pistol fired, as now, by Captain Smart of the Fire Department. On this occasion there were fifteen starters, all of whom had agreed to abide by the rather unique conditions. At the crack of the pistol they were off in a bunch, with a contestant from High River slightly in the lead and the Olds entry close up.
>
> Running west up the avenue, according to the terms of the race, the contestants raced up to the Royal Hotel, where each had to drink a glass of whiskey at the bar; thence helter-skelter up the street to the Alberta, where a snort of dry gin was the next condition laid down; from there they flew around the corner to the Dominion to put away a schooner of beer, speeding on and on from bar to bar the whole length of Ninth Avenue, drinking horn after horn, no two alike. A corps of umpires followed the runners the whole length of the course. Rounding into Eighth Avenue, it was noticed that only three were left in the race, and these just barely managed to make the Queen's Hotel. Only one emerged ten minutes later to finish the race. He had just one block to go, and it was indeed fortunate for him that Eighth Avenue is a narrow thoroughfare, for he came along bumping against the buildings on either side and stotting from one side of the street to the other. This was the only thing that kept him on his feet. He was the Macleod entry and had been training for just such an event as this for years. (December 25, 1920)

The *Eye Opener* carried lots of levity about liquor, but it was not intended as a defense of either the drink or the editor's mistakes. To the curse of drink in his own life he confessed many times. It worried him and he wasn't fooling himself when he wrote humorously about it. But a long and mournful face or an unrealistic approach to a thing with some of the characteristics of disease would not make it better. Perhaps, he reasoned, there would be less of stilted thinking and more of sensible planning if people paused to laugh at the demon in whisky. Moreover, there is a time for fun as there is a time for seriousness; and the person who will treat a serious topic seriously when seriousness would do some good, has license to treat it lightly at other times.

There was another and more determined reason for the jocular treatment of liquor questions; much of the humorous writing was Bob Edwards' scornful answer to the narrow way in which some pious prohibitionists approached the problem. The age-old liquor conundrum would not be resolved adequately by either the liquor interests or the fanatical prohibitionists, and Bob Edwards was ready to castigate both groups. Yes, and he would criticize a third group — the numerous people with independent views who seemed reluctant to speak above a whisper on the subject. Altogether too often people gave the impression that even the discussion of liquor was "forbidden fruit."

When people said, "It's too bad, but Bob is an alcoholic," he didn't deny it. He did say that "alcoholism isn't as contagious as leprosy but is equally vile." No doubt the constant flippancy in writing about booze made many readers think he was just another drinking man obliged, from time to time, to seek hospital care in order to recuperate from excesses. Certainly that manner of writing gave no clue to the mental agony that followed his periodic drinking bouts or the deeply thoughtful convictions which were his.

E. A. Shelley of the Alberta Hotel was one person who understood the weight of the cross Bob Edwards had to bear. Lots of times Bob came to Shelley's room after the latter had retired at an hour past midnight. "I'm fair choking for a drink," he'd say. "Will you get up and open the bar for me?"

Shelley would accompany Bob down the flights of stairs, unlock the door of the bar and pour the suffering man a drink. Holding the glass in two shaky hands, Bob would take down the contents in an unbroken drink. At once he would feel relieved and ready to return to his office to finish the night's work or perhaps sleep out the balance of the night in his chair beside the big roll-top desk. How could a man with such habits have lofty ideas about temperance? Even though he had two quarrels, one with the evils of alcohol and one with the intolerant attitude in which many prohibition workers conducted their campaign, how could such a person be magnanimous in his thinking?

The crucial test came in 1915. Nothing less would have convinced a multitude of skeptics. Calgary had been a battleground for "wets" and "drys" for years. Nowhere in the West were the liquor interests more vigorous, and nowhere were the prohibitionists imbued with more of crusading determination. The provincial referendum of 1915 promised to be the battle of the year, outclassing even the boisterous political frays for which that section was famous.

Where would the *Eye Opener*'s editor stand in this major test? Would he be on the side of the hotelmen, liquor wholesalers, and the rank and file of drinking people, many of whom he knew intimately, or would he, by any chance, be with the temperance workers and churchmen whom he had so often and roundly criticized?

About his influence in the community there could be no doubt. The fact of 10,000 copies of the *Eye Opener* being sold inside the city of Calgary alone every time the paper came off the press was enough to make both sides in any democratic contest covet the editor's support. Numerous people who would not admit admiration for him were visibly anxious to know his views and his reasoning.

The hotelkeepers who saw him drinking at their bars expected confidently that he would be on the side of the "wets" where he had lots of friends. They knew very well that if he followed unrestrained inclinations, he would be with them.

But Bob Edwards' sense of public responsibility was more highly developed than most people realized, and his conclusion was that the time had come when John Barleycorn should be struck down. The rumor went about the city: "Bob Edwards, of all people, is coming out in opposition to the liquor interests." It wouldn't have seemed more strange to hear that Henry Ford was advocating the use of horses to pull carriages.

Drinking friends were surprised, and the organized whisky interests were worried. Well they might be. "This man is powerful," said the anti-prohibitionists, "but he's a drinking man and we must have him with us." A deputation was selected and instructed to call on him, its purpose being to win him back.

The delegation called at Bob's office, and politely the members related the amazing rumor that he might not be with them in this campaign. Bob listened with the subdued attention of a jurist. One thing of which the visitors could be sure was frankness; in stating his position, Edwards would not deceive or mislead. . . .

But members of the party believed they had a "trump card." One of them, so it is told, said: "Bob, you could use some money; wouldn't five or ten thousand dollars help you a lot?" . . . He replied with customary forthrightness: "Yes, I could use it, but I've never taken that kind of money and I would not accept it now. Gentlemen, my mind is made up."

It was but a short time until a delegation from the Temperance and Moral Reform League called on him. This time Bob Edwards opened the discussion.

"You're after my support? Well, the 'Wets' would pay me well. How much is it worth to you?"

The reply was: "We're sorry, Mr. Edwards, but we have no money."

"That's fine," responded the editor, "because I'm not for sale. I'm with you. The next issue of the *Eye Opener* will make that very clear."

But a lot could happen in a Bob Edwards week; and as time was to show, the strife had only started. Bob wrote his editorial copy on Tuesday night. It was the analysis of one considering two sides of the question and concluding that drinking of hard liquor should stop. Here it is, perhaps the most influential editorial penned in the New West up to that time:

Consider well. View the act and its consequences from every angle. Many hotelmen will be put out of business and placed in grave financial difficulties. They are to get no compensation. Engaged in an occupation which is legalized and specially licensed by the government and the city, they suddenly find the earth opening up at their feet and a yawning pit of utter ruin being prepared for them to fall into, held the while at the mercy of rapacious landlords, inexorable temperance workers and absolutely heartless bankers. Does this not excite your pity?

It does ours, but only to a limited extent, for a panorama passes before our eyes of women and little children in humble homes, shy proper food and clothing, lacking warmth in winter and bereft completely of the joy of living, going to sleep in misery and awakening to another day with the dull pain of hopelessness, innocent victims of the damnable traffic of booze; we see a multitude of downcast men, down-and-outers, panhandling for dimes on the street to procure more of that very booze which lost them every job they ever had; there appear in the picture men whom we knew in their more prosperous days, who before our very eyes day by day and year by year have kept gradually falling behind in the race until one almost forgets that they ever started at all; our mind's eye lights on poor devils of both sexes being yanked each night to the police station and chucked into cells, to meet further humiliation the next morning in the dock; we see in this mental panorama much wretchedness, but the most saddening is the pitiful vision of graves containing the remains of men, good men, who were jolly companions in their day, beloved by hosts of friends, but whose careers were brought to an abrupt and shameful conclusion by bad whiskey and by nothing else. In a word, there is Death in the Cup, and if this Act is likely to have the effect of dashing the Cup from the drunkard's hand, for God's sake let us vote for it.

Elsewhere in the same copy, he continued:

> The Drys should have invoked the co-operation of the Dominion Government and brought about a condition where whiskey and kindred hard drinks were put in the drug class and labelled "Poison," with licenses granted for the sale of beer and light wines only. ... The chief recommendation of the Act, of course, lies in the abolition of the bar. So long as there is a bar there will be treating and treating is the progenitor of every toot. ... The jollity around a bar is absolutely bogus, booze-begotten jokes being invariably rotten. (July 17, 1915)

The editor's copy went to the *Albertan* for printing. Thursday was the day on which the *Eye Opener* customarily went to press, with sales starting early Saturday morning. But about midway through the week, Bob Edwards yielded to his old enemy and lost all interest in publication. Indeed, it had not been overlooked by one of the plebiscite groups that if the editor could be led to intoxication, the *Eye Opener* would never reach the streets.

Nobody knew what happened from that time forward better than Arthur Halpen, the young Irishman who was assistant foreman in the composing room of the *Albertan* printing plant, normally located only a block from Bob Edwards' office (where Macleod Brothers store stood later). Thursday morning Jesse Rockley, manager of the Job Printing Department, came to Halpen saying: "Bob has seen his galley proofs but now he's half drunk; could you handle the make-up of his pages?"

Halpen replied that he was familiar with Bob's style and would do it.

Accordingly, the page proofs were made up and taken to the *Eye Opener* office, where the editor was sitting at his desk, christie hat on his head and a smile of irresponsibility on his face. Partially drunk as he was, he insisted upon reading the pages and ordered Halpen to play the player piano in the office while he did it. After an hour or so of ineffective reading, the editor, in alcoholic recklessness, dashed his marking pencil across the pages as if to "kill" the entire issue. As far as Bob was concerned, the matter was closed; there'd be no issue that week. He took another drink.

In due course the drunken editor went to hospital, as he had done many times before. The defaced pages which he, in his stupor, had repudiated, were taken back to the *Albertan* office; and the "Wets" who had been spying breathed with some relief. To others who witnessed it, the most recent event appeared as the inglorious climax to a noble purpose.

But hope should never be abandoned, especially in Calgary. W. M. Davidson, the *Albertan's* editor, was a loyal friend of Edwards, and he reasoned that once the type was set he had a mandate to see that the issue went to press. With Miss Hart, Arthur Halpen and W. M. Davidson joining forces for the final effort, the page proofs were read and corrected and the *Eye Opener* went to press there in the *Albertan's* temporary quarters in the basement of the Westminster Block, corner of 10th Avenue and 1st Street East, a fire having driven the printers from their usual location.

The *Eye Opener* would be published. To one side in the plebiscite issue this brought satisfaction; to the other, it brought fear. Two hotelmen visited the *Eye Opener* office on Friday and offered to bargain with Miss Hart for the purchase of the entire issue before it went into circulation. The object, of course, was to destroy the papers and prevent them from reaching the readers. Had they been successful, it wouldn't have been the first time that *Eye Opener* fans failed to receive their copies on the allotted day; but the reason would have been a new one. Miss Hart refused to enter into any "deal" and told her visitors very bluntly that Bob Edwards would never condone that kind of business.

Both sides seemed to be maintaining effective intelligence; and when the "drys" learned about the tactics attempted by their opposition, they appealed to Mr. Davidson. He agreed to see that the out-of-town papers were packaged and safeguarded, and that the balance of the issue for Saturday sale in Calgary would be given the security of his vault. That was a happy suggestion, and thus the precious supply for local distribution would not be exposed to risks which careless storage might invite. The possibility of a raid for the purpose of hijacking the issue was not being overlooked; and it has been told that several husky members of the prohibition forces, thinking that the *Eye Opener* office might be the object of an attack, volunteered to spend the night doing an inconspicuous guard duty. But there was no raid and no midnight clash between "wets" and "drys" to enliven the story. At seven o'clock on Saturday morning Miss Hart was at the office to meet the boys and see that they got their copies for the street sales.

Four days later, on July 21, voters went to the polls and gave prohibition a substantial majority both in Calgary and in Alberta as a whole. The provincial result was expected, but the heavy prohibition vote in Calgary came as a surprise. On the Sunday following, the temperance forces held a big thanksgiving service at the Grand Theatre, with Rev. Robert Pearson as chairman. Bob Edwards wasn't present; he was still in hospital and probably wouldn't have been present if he had been out. But when he came out, he approved of all that his friends had done and thanked them for completing publication. Arthur Halpen received a present of twenty-five dollars.

The Gandhi of the Prairies

MacEwan wrote this excerpt in the 1950s but had begun researching the subject years before. Once he learned of Maski-pitoon, he would tour the country interviewing Indian leaders he thought might be in possession of snippets of verbal history about this idealistic human being. That Maski-pitoon's story was rescued from oblivion and dramatized is due in large part to MacEwan. (From Fifty Mighty Men, *Saskatoon: Western Producer Prairie Books, 1958.)*

Two thousand years ago, skeptics were asking: "Can any good thing come out of Nazareth?" and in comparatively recent times the same sort of doubters enquired if any good thing could come out of the Indian tribes occupying the Canadian prairies. "Primitive" and "savage" were terms used to describe those native people but in various respects they were misjudged, and to suppose that the tepees produced no great thinkers, is in itself an injustice.

The Indian way of life was different, strangely different, but it wasn't all inferior and what becomes increasingly clear, some members of the native race had minds of philosophers. Of such were Crowfoot of the Blackfoot nation, Red Crow of the Bloods, Piapot of the Crees and Peguis of the Saulteaux tribe. And that the buffalo country of a century ago produced a native who, in his life and death, had quite a lot in common with the great Asiatic Indian, Mohandas Gandhi, may be seen as the greatest surprise of all.

Maski-pitoon was the name of the Gandhi of the buffalo country, whose adherence to the principles of nonviolence upset many of the story-book theories about prairie Indians. Not only was he a thinker but one who had the courage of bold convictions. By this performance he earned a place of highest honor in western story and, indeed, a monument set somewhere in that section of central Alberta which was traditionally a Blackfoot-Cree battleground.

Only a few whites knew Maski-pitoon and the student will be forced to conclude that they forgot him rather quickly after his death. The story was almost lost. From fragmentary bits of evidence gathered here and there, however, it has been possible to reconstruct the story of his life or, at least, an important part of it.

The pioneer missionary of the Methodist church, Rev. John McDougall, referred to Maski-pitoon in one of his books and the Regina *Leader* of December 10, 1885, referred to him as a "courteous, hospitable gentleman of nature." Best of all, some of the old Indians of recent years have been able to offer fragmentary information and Rev. Edward Ahenakew, Cree minister serving the Anglican church at Fort la Corne, Saskatchewan, and Augustus Steinhauer have furnished important help.

According to Rev. Ahenakew, grand nephew of Chief Big Bear, the name "Maski-pitoon" meant "One Whose Arm Was Broken." More important than that, however, Maski-pitoon, in his early years, displayed unusual courage. Without flinching, he faced the test of the Sun Dance — three days of feasting, dancing and torture, at which young men hoped to qualify as braves. An ambitious youth desiring to win the high distinction, cut slits in the flesh of his breast, placed skewers or thongs therein and from these tied himself to a central pole against which he strained and grinned at the pain until the flesh broke to release him.

Maski-pitoon passed all the tests of endurance and bravery; he could be savage and cruel; and in gathering scalps and stealing horses he displayed such commanding skill that he easily won the admiration of his people who were more impressed by horse thefts than by lofty ideas. More than that, this young man had an erect and muscular body and no doubt enjoyed the imperfectly hidden glances of all the Indian maidens.

It just seemed that this young man was born to be a chief and lead his people to victory against all enemies. In due course, Maski-pitoon did become a chief and his tribesmen were proud of him. And why shouldn't they be? On the hunt his success was extraordinary and when he returned from battle no brave could show more of the bloody evidence of slaughter.

But with the passing years, Maski-pitoon saw many things in Indian society to disturb him. Although he had blindly accepted tribal customs, he now concluded that many of the inherited practices were wrong. Tribal customs should stand the test of reason. He was worried.

He made solitary journeys into the hills in order to think things through. More and more he was convinced that killing was wrong, that violence simply bred more violence and evil. It was terribly unorthodox for that time and place but he dared to ask himself why the tribes could not adopt a policy of good will and devote their energies to something more constructive than killing and stealing.

Any young Indian whose bravery was untried would not dare to express such thoughts because they would invite scorn and he would be sent to work with the women. Only a man whose courage and daring were proven could afford to be bold. The young chief shared his views with the Medicine Man but it was a waste of time. The wise man of the tribe could not imagine living without war and cruelty; it would be like an eagle living without feathers or a buffalo without horns. Maski-pitoon turned to his thoughtful old father and there he found encouragement.

Together, father and son withdrew into the hill country to be alone and commune with nature. There the truth was more likely to be seen without disguise; there the spirits hovered more closely to man. The days were calm and the nights clear — perfect for meditation. Finally, convictions confirmed, the father collected four black feathers and set them in a row in the ground, calling them Dishonesty, Hatred, Cruelty and War. Collecting four white feathers, the old Indian set them in another row, giving the names Honesty, Friendliness, Sympathy and Peace.

"Decide now, my son," said the elder: "will you choose the way that leads to destruction and war or will you follow the way that can lead to peace and happiness?"

Maski-pitoon was ready for the important decision. He motioned toward the white feathers and asked his father to burn the black ones. The old Indian followed the instructions and after destroying the black feathers, he bound the white ones and handed them to the young chief with a father's advice to carry them always.

Thereafter, the way of Maski-pitoon was the way of peace. Though most of his people could not understand the change, at least he was able to hold their respect because of a record for bravery already made unquestionable. His devotion to the new and better way of life, however, was to be tested many times in the days ahead.

The Blackfoot stole his horses and savage war-parties took Cree scalps but Maski-pitoon remained steadfast in his convictions that violent reprisals would achieve no good and only add to suffering. The Crees were astonished; this was beyond their understanding, especially when it came from a chief who won his high rank as a fighting man.

The supreme test came when a Blackfoot raiding party murdered Maski-pitoon's father. Now, thought the Crees, the young chief will renounce his strange theories and seek revenge. But there was no attempt at revenge. The young chief continued to wear the white feathers as a reminder of his pledge.

Months passed and, one day, Cree scouts brought word that a small party of Blackfoot was seen not far from Maski-pitoon's camp, close to where the city of Wetaskiwin stands today. Moreover, the Blackfoot who killed Maski-pitoon's father had been identified in that small and comparatively defenceless group.

Chief Maski-pitoon ordered that the Blackfoot killer be captured and brought to him. Instructions were carried out and the murderer stood before the Cree chief. Then, addressing the Blackfoot who had every reason to expect death as his punishment, Maski-pitoon said: "You killed my father; you killed a good man. Once I would have sought your life as revenge; but I have found a better way. I will not kill you but I will ask you to think about the foolishness of Indians killing each other. Will you help foster a new feeling between our two tribes? Will you return to your Blackfoot and tell them that Indians can live in happiness without killing each other?"

Astonishment filled the Blackfoot slayer. Never did he suppose an Indian would miss such a fine chance to kill an enemy. But he seemed to catch the spirit of Maski-pitoon's words.

"Never have I heard such a thing," he said. "My people will ask, 'who is this young chief, so brave and yet so good. He stands alone.' "

Then came another test, when the life of the young Apostle of Peace was threatened. The traditional hate between the tribes had scarcely lessened but Maski-pitoon knew that if his philosophy was to serve any purpose and survive, he must be bold about presenting it.

As it happened, he and a few followers were travelling south to invite a discussion of peace with the Blackfoot. Early on the journey, they encountered a Blackfoot war party and were hopelessly outnumbered. The Blackfoot were in no mood for peace talks and massacre might have seemed certain.

Maski-pitoon's followers deserted while still there was a chance of escaping. Blood-thirsty Blackfoot braves with guns cocked and knives ready, came on for the kill, but they found only the young Cree chief standing erect, motionless, unarmed and alone.

The Blackfoot halted in their astonishment. What did this unusual performance mean? That it was part of a crafty trick to distract and destroy the attackers did not escape the Blackfoot leader's thoughts. Neither tribesmen in retreat nor tribesmen ready for battle would surprise the Indians from the south but, surely, a single and unarmed Cree would not challenge the warriors unless there was a subtle plot about it.

But before there was any violence, the Blackfoot recognized the Cree as Maski-pitoon and they remembered what they heard about his courage and his new teachings. Their lust to kill temporarily forgotten, they approached in curiosity. Maski-pitoon spoke quietly and his traditional enemies listened. The lone Cree invited them to send an envoy to discuss peace and promised safety for those who came.

About this time, Maski-pitoon met the Methodist missionary, Rev. John McDougall, and the meeting served to strengthen the Cree's convictions. McDougall was invited to be present when the Blackfoot representatives visited to discuss peace.

Indians on both sides saw this as a bold experiment and the atmosphere was charged with explosive danger. It was not a simple matter to hold young Crees in check when Blackfoot scalps were within reach. But Maski-pitoon was in command and the conference was a success; men of both tribes feasted, danced and smoked the Pipe of Peace. And Rev. John McDougall, sitting in the place of honor between Maski-pitoon and the Blackfoot leader, gave his approval. Indeed, the Maski-pitoon story might have been lost, had it not been for McDougall who set down enough information to make interested people want to search for more.

But peace treaties must be renewed and about the year 1865, Maski-pitoon invited the McDougalls, Rev. John and his father, Rev. George McDougall, to accompany him to the Blackfoot country. The McDougalls were glad to go and the party set out on the journey that brought these men to the Blackfoot camp, somewhere close to where the city of Red Deer is located today.

The arrival of foreign tribesmen was bound to create a stir and present moments of danger and this one was no exception until Maski-pitoon and the McDougalls were recognized. Alarm gave place to welcome. The visitors were escorted to the tent of Chief Three Bulls and the discussions which followed were cordial.

There was a feast and a dance and the most devoted friend Maski-pitoon had in the entire camp was the Blackfoot who led the charge that day when the Cree chief stood alone and unarmed. That Blackfoot, in pronouncing Maski-pitoon as "the bravest chief of all," was acknowledging that the unarmed man who stood firm for his ideals was displaying more courage than the fighting man loaded down with guns and knives. To be an Apostle of Peace called for courage of the highest order.

It was on such an excursion in the name of peace that Maski-pitoon met his end. As he resembled India's Gandhi in his adherence to the principles of nonviolence, so his death at the hands of an assassin was similar. For the information about Maski-pitoon's death, all thanks go to

Rev. Edward Ahenakew who obtained the story from Chief Thunderchild and jotted it down many years ago.

It was "the year before the small-pox," probably 1869, and Maski-pitoon was trying to arrange another truce between the rival tribes.

With six followers, he raised a Hudson's Bay Company flag and rode into the Blackfoot camp. Recognizing Maski-pitoon, the Blackfoot chief rode out to meet and greet him and the inter-tribal negotiations were about to get under way when, suddenly, "a foolish young Blackfoot arrives unnoticed and unsuspected; he rides around fast and shoots Broken Arm dead."

But Maski-pitoon's life was not wasted. The whites who lived in and about Fort Edmonton had a huge debt to that splendid Indian for the security they enjoyed. And in his thinking and manner of life, he was a fine example to both the natives and the newcomers to the country, a noble contradiction to the popular savage-race concept.

The Winter of Hungry Cattle

In this excerpt MacEwan achieves two main objectives: He illustrates the character of the man, John Ware, in action, and he delineates the challenges that faced western Canadian cowboys early in the century. Here there are both entertainment and instruction in full measure. (From John Ware's Cow Country, *Edmonton: Institute of Applied Art, 1960. Reprinted by Western Producer Prairie Books, 1973.)*

The next day was October 26, 1886, and snow blanketed the cow country from Calgary to Oldman River. With shocking suddenness, like a fall through river ice, the range was plunged from Indian summer into winter. Still, most people were undisturbed; October storms were not uncommon, and a chinook would soon clear the range just as it had done many times.

The Calgary *Tribune* (of October 22, 1886) had just published its comment about this area's "unsurpassed climate . . . very similar to that of Southern Europe." And Sam Livingstone — trader, Indian fighter and first farmer close to Fort Calgary, made news by setting out 350 fruit trees on his land close to the Elbow River.

Optimism was fashionable. Pessimism was akin to treason. The cattle bonanza born on Canadian soil when Sergt. Whitney of the Mounted Police had turned a few cattle loose on the public domain at Fort Macleod exactly ten years before, had experienced only a few reverses in that period of time. Men on the frontier were not inclined to dwell on dangers like long periods of snow. The cattleman's kingdom appeared about as secure as Caesar's.

The only visible uncertainty seemed to lie in the outcome of a war between the ranchers demanding open range and the "nester" fellows who threatened to wreck the old order, "turn the grass upside down," and enclose the land of their choosing — and sometimes good watering places as well — with their contemptible barbed wire.

Cattle numbers had increased rapidly; 100,000 head were feeding on the Canadian ranges south of the Bow River. Unfortunately, however, the summer having been hotter and drier than usual, some ranges showed signs of overstocking and overgrazing. Equally serious was the fact that only a few cattlemen had hay in stacks; many of them didn't even own mowers, hayracks and pitchforks.

"Ah don' lak t' be sad," John Ware told the boss in mid-November, "but ah've a mise'able feelin' in ma bones that ol man Winta's got it in fo us this yeah. We've justa nough hay fo the studs an a bit mo in case theah's some sick cwitters. Gollyme, boss, do you think yo could buy us a lil mo hay in case we have twoubles?"

Barter listened with silence betraying an anxiety he had recently come to share. "Damn it, John," he said finally, "we might have made more hay, but it's too late now and you can't buy the stuff today — unless you're willing to pay a fancy price like twenty dollars a load. No, I reckon we'll just take our chances like every other cowman between here and the boundary. But I wish we'd get a spell of warm days. Those young things from Manitoba are getting thin and it's too early for that."

"Ah'm worried bout ma own lil bunch a cattle scatte'ed all the way to Montana. If ah evah have a place of ma own, ah'll sho wide he'd on my own cwitters so ah'll know wheah they ah. An, Boss, ah'm wo'ied about yo bawlin little cow cwitters f'om Manitoba," John added. "Wheah is that place, Manitoba? Betta get these cwazy lil cattle gathe'ed up, ah'd say, cause theah's gona be anotha stom in about five days."

"Storm? In five days? What are you talking about?"

John's face was serious as he leaned momentarily on a six-tined fork behind the stallions. "Didn yo see that wing wound the old moon last night, Boss? An just five stahs inside that wing? Five days they'll be a stom."

Barter chuckled. He knew all the weather signs observed by Ireland's superstitious people — but did not believe in them. "Maybe those stars mean five weeks or five months till the next storm," he said jokingly.

But strangely enough, snow was falling heavily four days later, and then a wind arose to wrap the foothills and plains in blizzard. Hardy western cattle shook their long-horned heads and looked for shelter along the river, while the soft and infantile specimens from Manitoba and Ontario seemed ready to drift like tumbleweeds in a wind. Having neither fear nor cow sense, they refused to be turned or guided by men on horses. Now, with snow on their backs, icicles dangling from their nostrils, and expressions of hopelessness in their eyes, they scattered aimlessly in a southerly direction.

Cowboys tried to turn them and drive them to shelter along the river, but when one of the dogie cattle was being turned, a hundred others were going their separate and aimless ways with the snow-laden wind.

"We weren't doing a thing except wearing out our horses," a new hand explained that night. "Might as well have been trying to round up coyotes. We might as well sit here till the storm quits and then we'll have a chance to get those fool cattle back. But, by the way, where's that big slave tonight?"

Barter replied: "John Ware, you mean? Why do you say 'slave'? Sure he was a slave but that's no reflection on him. And sure, he's colored but what's wrong with being born that way? By God, don't you or anybody else in my employ speak disrespectful of John. Show me a white man who's half as good and I'll hire him too. But if you fellows who gave up and came home in the storm today want to know where he is, I'll tell you; he rode to the Highwood Crossing. The big stallion's been having colic off and on all day and John insisted he'd get some linseed oil and turpentine for him. I told him I'm paying some men who'd let a stud die before they'd ride in that storm. You might just consider that before you cast any reflections on John. But I hope he won't try to come back till the wind goes down."

It was sixteen miles by trail from Quorn Ranch to the Crossing on the Highwood but on this day, even with the wind blowing from the rear, it seemed more like twenty-six. John's choice of a mount for the trip was a mare known as Molly — big, white and awkward. Stamina would count for much on a journey like this, and Molly was thought to possess it.

With no beaten path to follow and no opportunity to travel faster than a walk, the mare took four and a half hours to cover the ground to the Crossing.

"What in tarnation brings you here on a day like this?" Buck Smith exclaimed after John had tied his weary horse in Smith's stable to feed on a big ration of oats, and then presented himself inside the stopping place in the hope of securing some food for himself.

"Gotta sick stallion at home," John replied while rubbing his cold hands. "Need some tu'pentine and oil fo him. But will yo give me a little bit a bwead and tea an then ah'll get ma oil and start home."

"Start back? Tonight? Man, you're locoed! You'd be stiffer'n a frozen carrot by morning. You'd never get there in a night like this. Hell, no, John; I'm not letting you leave here tonight. There's a spare buffalo robe — biggest one in the house — I shot that bull through the eye when he was charging me. You can make a bed on the floor and start north in daylight. As a matter of fact, you were damned lucky to get down here alive. Now get your oil and turps fixed up tonight, and you can make an early start in the morning — if the storm lets up by then. Now mind what I'm telling you and no arguing."

The warmth from Buck Smith's potbellied stove was as acceptable as nuts to a hungry squirrel, and John remained close to the heat while he munched a meal of tea, bread and cold beef. He mumbled something about Eagle Plume, the sick stud, but knew very well that Smith's advice was right. It would be folly to start back before the light of morning and perhaps never succeed in delivering the turps and oil.

"Ah s'ppose yo' wight, Mistah Buck," he said, stirring his tea with his jackknife. "Ah'd lak to be goin but ah'll stay till mo'nin. Ah must leave ea'ly though. Ah'll just go now and give ma Molly hoss some hay and get ma jugs filled an then ah'll woll up in that buffalo skin and do some of the dangdest sno'in yo evah hea'd.

Before the first rays of morning light, John was up and lighting a lantern in order to feed Molly. The weather had changed without improving. The previous day's wind, which John said was "the laziest ah evah saw — wouldn't go wound a fellow; just wanted to blow wight th'ough," had subsided and visibility was more favorable but the snow was deeper and the frost more intense. The sixteen-mile ride would, at best, be a hardship. John knew he'd have no trouble finding his way; but with so much snow, the journey would be slower and more tedious than ever. Moreover, there were the jugs of oil and turpentine, one to be tied on each side of the saddle; and they'd add to awkwardness and difficulty in travel.

Hurriedly John devoured the bread and prunes and tea Buck Smith set for his breakfast, and minutes later turned his saddled mare's head northward and waved farewell.

Bareheaded and shivering, Buck Smith watched as John's horse labored through the drifts, one heavy step at a time. "By gee, I'm not sure he'll get through to the Quorn," he whispered to himself. "I'm not sure a horse can carry that load and fight sixteen miles of snow and drifts too. But John knows he can come back here if he can't get through."

It was just as tough as Buck Smith surmised.

Molly wanted to go home; but she was still tired from the hardships of the previous day, and three miles away from the river the mare stopped, needing a rest. John dismounted, rubbed the icicles from her face and said, "Molly, yo old scamp; yo got a long way to go. Yo shouldn' get ti'ed yet."

Another two miles and Molly was again showing signs of fatigue and begging for a rest.

John was puzzled. Was this horse sick too? Or was the hardship of plunging through soft snow, with a heavy man on her back, just too much for a saddle horse? In any case, progress would be slow. At this rate of travel and the necessity of periodic delays for rest, John knew he'd be fortunate to be back at the Quorn by nightfall.

It was close to midday when man and mare stopped for the third time. John's fingers were now numb from cold, and Molly was coming ever closer to exhaustion. The mare's head, with frosted whiskers, seemed at times to be dragging in the snow, and her ears flopped irresponsively. Moreover, there was no shelter along the trail and no food for man or beast. Molly might have performed some equine pawing to reach snow-covered grass, but she was totally uninterested in anything calling for physical effort.

For the first time on the trip, John was worried. He was still six or seven miles from home and his mare was playing out. Of course, he could abandon the horse and all the animal was carrying, and walk on to save himself from freezing, but that wouldn't be good; he wanted to complete a task, to deliver mare and saddle and crocks of colic cure. New urgency spawned in his thought. Violently he swung his arms against his body and ran in a small circle to improve circulation of the blood to his cold extremities. Then, cutting the rest period to a few minutes, John shouted, "Come on, ol Molly, yo gotta try it again."

Back in the saddle, John concluded that his mare was refreshed. But any revival of strength which might have been noticeable was brief. Before going half a mile, Molly's steps were again becoming short and the poor brute was stumbling. The situation was now perfectly clear; with a heavy man and some crocks on her back — 300 pounds at least — and bad footing, the mare would not make it to Sheep Creek. And even without a man on her back, the outcome was doubtful.

At that moment John spotted the forms of two animals, with coats filled with snow, in a nearby clump of trees. He wanted to know more about them. Leaving Molly to stand and rest, he walked toward the objects and at once recognized them as red yearling heifers. Just as he had suspected, they were two of the stupid young cattle brought from the East and wearing the Quorn's Z brand. Objects of pity, the heifers were half-perished and half-starved. Momentarily John forgot about the seriousness of his own plight. He wanted to drive the heifers back to the ranch headquarters, but that would be impossible. Recognizing the futility of trying to save the yearlings, he considered using the revolver he carried on his belt and ending their suffering — but he reminded himself that the boss should be consulted before such drastic steps were taken.

When John returned to his horse, the unhappy creature was lying in the snow, satisfied to remain there and freeze. "Wall bless ma soul, Molly. Yo sick o' jus done out? Guess ah'm going to have to leave yo heah and tak myself home without yo. Gollyme, ah hate to do this, Molly, but ah can't see anything else to do."

John loosened and removed the saddle, placed it to one side in the snow, picked up the crocks — one in each hand — and strode away, taking as long strides as deep snow would permit. He'd make better time this way and be sure of getting to the ranch before dusk. But after going a few hundred yards he looked back, saw Molly's head raised inquiringly, and thought he could detect a pleading in the animal's eyes.

"Gollyme — ah can't do this," John said to himself while turning in his tracks. "Ah can't leave that ol hoss theah to fweeze. Maybe she can walk in ma twacks and we'll both get home."

Backtracking, John urged Molly to get up; and then, taking the reins as lead lines, he tugged gently, saying, "Come on, ol scamp, yo can make it if yo got nobody t' cawy on yo back."

Molly did follow, not very briskly, about like a man carrying a sack of potatoes through a pool of mud. But it was all right; and weighted down with oil and turpentine, John wasn't anxious to make fast time through the unbroken and unmarked sea of snow.

There was another halt for rest, and another. But even without a rider on her back, the mare's strength was not returning. Her gait was becoming steadily slower, and more and more she was drawing back — almost leaning against John's hold on the lead straps. And even John, with his well-nigh superhuman strength, was getting tired.

A few minutes before sundown the Quorn workers saw the figure of a big man, jugs in his hands, more or less pulling the exhausted horse through the snow.

Barter rushed out to take the heavy containers from John's near frozen hands. "Thought you'd know enough to stay at the Crossing till weather was better," Barter scolded. "Don't know whether you're a hero or a fool, John — blamed if I do. But if you weren't even stronger than a horse, by God you never would have made it. And you'd carry those bloody crocks! Carry them!"

"Sho did, Mistah Boss. That's tu'ps an oil fo ol Eagle Ploom. That's what ah went fo an ah wasn comin home without what ah went fo. How's ma ailin stud hoss?"

The stallion, Barter reported, was still experiencing spells of colic. "But see here, John, you go right to the house and get thawed out and get some food into you. They boys'll take care of the horse."

"Oh no boss — ah'll see ol Molly gets some feed afo ah do. An ah wants to give that stud some stuff f'om those cwocks. Then ah'll eat."

"Damnest fellow I ever saw," Barter remarked, half in admiration and half in annoyance at this man who should be at the point of collapse. "Pull a horse through the snow, carry a load of colic cure from the Crossing, go all day without eating, and still in no hurry to take care of himself! Beats all!"

John smiled much as usual and went about the tasks of drenching the ailing Thoroughbred and making sure Molly had plenty of hay and bedding. When there was nothing of consequence left to do, John Ware sauntered to the ranch house to wash and eat and fall asleep on a chair beside the long ranch table.

After being left to sleep, balancing on his chair for an hour, he was awakened by Barter and told to go to bed. In the meantime, as John was quick to observe, somebody had removed his heavy boots and placed on his feet a pair of soft slippers. It was a considerate and kindly thing to do. But who had done it? It was the new ranch hand known as Slim — the one who on the day before had inquired in a tone of disrespect, "Where's that big slave tonight?" The "big slave" had made another conquest.

Sure it was a tough winter and it was just starting. For weeks after the November storm, there was no chinook to ease the cow-country hardship. The snow persisted; and cattle, rustling only a fraction of the feed they needed, grew steadily thinner. Many of the Manitoba dogie cattle were known to be dead already, having drifted and piled up in remote coulees. Some had traveled south to the Bar U and OH ranges, and Fred Ings sent word to the Quorn for somebody to come down and take care of them.

John Ware told Barter he was willing to go if there was a reliable man to tend the horses. The arrangement was made, temporarily, and from the OH headquarters John and Ings rode together and found plenty of the Quorn dogies — many in drifts and too weak to get up. None had enough strength to carry them back to the home quarters. What could be done? Barter had authorized any action John considered proper and John Ware was a man of action. He hated to see an animal in needless pain; and where there seemed to be no hope of saving a steer or heifer, he resorted to his six-shooter and speedily put the animal out of misery.

Christmas and the 1887 New Year came, and still there was no relief such as a good chinook would bring. What little hay was available soared to thirty dollars a ton. Ranchers generally were in trouble, but those near the Highwood and around Medicine Hat and the Cypress Hills were suffering the biggest losses. Near Calgary, where the snow was light, the losses were correspondingly less; and Walter Huckvale, wintering his "fiddleback" cattle on the Blood Reserve, experienced relatively good fortune. But A. E. Cross, having made a beginning on Mosquito Creek, knew that his losses would be around 50 per cent. And Ezra Pearson, at Medicine Hat, lost not only half his cattle but almost lost his own life while traveling in a storm from the "Hat" to his ranch.

At one time, according to Mounted Police estimate, there were 40,000 near-starving cattle within twenty-five miles of Fort Macleod. And the STV outfit south of the Cypress Hills lost nearly all the cattle driven in from Texas just a couple of years before. By February the Quorn men knew that all or nearly all of the Manitoba and Eastern dogie cattle brought to the range in the previous summer were dead. As for

John Ware's friends, John and Mrs. Quirk, they, with Sam Howe's help, kept their herd from disaster by cutting and gathering willow twigs for feed.

Even the wild animals like deer and antelope and rabbits died by the hundreds. Only the Indians and coyotes, eating sumptuously from the thousands of beef carcasses strewing the ranges, fared better than usual. Ranchers found it difficult enough to keep themselves alive at times, and anything resembling optimism had the appearance of being forced and artificial.

Even when winter departed in March there was new trouble for the cattlemen — floods on all the foothills streams, and a drop in cattle prices. All of this, coupled with the foul stench of rotting carcasses rising from the range when weather became warm, intensified the gloom.

The statistics from the spring roundups confirmed the crippling losses. Nobody with cattle on the open range escaped. John Ware's little herd was reduced to half the number branded 9999 in the previous season.

"Is this the end of cattle ranching?" people were asking. Many observers believed it was. "The present blow will hasten the obliteration of the large cattle companies," an editor wrote, and according to another: "The present paralysis of the industry heralds its end."

With the great pessimism pervading the cattle kingdom came a new interest in horses. With an inherent ability to paw their way to grass beneath the snow, horses would be less of a risk than cattle on the Canadian ranges. Stockmen as far away as the foothills nodded understandingly when they heard the story about a Medicine Hat settler who brought his oxen and horses through the winter by tying an ox to each horse and turning all loose. The horses pawed the snow and both oxen and horses got enough grass for survival.

Moreover, there was a promise of a good demand for horses. Farm settlers needed more horses than the farming districts would ever produce; Mounted Police needed them; the British War Department would be looking this way for cavalry horses; and, altogether, it was easy to see the hardy horse stock as offering more than cattle on ranges where winter climate held the seeds of disaster. Horse ranching was bound to profit from the failing popularity of cattle ranching, and the demand for breeding mares improved immediately.

"Guess ah'll get me some hosses," John Ware told Mike Herman. "But ah'm not agoin' t' quit cows. Ah've gotta get me a place wheah ah can cut hay fo bad wintas; an ah've gotta show that an ol slave boy can be a good wancha an a good Canadian. Sho, ah should get me some hosses."

"You've got one you can call your own right now, you know," Barter said. "I'm giving you that Molly mare you carried home through the snow."

John giggled. "Ah didn cawy the white maah home; ah just dwagged her. But thanks, boss, ah'd sho lack t' have a foal f'om Molly an Ol Ploom."

Adam and Eve of the Cattle Kingdom

Many of MacEwan's early sketches became part of book-length accounts later on. This one contributed to the larger work Cornerstone Colony, *the story of the Selkirk settlers. It is an excellent example of the writer "writing to space," that is, trimming his account to fill a page in* The Western Producer *tabloid magazine, leaving room for a title and illustration. All of which was secondary in the writer's mind — entertaining the reader taking first priority. (From* Blazing the Old Cattle Trail, *Saskatoon: Western Producer Prairie Books, 1962.)*

Adam and Eve were the first cattle in the Selkirk Settlement at Red River and, of course, the colonists hoped fervently that they'd be "fruitful and multiply and replenish" the new soil with oxen and milk cows. With three other cattle specimens they may share the distinction of being the first of their race in all the area now marked by four western provinces. Understandably, they were not delivered at the remote point where Winnipeg stands today without great effort and ingenuity.

There is reason to believe that the beginning of the 19th century — a dozen years before the Selkirk colonists arrived — found the present agricultural section of the West a complete vacuum as far as domestic cattle, sheep and pigs were concerned. Beyond the area, Albany Fort may have had a few cattle, sheep and goats surviving from early importations and Moose Factory *Journal* reported the slaughter of two cows and three pigs on March 24, 1783. But those posts were on James Bay and far from the present day farm belt where Indian dogs of many colors and horses held uneasily by horse-stealing tribesmen were the only domestic animals.

In bringing the initial foundations of domestic livestock to the new land, animals could be driven overland or carried in canoes. There was no other way. But one thing was certain: a farming community without cattle and other livestock was unthinkable, especially to settlers with British ideals concerning agriculture. Cattle had to come.

The first of the Selkirk people, under the leadership of Highlander Miles Macdonell, sailed away from Stornoway, Scotland, in July, 1811, leaving behind on the quay, eight young cattle provided by Lord Selkirk. The obstacle to taking the cattle was the necessity of carrying enough fresh water for the long voyage — one which took sixty-one days.

Macdonell and his advanced guard wintered on the cold and inhospitable shores of Hudson Bay and in the spring of 1812, the twenty-two courageous trailblazers started up the Hayes River in their long and shallow canoes, knowing their destination beside the Red River to be some seven hundred land and water miles — including thirty-six portages or carrying places — to the south.

Macdonell had been warned: this was a tricky route with confusing water courses, formidable waterfalls, deep lakes, shallow water with the character of swamps and many miles of fast current demanding the use of tracking lines. But after about two weeks of paddling on rivers and lakes, Macdonell and his men came to Oxford House, a small Hudson's Bay Company trading post encompassed by a sturdy stockade made from upright pine logs with tops sharpened like pencil-points. Built on a grassy hill rising from the shore of Oxford Lake, the setting was a pretty one where about the only noises ever heard were those made by wind or wolves.

The men were still less than halfway to Red River but they stopped to relax and there, to their very great surprise, were two young cattle, a bull and yearling heifer, contradicting their belief that no cattle existed in all of Rupert's Land. Evidently the animals had been brought from the Old Country as calves in the previous year. But where they came from mattered little; the Selkirk men, with the practical minds of Highlanders, were thinking more about the animals' destiny than their origin. Why let these young kye be wasted at a northern trading post when they could serve a most essential purpose in the new farming venture?

The men resolved to take the two cattle along to Red River and the Hudson's Bay Company trader surrendered wisely to the combined determination of twenty-two resolute Scots and Irishmen. The two young cattle — christened Adam and Eve — may have remembered calfhood experiences in boats. Anyway, they accepted the necessity of travelling again and two canoes with a yearling critter in each rode lower than usual in the water. Nobody could overlook the increased danger of upsetting if a bull in a canoe became obstreperous, especially in fast or tricky water.

Fortunately, Adam and Eve, on their best bovine behavior, learned to step into and out of their boats with exercised care and they grazed quietly when men were carrying bales and boats over the numerous portages. No hay was taken from Oxford House and stops — at least two a day — to allow the animals to forage, became routine. Finding satisfactory grazing and suitable places for loading and unloading demanded almost constant attention.

After leaving Oxford House there was the deep water of what the voyageurs called Holey Lake, then a sluggish, grassy section of river and more portages. At Hill Gate, rocky and picturesque cliffs rose sixty or eighty feet to wall the stream for three-quarters of a mile, and at what was called Painted Stone Portage, travellers saw a long, low rock which divided marshy waters flowing respectively to Hayes and Nelson rivers. Indians with spooky superstitions painted the stone and deposited gifts for members of the spirit world in the surrounding water. Such gifts dropped beside the big stone were like premiums on Indian life insurance.

Less than a week after leaving Oxford House, the Selkirk men passed Jack River House on Playgreen Lake and knew that the laborious experiences of portaging were nearly all behind them. The next stop was at the top of Lake Winnipeg and then there was the long stretch of generally still water, terminating at the marshy mouth of Red River. On August 30, exactly fifty-five days after leaving Hudson Bay, Miles Macdonell and his advance guard camped on the banks of the Red River, where Winnipeg stands today. In its primitive state it was no Garden of Eden but, nevertheless, Adam and Eve must have found the grazing far superior to anything they had seen at far-away Oxford House. There, in their new surroundings, they were to bring practical comfort to the settlers arriving a few weeks later.

The following winter was a hard one for both settlers and cattle. It was long and famine was a constant threat. But in the spring of 1813, Peter Fidler, faithful and prolific servant of the Hudson's Bay Company, learned about three other cattle in Rupert's Land, a cow, a bull and a heifer owned by the rival North-West Company at its post on the Assiniboine. Presumably, the cow and bull had been brought as calves from Montreal and the heifer was born in the west country. Anyway, nobody needed such stock as much as the new settlers beside the Red River and Fidler journeyed up the Assiniboine and succeeded in buying the three head for one hundred pounds.

By this time, Eve had a calf and the Selkirk Settlers could count a total of six cattle. These western provinces which today have around five million cattle, may have had exactly six head in that spring of 1813.

But cattle raising was never without disappointments. The bull bought from the North-West Company became vicious and had to be slaughtered in the fall of 1813. That in itself was not serious because the masculine Adam remained to fulfill all duties as head of the herd and bull beef could be used most acceptably by the settlers. But with the approach of spring, Adam yielded to a temptation to wander. Straying from the home corral was a sin long common to bulls and before Adam had time to repent, he was completely lost in the woods south of the settlement.

A search was organized but all efforts to locate the delinquent bull failed. Worried settlers hoped the wayward fellow would wander back in his own good time as he had wandered away, but Adam didn't come back. Nothing was seen of him until break-up on the river when the still-frozen body of a bloated bull was observed floating down the Red on a big cake of ice.

Now, the only herd of cattle in Rupert's Land had no bull and cattle outlook was bleak indeed. Not until after the bloody Battle of Seven Oaks on soil which is now in the city of Winnipeg were cattle numbers augmented. Lord Selkirk's private army on its way from the East to the relief of the oppressed colonists, seized the Rainy Lake Post, property of the hated North-West Company. At that fort, situated in what is now Western Ontario, the soldiers found three oxen, three cows and a young bull. Here were prizes of war, too good to be left behind — almost too good to be true — and plans were made to drive or lead the animals to the Red River.

It was winter. Two of the oxen were shod so that they might assist the five horses already in the party to haul the sleighs. The third ox, unshod, promptly slipped on ice and so injured himself that it was thought wise to slaughter him and salvage the meat. When additional work stock was needed on the trail, the young bull was hitched and even the cows were drafted to do a share in pulling the loaded sleighs.

Finally, the rescue force arrived at Fort Douglas beside the Red River where, according to Professor A. S. Morton (Notes to the author): "The bull and cows, discharged from the army, were now like Adam and Eve of five years back, to multiply and help build a farming community."

But Red River colony seemed a hard country to those pioneers who were planting the seeds of an agricultural industry. The bushel and one-half of seed wheat carried by Macdonell's men and planted beside the river proved unsuitable and the crop did not mature. Wheat planted in 1814 was lost from frost and local warfare between settlers and the Nor'-Westers prevented the harvesting of crops in the next two years. In 1817 it was frost which again destroyed the chance of harvest and then there were two years of grasshopper attack. It would have been easy to conclude that further attempts to till the unfriendly soil were futile.

And success with cattle was proving no better than with wheat.

Before a year elapsed, the Rainy Lake bull was dead and some of the other cattle had been killed and eaten by hungry Indians. When Lord Selkirk visited his colony in 1817, he was visibly disappointed at the absence of progress. There was extremely little to show for those first trying years of farming. Only the big annual harvest of buffalo meat, dried for winter use or blended with crushed saskatoon berries and melted fat to make pemmican, saved the settlers from starvation.

But with Scottish and Irish ideas about good farming practice, the settlers lost none of their longing to have livestock. Cattle could and would mean milk, butter, cheese, meat, draught power and security. Lord Selkirk agreed and admitted that he had already enquired about the possibility of driving a really worthwhile herd from the East or South. He would provide the money for fifty heifers, he said, and a thousand dollars for the expense of bringing them in. It was a prospect appearing almost as attractive to Scottish settlers as Selkirk's promise to send them a Presbyterian minister.

But where within driving distance could such a herd be bought? To drive from Montreal would be nigh impossible. Driving from the South might be easier but nobody was sure the cattle were available there. And where was there a man who cared so little for his own comfort and safety that he would accept the task of finding and delivering a herd — perhaps driving it halfway across the continent?

As for the good cow, Eve, there is reason to believe she was still alive when Selkirk made his visit — also one or two of her offspring — and it may be possible that progeny, far removed, are even today scattered across the farming country.

Pacers and Preachers

When it is made known that MacEwan was brought up in a Presbyterian family, it is often assumed that his early life in Manitoba was a grim and strict affair. This account rectifies that notion. It deals with just such Presbyterians reacting like the good natured humans they were to an otherwise solemn occasion. We are fortunate that the boy who heard the story remembered it and eventually became a writer to put it all down. (From Hoofprints and Hitchingposts, *Saskatoon: Western Producer Prairie Books, 1964.)*

Until gasoline motors brought more speed and more heart failures, roadster horses of Standard Bred type and breeding were considered as sheer necessities — like sheepskin coats in winter and sulphur and molasses tonic in spring. They pulled buggies and cutters over all sorts of roads, hauled doctors, farmers, machinery salesmen and ministers without discrimination. Farmers favored trotters; preachers preferred pacers.

To excel in road speed was everybody's aim. A good horse and shiny buggy with rubber tires placed an owner in a category identified in later years by a Cadillac. And if a man's driver was fast enough to pass other nags on the trail or in a matched race, so much the better.

Racing was a popular pastime in every community. In the absence of something better by way of race tracks, town and city thoroughfares were the scenes of rousing contests. Editors raised protests against street racing on the pretext of danger to pedestrians and local governments piously passed bylaws to make it illegal but policemen looked the other way and speeding continued. Anyway, who was to say that two trotters or pacers dashing up the Avenue — neck and neck — were not taking their drivers for emergency calls at the doctor's office?

Winnipeg's Main Street was a favorite meeting place for horsemen and warnings like the one issued by the Winnipeg *Sun*, August 17, 1881, went unheeded: "Some measures will have to be adopted to check driving in this city. Some gentlemen sporting fast horses indulge in a rate of speed on our principal streets which may be fun for them but terribly dangerous to pedestrians."

At Moosomin, ever a horse-loving community, the racing crowd practically took over the main street each day at noon, now and then varying the program, as on "Wednesday last" when, according to the Moosomin *Courier* of October 9, 1884, "Mr. Arnold of Ellice and a Moosomin sport got into a race, the Moosomin man betting $100 that Mr. Arnold's native pony could not trot to Ellice in three hours and a quarter, a distance of thirty miles. The Shaganappie took the money, with fifteen minutes to spare."

And at Brandon where horses ranked next to home cooked meals in filling men's lives, a race could start on Rosser Avenue at any daylight hour. Citizens would leave their work to watch the trotters and pacers display their courage and watch the horsemen add to their reputations. Sometimes the Brandon stakes were high, as when J. D. McGregor brought in the successful trotter, Dalton McCarthy. But pioneers recalled another McGregor horse which won more fame than success, this a California trotter with fashionable pedigree and pronounced disposition to laziness. The only command to bring unfailing obedience was "Whoa" which some transgressor on the sidewalk shouted in the middle of a Victoria Avenue race on one occasion to bring the high priced horse to a dead stop.

Dealing with heavy horses was a major Brandon industry and harness racing was clearly the chief entertainment. Children raced ponies as they drove home from school and fathers raced as they returned from church services or Christian Endeavor. And nobody had a stronger dislike to being passed by a faster horse than the country minister. Understandable was the satisfaction in being able to leave a boastful church elder or smug choir leader behind in dust.

One of those unscheduled races the local people could not forget, took place at a funeral. There were those citizens who considered it disgraceful that a funeral procession would arrive at the graveside in a cloud of dust and feigned a wish to suppress the story. Others, knowing how the deceased farmer loved a horse race, took the view that this manner of conveying the remains to its last resting place was, after all, entirely appropriate. But by whatever moral standard it was judged, it was the most exciting funeral in the history of that rural municipality, with preacher playing the leading role.

A certain Brandon livery firm commonly furnished the horse-drawn hearse for local funerals and one of the partners drove it. A reliable and slow-going team was kept for the purpose but on this occasion the team was not back from a trip to Rapid City. The hearse driver recognized no choice but to hitch a Standard Bred which had seen some racing along with a young broncho known to be without moral compunction.

The funeral service was to be conducted at the farm home of the deceased and burial at the country church cemetery another two miles beyond. With country road to himself, the experienced teamster had no difficulty in handling the obstreperous horses. At the farm, he might have stabled the team until the service had ended but hoping to eliminate unrest that could result from a strange stable, he decided to keep the horses hitched and simply drive them around the yard now and then to relieve excesses of nervous tension.

The service was long, or so it seemed to a man who had cause to be anxious about the behavior of his horses. With foamy sweat dripping from its overheated belly, the broncho member reared time and again but the driver consoled himself with the thought that when back on the road, the animals would settle down and show some semblance of respect for the occasion.

Finally the service ended and with proper solemnity the coffin was placed in the hearse. But the growing stir caused the unhappy horses to become more fractious. Then there was further delay while neighbors hitched to buggies, carts and democrats. The hearse would lead the slow-moving parade and the Presbyterian minister, driving his own horse, would be next in line, then mourners and others.

The hearse driver felt relief when the minister, with the air of a commanding officer, gave the instructions to move. The procession started with dignity befitting the sad moment although the hearse driver was not finding it easy to hold his team to a slow gait; the Standard Bred's instinct was to trot and the broncho's to run. Nobody in the long cavalcade of vehicles was worried however because the liveryman was known to be one of the best teamsters in the community.

But as events were to show, it was too soon for complacent thinking and at the moment the nervous young broncho on the off side turned his head to glance past bridle blinkers and see the great line of vehicles in pursuit, he reared and lunged forward while his Standard Bred mate showed no disposition to stay behind.

Despite the driver's best efforts, the hearse was now rolling forward at a disrespectfully fast rate. The minister's pacer, ever ready for a race and forgetting the funeral atmosphere, dashed ahead, overcoming any indifferent restraint from the reverend gentleman holding the reins. Those who followed could see no reason for a big gap in the procession and the pace quickened all along the line.

But the forward end of the procession was holding the centre of interest. With the minister's own horse gaining ground, the task of holding the hearse team became nigh impossible. The Standard Bred on the nigh side accepted this as a race; the broncho regarded it as a runaway and, either way, the teamster was having trouble. But the minister's noble pacer, knowing the shame of taking dust from other wheels on the trail, forged forward with the best of intentions. Torn between two instincts, the urge to race being slightly stronger, the churchman made an impressive show of inability to hold his fast horse. But how ineffective it was!

Any way one looked at it, here was a horse race and those who where far behind felt a stong desire to advance sufficiently to witness the finish. All along the line, buggy whips were taken from their holsters and applied to horses showing signs of lagging. Nobody wanted to be left behind.

At the forward end, where the principal contestants were now close together, dust was rising in generous clouds. As the hearse sped over rough spots on the road, the coffin and contents bounced until there was every prospect of it leaving the vehicle and coming to rest on the trail. The dead homesteader had taken part in a fair number of races but never one as closely contested or as eagerly followed by his neighbors as this.

The hearse team had the centre of the road and was showing no inclination to share it. The minister's horse had the left ditch, with two wheels on the unmarked sod. The buggy was coming alongside. Now the three horses were exactly abreast with still a quarter of a mile to the graveside.

By this time, no spectator could have been certain whether the community's spiritual leader was pulling or pressing forward on the reins he held, but with jaws clamped securely together, lower jaw protruding slightly, his august black beard swaying in the wind, plug hat tilted forward to anchor it on his head, and one foot braced against the metal foot-rest, he was driving like a master and revealing as little as possible of what was passing through his mind. It was a reasonable conclusion that he was not rehearsing his graveside committal.

There were now two questions in every mind: who would win the race and could the leading horses be stopped at the cemetery? For answers, nobody would have long to wait. The horses were tiring but if the drivers were suffering from anything more than race track emotion, they were not revealing it.

With a hundred yards to go, the wild pace was scarcely slackened and the leaders were still travelling neck to neck. But the experience of some other roadside races in which the ministerial gentleman had taken part was not wasted and he and his pacer were saving something for the last dash. Smoothly and expertly, the minister moved into the lead, made a gentle swing into the graveyard, crossed an imaginary line beside the open grave and was undisputed winner by half a length. From those close enough to witness the finish came a shout which on such premises at any other time would have suggested nothing less than the resurrection morning. It was a cheer for the minister and his roadster.

If anybody had a fear about a crisis at the end of the drive it was quickly dispelled. The winner made a loop turn to the right and came to a stop beside the open grave. With the same sort of expert driving the hearse team made a loop turn the other way and stopped like gentle horses at the allotted spot.

There was still the burial. Some of those in attendance seemed to have lost interest. As the mourners and others assembled at the graveside it was not easy for the minister's admiring friends to contain themselves in silence while the last rites were performed. It was probably no easier for the minister to forget his roadside victory and devote his thoughts to the solemn responsibilities.

There were those who took a dim view of the day's events but before the drive home was commenced, the minister's pacer was receiving embraces rather than punishment. The reverend gentleman had no comment but when a horse trade was suggested, he replied: "No thanks, not even if you throw in the Pearly Gates."

Professor to Politician

Rarely has MacEwan written so personally and at such white heat as in the following excerpt. It is of interest not only because of this revelation but also because it describes a situation that will seem strange to the contemporary reader, impossible as it is today. It was also the prelude to possibly the most far reaching failure in the writer's life. (From Poking into Politics, *Edmonton: Institute of Applied Art, 1966.)*

Politics, like certain varieties of worldly wickedness, held undeniable attraction for me but, as I discovered, active participation while pursuing an academic career was not as simple as smoking cedar bark behind the barn. My University employer, like the Civil Service and the business community did not want its servants dabbling conspicuously in politics. Between the University and the practice of party politics there existed a great gulf; compatability ranked with that of Capitalism and Communism and there was no hope of a young fellow being both a professor and a politician. It could be one or the other — certainly not both.

When I accepted a post on the staff of the University of Saskatchewan in 1928, I knew I would be expected to keep politics well to myself. As might have been expected, however, a University man in the public gaze was sure to be confronted with opportunities for political pursuit. I was invited to stand for nomination in the Federal Constituency of Melfort; later, to enter provincial politics by accepting a post in the Saskatchewan Government and run for a seat at Kinistino. The next invitation was to lead the revamped Conservative movement in Saskatchewan and, still later, when associated with the University of Manitoba, to accept the portfolio of Agriculture in the Manitoba Government and seek a seat in the Legislature through a by-election to be arranged.

In each instance, the attraction was great but to have accepted would necessitate a complete break with University work because University Boards of Governors took a dim view of professors and deans being mixed up with anything which might bring needless controversy to the institutions of learning. Moreover, it was a popular concept that any University professor who would consider leaving the gentle environment for the roughhouse of politics was either radical or crazy. University Governors wanted their men all to themselves or wanted no part of them. Having a professor or dean making political speeches would not do at all. When Professor Frank Scott of the McGill Law Faculty was National Chairman of the C.C.F., Governors squirmed and passed an extraordinary resolution, emphasizing that an active part in party politics by a faculty member was "not in the best interests of the University."

That it might have been in the best interests of the nation to encourage more trained minds in politics did not seem to be considered. Had those University-employed men like Hon. John Bracken who became Premier of Manitoba and then national leader of the Progressive Conservative Party, Dr. Sidney Smith who entered the Federal Government as Minister of External Affairs and Hon. Milton Gregg who went from the presidency of the University of New Brunswick to the Federal Government been imprisoned in the ivory towers, Canada would have been poorer. It may be understandable that University Governors do not want their people to be serving two masters, but the great injustice was in the rule that when a faculty man went actively into politics, he was considered beyond readmittance to academic life.

Anyway, after 23 years in the shelter of two western Universities, I faced another challenge and, this time, with full understanding of the impact upon my career, I plunged headlong into the muddy waters of politics.

Some of my friends could see a dozen reasons — all practical and valid — why I should not accept nomination in the federal by-election at Brandon. As a Member of Parliament, which high office I expected to gain, I would receive less annual salary than as Dean of Agriculture at the University of Manitoba. Worse still was the sure promise that transformation from a University Dean to a common politician would be unbecoming, equivalent to demotion from rank of Colonel to that of Sergeant.

I understood all that. I knew that I could have continued at my old post with loyal people on my staff and have lived comfortably until superannuated. I could recall my father's dictum that to render the highest in public service to the nation, one must become active in politics and to achieve the ultimate in easy living, one must stay out of it.

My friends were not in agreement. Perhaps I should have known better than to seek the advice of a man who had been in the House of Commons for 20 years. If it followed that politics has a hardening and evil effect upon a man, this politician friend should have been a hardened sinner. After two hours of discussion, I asked bluntly: "If you were in my place, what would you do?" His answer was not the one I expected. He replied in three words: "Grant, I'd pray."

Well, I accepted nomination at what the Brandon people said was the best political meeting they could recall. It was a good sign and my election was said to be certain. Immediately, my incoming mail mounted. Of scores who wrote to express their views about my impending change of life, over half offered congratulations, 15 percent said the rough equivalent of "a sad mistake," or "you should have known better," and the balance simply hoped for the best. One of those correspondents wrote: "Dear Grant, I once thought you were too honest for politics but now that I know you better, I think you will do just fine."

Some of the letters reminded me once again how reckless and unjust is much of the common criticism directed at public officials and how totally inadequate the thanks to leaders and governments when a job is well done. Said one of my correspondents: "Grant, your work has been with scholarly University people. Do you think you can adapt yourself to the roughnecks in Government?" And still another said: "Politicians, with very few exceptions, are ignorant and stupid and most of the clever ones are rogues."

The friend who pleased me most, wrote: "Grant MacEwan, you'll need your mother's faith, your father's courage, Sir John A. Macdonald's sense of humor, and you'll have my prayers." The same writer guessed that I would regret the decision to exchange the cozy shelter of a University for an exposed position on the "firing line" of public life.

"But we've heard it so often," my friend continued, philosophically, "that not enough people possessing training and leadership and a zeal for just administration go into politics. It's really not surprising, though, when you consider how damned miserable we make it for public figures, no matter how much they try to do the right thing. You will probably discover that even your noble University institution will forget its favorite platitudes about Democracy and service to country when you formally enter that uncertain and thankless business of serving the nation. Don't be surprised if you are whisked out of the University as though you had been convicted of treason."

Events moved quickly. I was soon to discover the real power of politics. It had taken many years of intensive study and specialization to get into University work but two working days of politics were enough to get me out.

The press reported that MacEwan was being approached to accept nomination for the forthcoming by-election and University Governors were filled with horror at the thought. Not waiting for my decision about acceptance of such a challenge, the uneasy Board members met and ruled that if and when such nomination is confirmed, the Dean's resignation would be accepted "ipso facto." Not being particularly proficient in Latin, I consulted my friend, the University Controller, whose command of the classical language was no better than my own. But he had been present at the Board meeting and I enquired: "Walter, if I accept, I must resign. That's understood. But what do they mean by 'ipso facto'?"

The Controller looked solemn and replied in words I could comprehend: "It means you resign damned fast."

The University President wrote me a delightful letter, told how magnificent I had been but said nothing to change a conviction that with the taint of politics upon my character, I could never return to the University. A father may take back a prodigal son and the church will accept a backsliding sinner but for a proud University, a politician would be forever an outcast.

I gathered books and personal files, said "good bye" to colleagues and, with a certain feeling of guilt, escaped by way of a back door. Perhaps I had made a mistake; perhaps the 23 years of University work had reinforced my need for security, making me unfit to live without it. But I reminded myself that too much security may be like too much rich food. The University experience had been good but it would be invigorating to live dangerously for a while.

In policy toward employee participation in politics, the Universities were not alone. Most business executives, although free with their criticism of government, refused to enter openly into politics and refused to allow their employees to accept nominations. They would contribute to campaign funds and furnish behind-the-scenes assistance but shrink with horror at the prospect of offending customers by openly supporting one candidate or another. Fortunately, there were exceptions; the Ford Motor Company and Bell Telephone Company of Canada were examples of organizations taking a broad and generous view of political participation. The latter company, in its manual, says the organization itself cannot be involved but individual employees may take active parts in government and in political parties of their choices, even to the point of running for office. The granting of leave of absence for the purpose of holding office would be considered.

Politically minded employees who have been told to forget politics or resign, found satisfaction in Province of Quebec legislation of 1965 to protect individuals running for public office. Under the amendment to the Quebec Election Act, employee candidates can claim leave of absence without pay for the period of the campaign and cannot be dismissed for participation. An infraction would make employers liable to fine or imprisonment.

Obviously, the Quebec legislators entertained less fear of politicians and more respect for them than the University Governors had shown. The legislators stood by a principle. If our way of government is so important, it becomes a serious matter to deprive anybody of full rights of citizenship or to discourage anybody from accepting fullest democratic responsibilities.

In any case. I had taken the precarious plunge from high on the Ivory Tower into the polluted pool of politics.

Loaned for a Season

MacEwan began writing about conservation when it was a word strange to the ear of the general public. In this excerpt he reveals the origin and inspiration of his deep interest in a subject that has occupied his thoughts and writings over the years. (From Entrusted to My Care, *Saskatoon: Western Producer Prairie Books, 1966.)*

According to an Oriental proverb, "God will not enquire of thy birth, nor will He ask thy creed. Alone He will ask: 'What hast thou done with the land I loaned thee for a season?'"

If natural resources are on loan, much of the accounting will bring no compliments to the borrowers. On his longtime record, man will appear as a careless fellow, a waster and a predator. It has suited his arrogance to believe he was created to have "dominion over the fish of the sea and over the fowl of the air and over every living thing that moveth upon the earth." Having inherited special privileges, why shouldn't he be free to amend Nature's laws and consume Nature's bounty to suit his convenience, pleasure and lust for luxury?

To enjoy the full benefit of an exalted position, he plundered soil, grass, trees, minerals, wildlife and other natural gifts, forgetting that they were his "for a season" only. Knowing his life span was short, haste seemed imperative. That succeeding generations with expanding populations would have more rather than less need, conveniently escaped his notice.

To give his exploits a mantle of respectability, he called it development but went right ahead to market natural gas as though the product sealed in rock for millions of years should be liquidated in a generation or two, as though it was perfectly right to take Niagara peach land for industrial use or take as much as possible from agricultural soils while returning little.

It doesn't mean that Nature's treasure has been suddenly or drastically depleted. Notwithstanding what happened to passenger pigeons, Eskimo curlews, cedars of Lebanon, soils of North Africa, blue whales and the mines of Rome, rich resources remain. It would seem that greedy humans failed to discover all of them or found themselves incapable of eating all, selling all or burning all.

It is wrong to suppose the world was created primarily to serve mankind's purposes and pleasures. A conviction about having dominion over land and water and living things breeds ideas of unwarranted self-importance, even worship of self more than the Creator. It's a sobering thought that man's place in Nature's scheme is, after all, a small one. If through war or disease or race suicide, human kind were to disappear from the earth, there is no reason to believe the remaining species of plants and animals and the planet itself would not go along fully as well, perhaps better than before. Spring would follow winter as usual; plants would grow and seed and die as always; ducks would nest in the North and winter in the South and, apart from a few parasitic animals like English sparrows and Norway rats, no living creatures would miss the absence of humans any more than the Labrador duck is missed. Man is not an essential spoke in Nature's balance wheel. If anything, his predations and greed have made him a disturbing force more than a balancing influence.

More than any other animal, man is a stranger and foreigner in Nature's community. He's the one guilty of leaving parts of the earth in waste; he's the trouble-maker, the one inspiring the most fear and terror in fellow-creatures. If the wild things could speak, they'd agree; the sight or smell of man is enough to send any wild animal to flight. From the time the civilizing white man arrived on the North American continent, many wild things have been trying to escape from him — like grizzly bear and whooping crane — retreating farther back to avoid his dangerous and repulsive ways.

Nor is there reason to think that people of modern times have found a much better conscience towards resources. History may have some harsh things to say about the present generation. As world population goes from three billion to four billion and then five billion and the planet becomes more and more like a human anthill, wise use of resources becomes a matter of ever greater urgency. The prospects for grandchildren and great grandchildren are ever more uncertain. A benevolent philosophy of conservation should be cultivated.

But what is the meaning of conservation? The "developers," eager to make their millions, the trigger-happy hunters and the aspostles of unrestricted free enterprise continue, in many cases, to misconstrue the meaning. They have been inclined to look upon those taking up the challenge of conservation as hoarders and misers. But nobody suggests that resource gifts should remain untouched. They are for using. Hoarding would be folly. Conservation means managing resources so they will continue to support the human family. Envisaged is a state of harmony between people and the natural treasures around them. In contrast to exploitation for the sake of getting rich quickly, conservation means using in such a way that resources will bring the greatest good for the greatest number. The conservationist is not a miser, not a hoarder, not an apostle of gloom; rather, he holds to the wisdom of Nature's time-tested order and believes that a generation occupying but a speck in eternity's span should work with Nature, not against.

Surely it could not have been part of the Master Plan that natural resources should be consumed or plundered by the first generation of human creatures to discover or reach them. Recognizing responsibilities to generations yet unborn, thoughtful people will demand the renewing of renewables like soils and forests, and the administering of non-renewables so they will serve mankind to the best possible advantage. What greater challenge than that of bringing wise and generous guardianship to the natural heritage?

Much of the achievement in rapid development of North American resources was at a high price in waste. Nobody can condone waste and extravagance in resources, even though reckless haste may enlarge the immediate dividends. Canadians saw irretrievable waste in various fields of resource exploitation but in a period of enthusiastic expansion, the voice of the conservationist was lost. Men in a hurry to recover fortunes saw no wrong in slashing forests, flaring gas from oil wells and selling birds by the barrel; and others in the new land were so overwhelmed by a false concept of inexhaustibility that they remained silent.

The fact is that every year since the white man forced his ways upon a simple but lasting Indian order on this continent, there has been some shrinking in the "bank account" of resources, even the renewable kinds for which nothing less than production on a sustained yield basis should be demanded.

Little wonder that the aged Indian at Sault Ste. Marie had strong feelings when he watched white men rushing to his part of the country to stake uranium claims. "White man," he was reported as saying in amazement, "come long ago and take all the beaver furs and other furs; come back and build sawmill and take all the big trees; come back still later and build a pulp mill and take all the small trees; now, he comes again to take the rocks."

There is a moral side to it. Indeed, conservation is largely a matter of morals. It is agreed that the man who deliberately contributes to human hardship and poverty by any means is an immoral fellow, a knave and sinner. Is he less the sinner if he makes it difficult for his fellow humans of a generation hence — or five generations hence? Are the horse thieves any more guilty than men, who by greed or carelessness, would take bread from the mouths of grandchildren or deprive them of trees or natural gas or whooping cranes or clean water or some natural land-scape?

For that matter, are the horse thieves guilty of any more serious crimes than those people who would pass on to future generations huge burdens of public debt with less of resources from which to make the payments?

Perhaps man's highest purpose is in the role of guardian or caretaker of Nature's gifts, "loaned for a season." Ruskin seemed to agree, saying: "God has lent us the earth for our life. It is a great entail. It belongs as much to those who come after as to us and we have no right, by anything we do or neglect, to involve them in any unnecessary penalties, or deprive them of benefit which was in our power to bequeath."

The principle is the same as that which guided one of the conscientious pioneers in Canadian agriculture. His highest worldy purpose, he confessed, was to try by all the means in his power to leave things better than he found them. If that proved impossible, he would at least leave everything entrusted to his care with the very minimum of deterioration. That was the way he conducted his farming and used his fields. When asked: "What hast thou done with the land I loaned thee for a season?" he would be able to reply that after using his fields for most of a lifetime, they were as productive as when he grew his first homestead crops. His guiding purpose — striving to leave things better than he found them — was close to the Golden Rule.

The cause of conservation is not exciting or glamorous, like guiding rockets through the unknown reaches of space but, for the human family, it may be more important than winning the race to the moon. It invites the support of intelligent and reasonable people. If certain of the tragedies which overtook a score of ancient nations are to be avoided in the western world, a philosophy of wise and conscientious use of soil and other resources must be adopted and followed — before it is too late.

In opening the Resources For Tomorrow Conference in Montreal in October, 1961, Hon. Walter Dinsdale, Minister of Northern Affairs and National Resources, said: "Man, because of his egocentricity, is inclined to take a short-sighted view of things. To use the vernacular, 'he wants what he wants when he wants it.' Yet, here we have a group of Canadian leaders deeply concerned about the future. Surely, this is an encouraging development in the Canadian body politic for, in the final analysis, conservation is a moral issue, as all issues are moral issues.

"It is a particularly significant development in a country like Canada where, up until recently, we have been motivated by a frontier philosophy in our exploitation of resources. In North America, there have always been new worlds to conquer, whereas, the truth of the matter is that we are now well on the way to occupying our last frontier, the huge, vast territory 'North of Sixty.' Perhaps it is this new northern orientation which, for the first time, has made us aware that, even in God's own country, the natural endowment is neither inexhaustible nor indestructible."

Gold in the Interior

While MacEwan wrote mainly of the western prairies, he also on occasion stepped across the border and dealt with British Columbia as this excerpt reveals. All the elements he prefers are here — the Overlanders, the riverboats, and the rough frontier and the courageous characters it attracted. (From A Short History of Western Canada *by J. W. Grant MacEwan and Maxwell Foran, Toronto: McGraw-Hill Ryerson, 1968. Reprinted by permission of McGraw-Hill Ryerson Limited.)*

British Columbia gold became a topic of conversation for the first time in 1850, when a discovery was reported in the Queen Charlotte Islands. More important and fantastic, however, were stories from the Interior, telling of Indians who had taken nuggets to Hudson's Bay Company posts, offering to trade them for beads.

The discovery strike was made at Hill's Bar on the Fraser, between Fort Yale and Fort Hope, in March 1858. This was the placer works which filled men with dreams of riches and started the famous rush. During the last half of the year, the Hill's Bar sand yielded over a half a million dollars in gold.

News travelled slowly at a time of primitive communications, but stories of gold on the Fraser and its tributaries ultimately reached distant parts, and people of many races prepared to seek their fortunes. Thousands came from San Francisco and other points in the United States; some came from England, Scotland, and Ireland, sailing round the southern tip of South America and up the west coast; others came from Upper and Lower Canada and Nova Scotia by various routes. At least 25,000 of them came to a part of the world which was far from being ready to receive them. There had been nothing quite like the gold rush to the Cariboo.

The incoming miners went from one river bar to another, prospecting and panning. A few were striking it rich, while the majority were recovering less than enough to pay their expenses. One of the strikes widely discussed at the time was at William's Creek, where William

Dietz was the discoverer. In two years, almost four million dollars' worth of gold was taken from William's Creek area alone. Still, the search spread and important finds were reported from Vancouver Island, Okanagan Valley, and points well to the north.

News of fresh discoveries reached the outside and the rush revived. The new interest was in William's Creek, and wave upon wave of fortune-seekers came in. Men in the Canadian East and the eastern United States sensed a possible advantage in a direct route across the continent. They could travel by rail to St. Paul in Minnesota, by stage coach to a point on the Red River, and then by steamboat to Fort Garry. That was the course chosen by the group known as the Overlanders, but it was not as easy as the map made it appear.

The completely new riverboat, *International,* which was 150 feet long and which drew 42 inches of water, arrived on her maiden voyage in May 1862, with a cargo of freight and a crowd of eager miners on their way to the gold fields of the Cariboo. There, at Fort Garry, about 130 of them, dreaming about scooping up fortunes in gold, prepared for the long and trying trip across a thousand miles of prairies and some hundreds of miles of mountain country.

It was June when they started overland. With an Ontario man, Tom MacMickling, as leader, the party left the Red River settlement in horse-drawn and ox-drawn carts. In the party was one woman, Mrs. August Schubert, with three children. It was a poor place for a woman, but there she was, showing no less courage and determination than the men. They knew there were dangers ahead. The temper of prairie Indians left much to be desired and there was no guarantee of food supplies, but the men were armed and ready to use their guns.

Each night the travellers camped within a circle made by carts. Guards were posted to maintain constant watch for attackers. Each morning at two o'clock, the camp was roused for the day's journey. Periodically, the men hunted buffalo and made pemmican, prairie-style.

The Overlanders reached Fort Edmonton about a month after leaving Fort Garry and faced a delay of several weeks while preparations were made for what was recognized as the most difficult part of the expedition: their advance into and beyond the Yellowhead Pass. Carts and wagons were abandoned in favour of pack horses and pack oxen, 140 animals altogether, each loaded with about 200 pounds of equipment and supplies. By the time they reached the pass, pemmican and other food reserves were depleted, and the travellers were obliged to fall back on meat provided by the slaughter of work oxen.

At this point, they faced an important decision about their route. Indians told them they might follow the Fraser River as it swung northward before bearing south again. Other advice was to go overland and cross some mountains with the idea of coming to another river, the North Thompson. Members of the party could not agree, and they divided their resources, separating into two groups. One group set about building rafts 40 feet in length, with which to float down the Fraser, while the others in the party took the 130 remaining horses and oxen and set out through the forests and over mountain obstacles, heading mainly southward.

Those following the Fraser reached Quesnel on September 11. The others encountered more obstacles, but after rafting down the North Thompson, they arrived at Fort Kamloops on October 13, thankful to be nearing the end of their journey. On the morning after arriving at Kamloops, Mrs. Schubert's new baby was born, the first white child born at that old trading centre.

Altogether, it was a rough trip, and lives were lost on the fast waters of both the Fraser and the Thompson. The original enthusiasm for gold had subsided, although a few of the famous Overlanders continued to the diggings at William's Creek. Some went on to the coast; others settled to farm in the valleys. They had hoped to make a long trip in two months. As it was, the journey which began in June ended almost six months later, rating as one of the most adventuresome in Canadian history.

Barkerville, ultimately the terminus of the wagon road from Yale, was the undisputed capital of the gold rush by the time the Overlanders reached the end of their travels. The famous town took its name from Billy Barker, a sailor who was absent without leave from his ship on the west coast. Luck was with him, however, and after sinking a shaft on a benchland location between the creek and a steep hillside, he took gold said to have been worth half a million dollars. A town sprang up around the shaft, and it was called Barkerville.

One year after the young sailor found wealth, more than 5,000 men were working at or near the fabulous town, and fortunes were being made and lost daily. With the miners came merchants, drifters, gamblers, criminals, and dancing girls, all ready to help the miners get rid of their money. Billy Barker, according to legend, lost his half million dollars, mainly at the bars. People who were there told about a Barkerville man who entered a saloon with $50,000 in his pockets and did not leave the place until the last dollar was spent. Then, no doubt, he went back to shovelling gravel in the hope of finding more gold.

One of the strangest stories from the Cariboo gold diggings concerned John A. Cameron, ultimately known as Cariboo Cameron. From his home in Glengarry, Ontario, he went to the west coast, taking his wife and infant daughter. The little girl died at Victoria, but the parents went inland where Cameron conducted a trading business and then took to mining. The first shaft in which he was interested on William's Creek yielded nothing, but the next one held a vein with a million dollars' worth of gold in it.

Then tragedy struck again. Cameron's wife died, a victim of typhoid fever. Winter was just setting in, but the sorrowing husband was determined to take the body back to Glengarry for burial. It is said that Cameron had the coffin placed in a metal box which could be sealed and instructed that it be hauled on a hand sleigh as far as Beaver Lake where a horse was obtained to pull it the rest of the way to the coast. The coffin reached Victoria in early March, more than four months after the journey was started, and there the metal container was opened, filled with alcohol, resealed, and buried.

After another summer at the mines, Cameron was ready to complete his self-assigned task, and returning to Victoria, he obtained permission to move the remains of his late wife. Accordingly, the coffin was placed on a steamer for the long trip to Montreal and then to Glengarry. There, in the Ontario community, suspicions arose. Mrs. Cameron's father wanted the coffin opened so that he might see his daughter's face again, but Cameron refused to allow it, and the body was buried again. This did not end the rumours that the coffin contained a totally different body than that of the late Mrs. Cameron. There was even some gossip about the bride who went from Glengarry having been sold to an Indian chief. Only after nine years did Cameron agree to having the casket raised for identification. Interest was intense, but when the coffin was opened, there was apparently no doubt that the remains were indeed those of Mrs. Cameron. Again the coffin was buried, but the story of Cariboo Cameron was not forgotten. As for Cameron, he lost his fortune, returned to the Cariboo to hunt for gold, and died there before he found it.

Barkerville retained its place of prominence and its salty characters for a few years, but the town, built on a single street, was never very beautiful. The big buildings, built in a hurry, were not all symmetrical nor level. Shafts in the ground could be seen everywhere, and since diggers dumped clay and tailings in the creek, the dammed-up water might leave its channel and run down the street. No one cared. Some buildings were erected on stilts, and as they settled, they seemed to slouch like carousing miners.

Freight vehicles and beasts of burden must have been about as varied as the personalities seen at Barkerville. Some of the miners walked the 600 miles from the mouth of the Fraser; some went by ship as far as Yale and walked from there or caught a ride on a freight wagon. Some of the wagons were drawn by horses, others by mules or oxen. Mule teams were favoured over horse and ox teams, but in 1862 camels made their appearance: humps, smells, sour faces, and all.

The Cariboo Trail was the only roadway in Canada on which camels were employed seriously for transportation. Frank Laumeister was credited with, or blamed for, the idea that they would travel more miles per day, carry bigger loads, and require less attention for feed and water than other draught animals. On these points, he was quite correct, but on two other counts the camels were disappointing: their relatively soft feet could not stand up to the rough and rocky roads, and furthermore, it was found almost impossible to work horse and mule outfits on the same trail as the camels.

It may have been the musky smell from the camels more than appearance that filled horses and mules with terror. A few freight shipments, one of them a cargo of rum, were lost when frightened horse and mule teams ran away, and faced with the prospect of litigation, the camel owner decided to take his imported beasts off the road. And what happened to the camels brought in to serve the gold rush? Some were sold and sent out of the country, and others of the original 23 were turned loose beside the Thompson River where they managed to survive in the wild state for a number of years.

After some more years, the lively town of Barkerville began to decay. It became a ghost town until 1958 when the province was celebrating the 100th anniversary of the birth of the Crown Colony of British Columbia, and Barkerville was marked for restoration and given the status of a park.

The West in Confederation Year

This second excerpt from the same source is included as it presents the writer dealing with a subject much on the minds of contemporary Canadians. (Continued from A Short History of Western Canada, *1968.)*

Confederation must be seen as a great stride in national development. In its initial stage, however, it was strictly an eastern operation. People living in the Northwest had no part in it and no particular interest. Most of them had not heard about those great struggles which were bringing four provinces into union, nor did they care.

To residents on the Atlantic side of the Great Lakes, the West of 1867 was like a foreign land, with which there was no means of direct communication except over the long canoe route finding less and less use. For western people, the lines of communication were by water through Hudson Bay to the Old Country and by cart trail to St. Paul, also known as Pig's Eye, in Minnesota.

Those who sat in the government at Ottawa had no jurisdiction in the Northwest. What is now western Canada was Rupert's Land and still in a primitive state, without settlements except at a few trading posts, without agriculture except at Red River and Fort Edmonton, without laws except those laid down by the Company, without schools except for a few at Fort Garry, without government except for the Council of Assiniboia and the fantastic "Republic of Caledonia," without means of transportation except by canoe, Red River carts, and a few steamboats on the Red, without industry or the prospect of industry except in beaver skins and buffalo robes.

The fact was that no sense of political destiny existed. The West had changed but slightly in the century after Anthony Henday trekked overland to spend a winter within sight of the Rocky Mountains, and most people in the fur trade were happy to see the country remain without change.

During the year immediately prior to Confederation, the island and mainland colonies on the Pacific side of the continent were joined to form the colony of British Columbia, an entity with an uncertain future. The gold rush was fine while it lasted, but as gold returns declined, miners went away, leaving the area which was to become the sixth province of Canada with a pronounced letdown. Something was needed to make up for the dwindling gold, and interest turned to forests and fish. The first sawmill was built on Vancouver Island in 1848, but by Confederation year, the colony had dozens of mills cutting Douglas fir, cedar, spruce, hemlock, and pine, in which the area was fabulously rich. Commercial fishing was starting in about the same way. Although coastal Indians had speared and hooked salmon and other kinds of fish for generations, Confederation year found immigrants from afar making exploratory attempts at canning on the Lower Fraser River.

What is now Alberta, Saskatchewan, and Manitoba was still the vast preserve held by the Hudson's Bay Company as an exclusive trading territory. Was it not the attraction of wild furs that led to the Company's formation in the first place, with its charter from King Charles II? For almost 200 years the Company administered the country as a piece of privately-owned real estate. When the United States purchased Alaska from Russia in 1867, paying $7,200,000 for it, the transaction suggested the possibility of the Hudson's Bay Company selling Rupert's Land to the highest bidder. As long as they owned it, however, Company men were satisfied to keep it without change.

The gold rush west of the Rockies drew public attention and thousands of fortune-seekers, but nothing of the kind had happened to change the tenor of life in the prairie area. It was, indeed, a primitive community. The first steamboats had not ventured into the North Saskatchewan River, and for anybody making the journey from Fort Garry to Fort Edmonton, the only alternative to walking was a trip by oxcart or canoe, tedious in either case.

It seems safe to presume that the Bow River country, now marked by the city of Calgary which boasts more motor vehicles per thousand of population than anywhere else in the world, had not, in Confederation year, emerged from the *travois* stage or felt the imprint on its sod of the first wheel.

A few thousand people lived in and around Fort Garry, with the French-speaking Métis outnumbering all others. A few hundred people lived in and around Fort Edmonton. Apart from these two, no settlement between the Red River and the Rockies had more than a few dozen inhabitants. Archdeacon Cochrane went to Portage la Prairie in 1853, and Rev. James Nisbet, in 1866, led a few followers to found a community which was to become the city of Prince Albert. Métis settlements existed at places like Willow Bunch, Batoche, and Tail Creek, the latter on the north side of Red Deer River.

In what is today southern Alberta, the first white man to build a permanent habitation had not yet arrived on the scene. The whisky traders from Fort Benton, Montana, were beginning to venture as far north as the Oldman River, and in the year after Confederation, they built Fort Hamilton at a site a few miles south of the present city of Lethbridge. Although destroyed by fire in the same year, it was rebuilt on a grander scale and given the name, Whoop-Up. There the Indians were invited to trade furs and robes for a strange kind of liquor, appropriately called fire-water. Fort Whoop-Up became notorious for drunkenness and murder.

It was also in the year after Confederation that the first home was built by a white man in what is now southern Alberta. John George Brown, better known as Kootenai Brown, was the man, and his story should not be ignored. This dashing character, who became the first warden of Waterton Lakes National Park, was born in Scotland, and after his formal education at Eton and Oxford, he served in the Queen's Lifeguards. His tall and athletic figure carried a uniform well, and with bearskin busby on his head, he was a commanding-looking officer. Even the ladies in the royal household could not hide their interest, and superior officers thought it best to post him to India, a safe distance away. There, according to stories, somebody was shot, and John George Brown showed an immediate interest in seeing South America.

Before long, Brown was making his way northward, passing Panama, and joining the 49ers going on to the California gold fields. From there, Brown hunted, traded, and quarrelled with western Indians, ultimately arriving in British Columbia with a band of irritated Indians in hot pursuit. With them still following him, he came through a mountain pass and looked down upon Waterton Lakes, convinced they presented the most beautiful picture he had ever seen. "When I am free of these pursuing Indians," he said to himself, "I will return and build a home beside that water."

Sure enough, with a Métis girl as his wife, he returned in 1868 to the unforgettable wonderland beside the mountains and built a log cabin, the first of its kind in a very big area. Brown became a prominent and useful citizen, cultivating some land, acting as a guide in Northwest Rebellion days, succeeding in finding the first evidence of oil in southern Alberta, and furnishing advice for cattlemen coming to establish themselves in the kingdom of range grass, where the prairies met the foothills.

A few missionaries had ventured as far as Fort Edmonton before 1867. Rev. Robert Rundle, the first Protestant missionary, was there in 1840, and Father Jean-Baptiste Thibault was sent there by the Bishop of

St. Boniface in 1842. Father Albert Lacombe went to Fort Edmonton in 1852, and Rev. John McDougall followed in 1862. In Confederation year, however, it would have been impossible to find a doctor, dentist, fireman, or policeman in a million square miles of country west and northwest from Fort Garry.

When an aching tooth tormented Rev. John McDougall, and there was neither dentist nor dental forceps within a thousand miles, he tried to extract it with a pair of mechanic's pincers, but the tooth broke off, leaving the root to generate as much pain as ever. Only after nine years, when visiting in the East, was McDougall able to have the offending root dug out by a dentist.

The Hudson's Bay Company had attempted to discharge a duty in providing something in the nature of law and authority by setting up the Council of Assiniboia. Nevertheless, this could not be considered a democratic body, and its effectiveness was negligible except in and around Fort Garry. The judgement of Canadians of later years was that the country lacked government, and it was in an administrative vacuum that the strange thing known as the Republic of Caledonia was born.

It was the brainchild of Thomas Spence who was at Fort Garry for about a year, long enough to make himself generally unpopular, and who, in 1867, went to Portage la Prairie, where a man could be completely free to act as he pleased. Spence craved authority and Portage la Prairie offered opportunity. Therefore, at precisely the time John A. Macdonald and the other Fathers of Confederation were producing a dominion in the East, Thomas Spence was setting up his prairie republic.

Who would be the president of the republic? Naturally, the position would go to Spence. No one challenged his scheme at the outset; Spence plunged right ahead with plans. Portage la Prairie would be the capital; Spence's friends would be cabinet ministers and serve part time as constables. There was the matter of boundaries for the republic, but the president had no hesitation in fixing them: the 49th parallel would be the southern boundary, the Rocky Mountains on the west, the Arctic Circle on the north, and some unclear line on the east, this latter meaning as close to Fort Garry as Spence considered it safe to go.

Then, there had to be money for the republic, and Spence, backed by his cabinet, ruled that customs duty would be collected on all goods coming into the republic and all goods going out. Apparently, officers appointed by Spence did manage to collect some duty money, and he was able to maintain a perfect balance of budget. The secret formula was simple enough: all income was spent on whisky for the president and members of his cabinet, and there was neither surplus nor deficit.

Everything was going fine for a while; however, it seems to be the fate of potentates and autocrats that sooner or later they make the errors which are their downfall. Spence's mistake was in picking a quarrel with a MacPherson. This Scot, a shoemaker living at High Bluff, not far east of Portage la Prairie, took a contemptuous view of the republic. What he had to say about the necessity of paying duty taxes to a republic which did not really exist reached the ears of the president. An order went out for MacPherson's arrest on a charge of treason.

It was wintertime and snow was deep on the Portage Plains. Two of the republic's constables drove out to High Bluff to bring the alleged criminal to justice, but the accused man was most uncooperative, and there was a scuffle in the snow before the officers overpowered and handcuffed him.

On their way to Portage, the police constables with MacPherson passed John McLean, first farmer on Portage Plains. Seeing his fellow Scot, McLean wanted to know what it was all about. MacPherson furnished a convincing summary and McLean's sympathies were aroused. At first McLean was going to use force to free his friend, but on further thought, he advised MacPherson to go along quietly, promising that he would be on hand at the trial in Portage that evening.

On his way to town after doing his farm chores, McLean invited two friends to accompany him. Their arrival at the place of trial coincided with the reading of the charge of treason against MacPherson. It was "treason against the laws of the republic." Seeing President Spence sitting in judgement, McLean could not hold his tongue. "What d'ye mean? Laws o' the Republic? We hae no laws and hae no Republic. Come oot o' it, ye whited sepulchure," he called defiantly. "Ye canna be baith accuser and judge."

To President Spence, it sounded like more treason, and he ordered another arrest. McLean was in no mood for more nonsense, and his fists began to fly. The table on which the lamp rested was upset, and immediately the room was in darkness. A free-for-all continued in the darkness until someone fired a revolver shot and then all was silent. After a few minutes, someone recovered the kerosene lamp and lit it. To MacPherson's surprise, the President was not to be seen.

The back of the iniquitous Republic of Portage la Prairie was broken forever, and the big country west of the Red River was still without democratic or constitutional government, a buffalo pasture waiting for men with the faith and imagination of nation-builders. . . .

Today and Tomorrow

The brevity of western Canada's recorded story adds to its charm. And a short story can be a good one. Canadians visiting the Old World and seeing where Abraham was supposed to have dug a well 4,000 years ago and where Pericles was at the peak of his political power in Democratic Athens 2,400 years ago might conclude that the history of their own West, which had not completely disengaged itself from the Stone Age just 100 years ago, is relatively unimportant. Such a conclusion would be wrong. It is the achievements and events which enrich the history of a particular area rather than the years.

Western Canadians celebrating the centennial anniversary of Confederation took stock of an area quickly transformed from a wilderness to a land with super highways, fine homes, superior educational facilities, challenging opportunities, and one of the highest standards of living in the world. These phenomenal changes in so short a time could only find explanation in a combination of rich natural resources and vigorous people.

As mentioned previously, Confederation year meant practically nothing to the scattered residents of Rupert's Land. They had more reason to be interested in the policies of the Hudson's Bay Company than in the efforts of the Fathers of Confederation to bring the eastern provinces into union. For those people who had adopted the western frontier, a more meaningful landmark date might have been 1869, when the Hudson's Bay Company relinquished its territorial claims in Rupert's Land; or 1870, when the province of Manitoba was created; or 1874, when the Mounted Police trekked westward to build Fort Macleod; or 1876, when the first wheat was sent from the West; or 1878, when the first railway tracks were laid to Winnipeg.

These dates are within the lifetime of some Canadians still living today and serve to illustrate the dramatic changes which took place in only a few decades. But the winning of the West was not easy. Pioneer years were trying in many ways, and there were many tests to be undergone. Some of the reverses were serious and might well have been more serious. Indian hostility posed a grave danger for some years; twice there was something resembling rebellion; and twice there was involvement in world wars. There was no greater blow to local progress than the years of extreme drought which accompanied the depression in the thirties and cast undisguised gloom and pessimism over a land which had been gaining fame for hope and optimism.

But crises were interspersed with triumphs. The country judged to be doomed to eternal sterility was found to be a virtual treasure chest of resources. The area George Simpson considered to be unsuited to cultivation because of the poverty of its soil turned out to be one of the world's best for food production. The privately-owned piece of real estate known as Rupert's Land, with no recognized future except in producing furs, was found to hold unbelievable riches such as gold, iron, oil, natural gas, coal, and potash, all of which added much to the area's economy.

It was not a country for faint hearts. There were those individuals who could not endure the frontier hardships and disappointments and who, with a sense of relief, moved to other regions where life was easier and more secure. Others, however, with determination and muscle and fibre, remained to impart to the frontier its vigorous character. To the resources like soil, forests, gas, and oil, of which Westerners were able to boast, one must add the priceless quality of pioneer fortitude supported by self-reliance and energy.

The change, of course, went far beyond the mere recovery of natural resources. In 1967, viewers of the western scene saw factories and industries of many kinds, contradicting the old dictum that "the West can grow the wheat; the East will keep the factories." With raw materials and the necessary skills, it could have been expected that diversified industry would emerge. The earliest manufacturing had its base in agriculture, forestry, and fishing. Understandably, the plants were abattoirs, flour mills, creameries, tanneries, sawmills, and canning establishments. With a higher level of production and a bigger population, however, factories became more varied and more numerous.

One of the best indications of the growth in manufacturing was the increasing demand for electrical power. Between 1947 and 1967, the use of electrical energy increased by 300 per cent. The Portage Mountain project in British Columbia, the complex Columbia River development, and the South Saskatchewan River operation, each of which cost a staggering amount of money, symbolized the change to a more advanced and complex economy.

But what of tomorrow? Is it inevitable that progress will continue in an uninterrupted manner as in recent years? Success gives no reason for complacency. Time and again throughout history smugness has been the forerunner of decline. Too often people who had the courage and will to cope with difficult pioneer problems failed in dealing with the problems accompanying success and wealth. Progress can and should continue, but there is no guarantee that it will. As long as natural and human resources last, progress and prosperity will likely go hand in hand with them. But for how long can they be expected to survive? All Canadians must be on guard to preserve those qualities which brought them to positions of comfort.

As for the natural resources, some of them will not last forever; indeed, some will not last many years. With proper care, the renewable resources may last forever. Regardless of early greed and waste in handling forests, the new policies based on sustained yield are sound and will win the approval of Canadians a hundred years hence. Likewise, the concern for soil in relation to world food needs should ensure safeguards for Canada's most precious natural asset. With understanding care, agricultural soils can be as productive in a thousand years' time as they have been in recent years, and the world's growing population will bring ever greater importance to those soils. Similarly, it has been proven that fish resources will respond to intelligent management.

Such, however, is not the case with certain other resources described as non-renewables: oil, natural gas, minerals from the mines. These should be used with the realization that waste and extravagance may mean depriving Canadians of a later generation of something to which they will feel they have a claim. They are easy to destroy and may be impossible to restore.

Anyone with concern for the future of his land must think seriously about protection for wild life, safeguards for forests, arresting soil depletion and erosion, prevention of pollution in air and water, preservation of parkland, and the minimizing of waste in all resources, none of which is inexhaustible.

The Dawn of a New Day

The reaction of readers to MacEwan's writings is most commonly, "He makes the history of our country live — he brings it to life." The reason for such enthusiasm is here to be seen in the following excerpt. It deals among other things with the first shipment of wheat from the West to eastern Canada, a subject that has often bored students over the years but which in MacEwan's hands is a different matter. (From Harvest of Bread, *Saskatoon: Western Producer Prairie Books, 1969.)*

October 21, 1876! A primitive sternwheeler splashed away from a shaky landing on the Fort Garry side of the Red River, carrying the most momentous cargo in western Canadian history — perhaps in Canadian or North American history. The boat, resembling a floating warehouse more than a sleek ship, was Jim Hill's *Selkirk.* The cargo consited of 857 bushels and 10 pounds of Red Fife wheat, the first to be shipped from the new West. For anybody with sentiment for Canadian history and Canadian industry, that October date would seem to justify annual recognition in one form or another.

In many respects, it was a year of unusual significance. It was the year in which the first cattle were released to rustle a range-living and test a western winter at Fort Macleod. This experiment marked the birth of prairie ranching. It was the year of the bloody Custer Massacre beside the Little Big Horn River, Montana, when Sitting Bull and his Sioux braves annihilated an imposing United States force under General George Custer. As the year of the first wheat shipment from the West, it had the character of a fresh start for the growers, a year of beginning again.

The supply of Red Fife wheat, brought in at great cost and even greater inconvenience, had been apportioned in small lots to as many farmers as wanted it. Nobody was interested in planting more than a few acres because the only market which growers had known was the one created by strictly local appetites. The demand for gristing grain was limited, and there seemed no purpose in growing more wheat than settlers and a few fur traders could eat. Most farmers had no thought of planting more than three or four acres. Any person with six or eight acres of wheat was seen as a big operator.

As if to give the new variety a chance to show what it could do, the grasshopper menace disappeared. Growing conditions were favorable. Even with the small Manitoba acreage it became apparent that farmers would have wheat to exceed what the local mills could take. Concurrently, the Ontario crop was poor, and farmers there concluded that their wheat was deteriorating and a change of seed was needed in order to recover vigor and higher yields. It was a principle similar to that of changing herd bulls every few years. Their preference was for seed from an area with northern climate, capable of transmitting early ripening qualities and vitality. Farmers in Illinois were asking for seed from Minnesota. Simultaneously, men directing the Toronto seed business of Steele Brothers resolved to secure a supply of Manitoba wheat for distribution in the eastern trade. It was a bold decision, bordering on recklessness, because of the time element and the unknown factors of quantity and quality involved.

Not until after the poor Ontario crop was harvested were the eastern seedsmen able to confirm their plan. By that time, lateness of the season coupled with total lack of railroads or other direct communications raised huge barriers. Any hope for success depended upon R. C. Steele, junior member of the firm and later president of Steele Briggs Seed Company, being able to get to Winnipeg quickly and make the wheat purchases with the least possible delay. He could travel by way of Chicago and St. Paul to the end of United States rail at Fisher's Landing in Minnesota, and from the latter point he could go to Winnipeg by riverboat. He obtained a ticket for passage, hoping to arrive early in October.

The river cruise, however, would take at least three days. Fearing river freeze-up before the needed wheat had been purchased and shipped out, Steele sought some way of reducing his traveling time and learned that he could save a few hours by abandoning the boat trip and taking to team and wagon. This he resolved to do. His first stop, after Fisher's Landing, was at Grand Forks in North Dakota, thirteen miles away, but the pause was a brief one — just long enough for feeding the horses — because Steele saw his trip as a clear race against time. Leaving Grand Forks at six o'clock in the evening, he drove the remaining 150 miles to Winnipeg, arriving at exactly twelve o'clock on the second night, precisely thirty hours later. They were thirty hours of continuous driving, save for the time taken to change horses.

In Winnipeg, where people were finding it difficult to accept the new name for Fort Garry, the young seed merchant made the acquaintance of

David Young of the local firm of Higgins and Young, "Dealers in Boots and Shoes, Crockery and Glassware" — and just about any merchandise promising profit.

Yes, David Young would accept the assignment to buy 5,000 bushels of wheat or as near to that amount as available supplies would allow.

From October 13 until October 21, the *Manitoba Daily Free Press* carried the Higgins and Young announcement: "Cash for choice wheat to export to Ontario . . . 80 cents per bushel."

For Higgins and Young there was a commission of five cents a bushel; hence the cost to Steele Brothers, as shown on the bill of lading, was eighty-five cents per bushel for the wheat, plus thirty-five cents a bushel for freight, and twenty-six cents each for cotton bags.

Manitoba farmers, hearing of the unprecedented cash offer, responded eagerly, assessed their wheat stocks, and determined how much they could spare. Wives, with no less enthusiasm, held the bags while husbands shoveled. As loaded carts converged upon McMillan's Mill on Post Office Street, close to the river, farmers wondered if the Toronto money, with which they would be paid, was genuine. Dealing in dollars was a new experience. Although the settlers saw little cash in any form, most transactions had been conducted in English pounds and shillings.

But nobody had much to sell and it became quite clear that the country stretching from Red River to the Rocky Mountains could not fill an order for 5,000 bushels of wheat, regardless of the amount of Toronto cash offered. The country of 1876 did not have that much wheat — just 857 bushels and 10 pounds.

The biggest single contribution to the historic order was made by G. R. Miller of Kildonan who delivered 204 bushels. He received settlement amounting to $163.20. His neighbors wondered what he would do with it all. Next in volume of sales were H. Soar of St. John, who was paid $123.20 for 154 bushels, and R. Black of Springfield, who received $81.60 for 102 bushels.

Others delivering wheat included: J. W. Carleton, Clear Spring (80 bushels and 10 pounds); D. McDonald, Springfield (94 bushels); John Spear, Springfield (44 bushels); John Reich, St. Paul (40 bushels); F. Dick, Springfield (35 bushels); Alex Gibson, Springfield (33 bushels); T. B. Robinson, Rockwood (32 bushels); Neil McLeod, Victoria (22 bushels); and John McIvor, Greenwood (17 bushels and 45 pounds).

According to the *Manitoba Daily Free Press* of October 23, 1876, "Mr. Steele who is a seedsman of long experience, is highly satisfied with the samples furnished." Glad to have a news story of such unusual character, the editor made the most of it. He noted that "wheat from a northern district where the season is short carries its habit of quick ripening with it when sown in a southern district where the season is longer." This would lead to bigger demand and bigger orders for "seed," the editor assured. "In the near future enterprising seedsmen will have to send their buyers here in time to make their purchases more leisurely and in time for large shipments before the close of navigation."

While praising Mr. Steele, as purchaser, and David Young, who acted on behalf of Higgins and Young in assembling the shipment, the editor displayed some of the vision to which all writers aspire. This, he told local people, might very well be a transaction of historic importance, something "worthy of remembrance when in the not far distant future, our shipments amount to millions of bushels."

The precious wheat was tied in 412 new cotton sacks and piled carefully on the riverboat. Then, with a feeble toot from the ship's steam whistle, the *Selkirk* drew away, upsteam. What the few bystanders witnessed on that slightly frosty October morning, whether it occurred to them as a possibility or not, was the first trickle of what was quickly to become a torrent of wheat leaving the West for distant markets.

By traveling long hours and making the best use of time, Steele just managed to get his wheat out before the river froze over; forty-eight hours after the cargo arrived at Fisher's Landing, Red River navigation ended for the year. But the Manitoba wheat was then well on its way, going by rail to Duluth, lakeboat to Sarnia, and finally, rail to Toronto.

Ontario people studied the quality of this Manitoba product and uttered words of surprise and admiration. Eastern millers were anxious to secure a sample for testing in their plants. The milling result brought astonishment. Could Manitoba furnish more wheat of this kind? men wondered. At once the proposals for construction of a transcontinental railway to link the East and the West assumed more merit.

Winnipeg's only tangible reminder of the initial shipment of wheat is a bronze plaque hanging in the hallway of the Legislative Building. When the Canadian Seed Growers' Association held its convention in Winnipeg in June, 1932, the loading of the first wheat on a riverboat was re-enacted and a suitable bronze plate fixed to a large granite boulder at the riverbank site of McMillan's Mill was unveiled with appropriate ceremony. But on two occasions, men with more sentiment for scrap metal than for the momentous events of Canadian history forced the plaque from its base and took it away.

Wisely, the third plaque was placed where there would be less temptation to riverbank denizens. The great stone upon which the original metal was secured became buried beneath one of the dikes constructed to keep "Old Man River" in its place.

The editor, in his wisdom, believed Manitoba's principal role would be in furnishing wheat for seed purposes rather than for milling. In this opinion he was wrong, but he was not wrong when he saw the initial shipment as one possessing great significance, both locally and nationally. The wheat trade was to grow at a spectacular rate and all of Canada was to benefit. Indeed, the twenty-first day of October in every year should not pass without a pause to recognize the birth of a great industry and its remarkable growth after 1876.

That historic shipment of Red Fife wheat provided the best advertisement the new country could have obtained, and immediately, there was an invigorated interest in those homestead quarter sections, said to be available at ten dollars each.

Man with a Message

This is an important excerpt as it is from a book dealing with one who was a strong influence on the writer's outlook and attitude toward religion. MacEwan has written much about Indians and their culture but never in the condescending manner that sometimes creeps into other accounts. (From Tatanga Mani: Walking Buffalo of the Stonies, *Edmonton: Hurtig, 1969. Reprinted by permission of Hurtig Publishers Ltd.)*

Unsaddling his bay cayuse and closing the corral gate, the aging Stoney Indian, Chief Walking Buffalo, greeted his visitors with a shy grin and then led the way to his weather-beaten log house sitting picturesquely in the long shadow of the Canadian Rockies. Close to the kitchen door, the pathway forked with one much-used branch pointing into the spruce and poplar trees standing on the south bank of the Bow River, the other leading directly to the house.

"Come in. I'll show you my chief's medals," our host invited in a low, clear voice. "Then we will walk down to the river, and I'll show you how I make a bow and arrows."

In the language of his tribe, he was Tatanga Mani, but as elder statesman of the Stoney Reserve, he was almost as well known by his Anglo-Saxon name, George McLean, given to him when as a small boy he was adopted by the frontier missionary, John Mclean. It was generally an advantage to have two or three different names, but when visiting in Scotland, he encountered difficulty in explaining his claim to the McLean tribe, especially in the presence of clansmen who argued with fierce Scottish pride that the exclusive McLeans had their own ark at the time of Noah's flood.

For years the Stoney chief was the amateur photographer's delight; no Indian of any tribe had faced more cameras. Even without the gay buckskin, bone-beaded trappings, and ceremonial headpiece set under buffalo horns, he was an imposing figure. Typical of his race, he was of medium height with full chest, small feet, short nose, high cheek bones, and heavy lips. His broad, bronzed face showed deep lines etched by the cruelty of many seasons, but his hair remained dark and thick, his eyes bright, his powerful body muscular and straight. Until the age of eighty-eight, his black hair had hung in long braids, his feet had known no protection except moccasins.

As he walked along the grassy path, feet turned inward Indian-fashion, his pace was as brisk as ever, although there was a noticeable limp, the result of, as he explained succinctly, "being bucked off my horse." But apart from the ignominy of losing out to a temperamental mount, the fall was of little consequence to a man who had been "bucked off" more times than he could remember, now and then in rodeo contests, more often on the reservation.

Inside the house the aroma of tanned buckskin blended with that of willow wood smoke. An ancient cookstove occupied the center of the sparsely furnished room. On the table sat a single plate, knife and fork, cup without saucer, half a loaf of bread looking dry and stale, a tin of honey, and a teapot. Before settling into his chair beside the stove to display treasures accumulated over many years and pictures taken in a score of countries while on a world tour, the Indian patriarch pointed to a few objects breaking the monotony of the log walls: the moth-eaten skin of a coyote taken with a single shot, a desiccated loon in full feather tacked to the wall, a ceremonial drum used in numerous tribal dances, and a picture of his father wearing little more than a ferocious expression.

After world tours totaling 150,000 miles — an enlightening few days at Mackinac Island, a visit with the Prime Minister of Canada, a warm reception in the United Kingdom, a presentation before the West German government at Bonn, a civic reception in his honour at Johannesburg, and happy memories of the Scandinavian countries, Switzerland, New Zealand, Australia, and other lands — Walking Buffalo was happy to be back on the reservation, living in the house he had fashioned from logs long ago and spending most of his days in the saddle. When he had visitors, he urged them toward greater sensitivity in dealing with Indian problems.

Proud of his Indian blood, the chief could still hunt, dance, and describe in vivid detail the grisly old pastime of scalping enemies. But on this day he wanted to talk about the white man's scorn for Indian customs, Indian religion, and Indian ideals. Because Indian culture was often strange and foreign to the intolerant white man, he dismissed it derisively as savage, primitive, and even evil. Having sampled two worlds, one called pagan and the other supposedly civilized, the chief could recognize good and evil in both. In the long run, he found that there were no great moral distinctions to be made between the two ways of life, notwithstanding the white man's offensive air of superiority.

"The red savages," he repeated with a benevolent grin, "can teach the white savages something about living yet."

Then he became more serious. "Long ago my people fought with bows and arrows, and only a few warriors were killed. Nowadays warring nations are not satisfied with killing a few; they aim to destroy millions. Every country is determined to have the biggest guns. They don't make those big guns for ornaments; they make them to be used. If we don't find understanding in this world, all mankind is likely to be destroyed."

The old man knew he had a sympathetic audience. "What you call civilization has a lot of foolishness about it. It needs a foundation of Indian common sense. You white people are the worst offenders in rushing about madly to make money you'll never live long enough to spend, using up the forests, soil, and natural fuels as though another generation won't need them too, and all the time talking about a better world while making bigger bombs to blow up the one you've got. My people took a few scalps from their enemies, but they were never guilty of scalping nature's resources from an entire country."

Who was in a better position to carry the Indian's message than this man who had enjoyed intimate associations with people of two races and two cultures during almost all periods of his life? Brought ' p in a tepee, he attended the white man's schools. As a young man, he .ried working in the city for cash wages, but the need of his people for I.adership drew him back to a lifetime in the heart of his native community. In time he became a tribal councilor, then a minor chief, and finally a chief and medicine man, the highest positions in Indian society. In his old age, there came the unexpected opportunities for travel in many countries followed again by a return to the simple, free life where he could listen to the changing moods of the Bow River, watch the coming and going of the birds, converse with the trees, and be close to the maker of hills and forests, of Indian and white man. Walking Buffalo's life was truly lived within two worlds.

Early in his life, as he saw poverty and degradation being forced upon his people by the new order, Walking Buffalo felt anger at the invading white race. Many times he wondered why the Indians had not united against the palefaced newcomers while their numbers were still small, either to destroy them or to drive them out of the country. In that way, the style of life of native Indians, as well as their opportunity ultimately for nationhood, could have been preserved. But the warlike tribes had never joined, and so before the Indians sensed their full, oppressive impact, the might and numbers of the strange newcomers were completely overpowering. Before there was either time or opportunity to understand what was happening, the Indian owners of the land were being relegated to reserves, like mustangs being rounded up and placed in well-fenced paddocks.

Yes, there have been times when the longing for revenge swelled in Walking Buffalo's heart. But even that had changed with passing time. No longer did he hate either white men or men of other colours. He was searching now for something more productive than hatred. Why should men hate each other because of such inherited differences as variation of skin colour or language? The Great Spirit, if he be Father of all, desired that men live together in tolerant understanding as did the various species of trees growing side by side along the Bow River. "See," Walking Buffalo pointed out, "there are black poplars, white poplars, red willows, and other trees growing close to each other. They live without hatred."

After a lifetime of searching, his mind was made up. Needed were not tomahawks, not bombs, not demonstrations of hatred or loud voices of anger; rather, the need was for more of the warmth of understanding, more thought to the purposes of the Great Spirit.

"Why hasn't the white man shown more of the tolerant understanding he talks about?" the chief wondered. "Remember, the Indian has a perfect right to be an Indian; he need never be ashamed of it. Don't try to make a white man of him. If those white people who want to help the Indian would get to know him and his background better, they would understand why he wants to keep his Indian ways."

Perhaps it was easier for the Indian to grasp the meaning of brotherhood under one Great Spirit or God, for those who preferred that name. For long ages, North American Indians recognized a kinship between themselves and all other living things — animals, birds, insects, flowers, and trees — all were children of one Great Spirit. "And nobody," Walking Buffalo noted, "tried to make the coyotes act like beavers or the eagles behave like robins." Christians, he observed, saw themselves as set apart from the rest of the animal and plant world by superiority, even as a special creation. Perhaps the principles of brotherhood which the world so urgently needed came more easily to the Indian.

With the air of a mystic, Walking Buffalo questioned his visitors. "Do you know that trees talk? Well, they do. They talk to each other, and they'll talk to you if you listen. Trouble is, white people don't listen. They never listened to the Indians, and so I don't suppose they'll listen to the other voices in nature. But I have learned a lot from trees: sometimes about the weather, sometimes about animals, sometimes about the Great Spirit."

There could be no doubt that throughout his long life Walking Buffalo had been an observant student of nature, his finest teacher. And his acute philosophical insights made the chief a living refutation of the white man's usual assumption that North American Indians were all poor thinkers.

"Oh yes, I went to the white man's schools," he reminded his listeners. "I learned to read from school books, newspapers, and the Bible. But in time I found that these were not enough. Civilized people depend too much on man-made printed pages. I turn to the Great Spirit's book which is the whole of his creation. You can read a big part of that book if you study nature. You know, if you take all your books, lay them out under the sun, and let the snow and rain and insects work on them for a while, there will be nothing left. But the Great Spirit has provided you and me with an opportunity for study in nature's university, the forests, the rivers, the mountains, and the animals, which include us."

At this point, one of Walking Buffalo's admirers from the city made a request: "Tell us about your own life, your adventures, what you have seen."

The old man stood, stretched, and moved to place the teapot on the wood-burning stove. "That would be a long story," he replied. "My first way of transportation, you know, was in a moss-lined bag on my grandmother's back. That's an easy way of getting around, but you don't see much of the world from a cradlebag. The next was a *travois*, a cart without wheels, you might say. Then think of the change in leaping halfway around the world in a million-dollar airplane. Yes, I've seen many changes, yet through them all the Great Spirit has blessed me.

"But the story of my life will take a long time to tell. You might as well ask for the whole history of my race. Where should a person begin? I suppose I can start by telling you what I believe to be the origin of the Indian people and follow with the story of how the Stoney tribe happened to come to these mountains and foothills a long, long time ago."

The Battle of the Breeds

Some years ago an old prize winner in the judging ring said that MacEwan was from the beginning "a Clydesdale man" but that he leaned over backwards to be fair to all breeds when called upon to select a winner. In this excerpt all the important breeds of horses are dealt with. It now remains for readers to judge his fairness for themselves. (From Power for Prairie Plows, *Saskatoon: Western Producer Prairie Books, 1971.)*

In building the agricultural empire of the West, no topic was debated more bitterly than that of breeds in draft horses. Sooner or later every farmer held loyalty to one particular breed and held to it tenaciously. Neither the cleavage produced by political parties nor church denominations rivaled it. Methodists and Presbyterians might seek the company of their respective kind, and Conservatives and Liberals could be expected to segregate at times, but it was on the merits of Clydesdales, Shires, Percherons, and Belgians that rural communities divided most fiercely. Nobody was neutral; either a man favored the flat-boned, hard-hocked, big-footed Clydes with straight and bold action, or he declared for Percherons or Belgians with their huge middles, powerful muscles, and phlegmatic dispositions.

Breed merits could be debated without emotion at public school, but when the question arose at the livery stable or during moments of neighborly conversation following the weekly Prayer Meeting or Christian Endeavor, tempers could flare like kerosene fires. Nothing, it seemed, could bridge the opinion gap between those who held to Clydesdales and those who favored one of the other breeds. Scottish settlers were irascible in their loyalty to the Clydesdale; people from England favored Shires but less furiously; and most settlers from the United States and mainland countries of Europe wanted Percherons or Belgians. The province of Ontario, having drawn its people very largely from the British Isles, was essentially Clydesdale country, and because many of the early settlers in the West were from Ontario, the Clydesdale held the advantage of an initial acceptance.

Until the beginning of the twentieth century, the massive, hairy-legged English Shires were the Clydesdales' only competition on the Canadian scene. At the Toronto Industrial Exhibition in 1900, with 875 horse entries, Clydesdales dominated overwhelmingly in the draft section and would have monopolized it had it not been for a few Shires exhibited. Percherons and Suffolks were known in some parts of rural Ontario and Quebec but were not sufficiently numerous to rate separate classes. Belgians were known only by pictures carried in farm magazines.

There was no doubt about the early West being Clydesdale country, just as in the East. Horsemen visiting the Winnipeg Industrial Exhibition held in July, 1900, saw hundreds of Clydesdales in the competitions, a total of two Shires and one Percheron. The Scottish horsemen could view the exhibits with smug composure, but the lone Percheron was a much bigger threat than anybody sensed. Two years earlier, George Lane, of the Bar U Ranch in the Canadian Foothills, bought the entire stud of purebred Percherons belonging to James Mauldin, Dillon, Montana — thirty-five mares in all — and drove them north to range west of High River. The importation was creating interest and giving the French breed a needed stimulus. But for most people attending the Winnipeg Industrial of 1900, the two-year-old Percheron being displayed without benefit of prize-list recognition, was the first representative of the breed they had ever seen. The *Farmer's Advocate* noted that the "black, blocky fellow of smooth pattern" was admitted for display in the judging ring and even in the absence of competition, was allowed, charitably, to take a first-prize ribbon which had gone unclaimed in the section for Shires.

At Brandon's exhibition, a few days later, breed representation was about the same: many Clydesdales, only four Shires, and no entries of any other draft breed. Until this time, therefore, most breed arguments were between the numerous supporters of Clydes and the outnumbered horsemen who favored Shires. Often it was a quarrel between Scots and Englishmen, where the fires of disagreement were never difficult to handle. Generally, the Scots had the last word. Shire supporters inviting argument could expect a broadly accented barrage. One of those foolhardy fellows, using the pen name "Claughbane," wrote to the *Farmer's Advocate* (May 20, 1895, p. 205), saying tauntingly that the Clydesdale's popularity had to be explained by the large Scottish element existing in the country, "for there is no doubt about it, Scotchmen like things which are Scotch, and not the least among these they like Scotch horses . . . . [But] the Shire is the largest breed of horses that we have and for that reason, if we would export draft horses to England, he is the sire we must use in producing them . . . . We should not breed for feet and legs but for the market."

"Claughbane," it appeared, could find good in all draft breeds except the Clydesdale and in a later issue of the *Farmer's Advocate* (June 20, 1895, p. 242), he insulted the Scot's beloved Clydesdales by ignoring them and praising Percherons and Suffolks. Of Percherons, he said: "There is a very strong prejudice against them — for what reason is hard to say. . . . They are always ready to work and easily kept in condition. Another point in their favor is that they are clean-legged. And here let me say something about feather. Of what use is it? Certainly none whatever to a farm horse. It is rather a defect for it gives extra work in keeping clean and it is also an indication of poor bone. . . . The Suffolk Punch is a horse of great substance and it is surprising that there are so few of them in Canada. Why these two clean-legged breeds [Percherons and Suffolk Punch] are not in greater demand, I am at loss to understand for they are undoubtedly most suitable for getting agricultural horses."

As "Claughbane" might have expected, his irreverent treatment of the Scotsman's horse drew fire in abundance. One of the responses came from a correspondent signing as "Scotland Forever," showing unmistakable anger at anybody who would challenge his favorite breed. *(Farmer's Advocate*, July 15, 1896, p. 1288). "Claughbane had the hardihood," wrote "Scotland Forever," "to compare the Shire with the Clyde. . . . Now, I call this nothing else but cheek. The idea of comparing a big, coarse, clumsy brute, with round bone, coarse feather and no action, with a horse that while large, has splendid action, is noted for flat, hard bone, and good feet. The Clyde is an ideal farm horse; can handle the plow and harrow in good shape and with ease to himself. . . . The Shire, on the other hand, is too slow and clumsy to be of any use on a farm. It is true, he can plow, but so can an ox, and for anything else he has not speed enough; in fact, I would advise farmers to use oxen instead, as they are just as able to get through the work, costing less, and they can be converted into beef — which the Shire cannot — a decided advantage in favor of the ox. . . . For one who finds fault with the Clyde, when compared with other draft breeds, does not know a good horse when he sees it."

The vitriolic exchanges began again when a correspondent identifying himself as "A. S., Daly Municipality, Manitoba," wrote to the *Farmer's Advocate* (February 5, 1900, p. 60) saying that he had no use for Clydesdales. "I consider them too soft for Manitoba," he said and then went on to explain why he wanted Percherons. A reply came from "Jas. M., Pipestone" *(Farmer's Advocate*, May 21, 1900, p. 270), delivering an elementary lecture on draft horse type and reminding all that "feet and legs are the most important part of the horse, for, with good feet and legs, even though the body is a little plain, you have a good useful beast; but a model body with poor feet and legs, and you have what I call a good-looking 'nothing.' . . . I really think the Clydesdales — straight-legged, clean-boned, and with good action — are what we want." In other words, farmers want or should want Clydesdales.

For Percherons, the best chance to advance their cause came in 1903 when the breed was recognized with show-ring classes at both the Winnipeg and Brandon exhibitions. At Winnipeg, where the continuing popularity of the Scottish breed was attested by the eleven mature stallions coming together in the first class, the Percheron entry was unimpressive. An editor (Farmer's Advocate, August 5, 1903, p. 812) reported the Percheron exhibit as "scarcely sufficient to justify its continuation. There is no question," he added, "but that good Percheron horses are being bred but the best do not appear to be finding their way to this country." It was part of that editor's continuing warning for horsemen to be on their guard against "fakers" from the south, offering "horses of a breed with which Canadian farmers are not familiar, asking from syndicates three or four prices, and giving all sorts of unreasonable guarantees."

Of the two mature Percheron stallions and two three-year-olds exhibited, the judge, Robert Ness from Eastern Canada, said, "a poor lot," and then awarded the breed championship to the winning two-year-old, a horse purchased by a Dauphin syndicate at a price said to be "about $4,000."

At the Brandon Exhibition a few days later, the Percheron display was neither bigger nor better. A stallion called "Archibald," shown by the Brandon Hills Syndicate, was the only entry in the mature class and two representatives appeared for the three-year-old class, one of them becoming the champion. Nobody was becoming very excited about that initial public appearance of Percherons in a notoriously strong Clydesdale area, but regardless of derogatory remarks, published and un-published, the massive frames and comparatively easy-going characteristics began to win the interest of many men on the land. And having accepted the Percheron and then the Belgian, they were ready to argue more determinedly than ever with those belligerent supporters of Clydesdales.

Some of the most bitter differences arose at local fairs where much of the show-ring competition was in interbreed classes. The sections for grade horses brought together animals bearing the characteristics of different breeds, and the role of judge took on a new occupational danger. The Scottish horsemen expected qualified judges to attach an overriding importance to quality in feet and legs and elevate the sons and daughters of Clydesdale stallions to winning positions. With no less determination, men of the "rebel group" were sure that any judge who failed to be guided by the powerful bodies and obvious utility in the offspring from Percheron and Belgian sires was prejudiced and unfit for the tasks of adjudication. Depending upon the distribution of awards, the judge was branded by the ringside observers as "a Clyde man," or "a Percheron man." As such, he was praised for good judgment by one group and damned by the other.

So strong was the feeling in some communities that friends of the Clydesdale breed sat or stood on one side of the judging ring and friends of the Percheron and the Belgian congregated on the other. When a half-bred Clydesdale colt or filly gained a first-prize ribbon, there was cheering from the side seating the MacLeans, MacEwans, and Campbells. When victory went to a black, gray, roan or chestnut showing its Percheron or Belgian breeding, shouts of approval came from the opposite benches, and the judge knew that whatever his decision, he would receive both commendation and criticism.

The keenest of rivalry between breeds was in classes for draft and agricultural mares and geldings shown with halter; and draft and agricultural teams in harness. In these, the Clydesdales, with stylish white markings and bold and snappy strides, continued to win most of the contest victories. In six-horse teams, for example, the Scottish breed had an almost unbroken record of winnings. But while the bonnie Clydesdales were continuing to dominate in the show ring, and Shires and Suffolks were disappearing from the Canadian scene, Percherons and Belgians were making fast friends back in farming communities where the only test of importance was in ability to do a day's work with a minimum of hardship and loss of weight. More and more men on the land were saying that Percherons and Belgians were "easy keepers" and the kind that could be entrusted most safely to inexperienced hired helpers. The result was that Percheron and Belgian popularity climbed to equal and then surpass that enjoyed by the Clydesdales.

By 1940, the number of purebred Percherons registered in Canada had passed the corresponding number for Clydesdales, and Belgians were gaining rapidly. Actual registrations for the year showed 865 Percherons, 786 Clydesdales, 420 Belgians, 13 Suffolks and 5 Shires. Twenty-five years later, all the draft breeds were down in numbers registered, but the Belgian was the leader, followed by the Percheron and then the Clydesdale; the Suffolk and Shire, by this time, had disappeared from registration statistics.

Breed rivalry lasted for many years, and while horsemen were berating each other on trivialities, they did not seem to consider that their chief concern should have been the new competition in the form of motor power, soon to force all breeds of heavy horses into decline together.

More Power, More Comfort, More Debt

This second excerpt from the same book is included because while a great deal of MacEwan's writings deal with the distant past, in this chapter he deals with the development of a problem now facing many producers on the prairies — the cost of modern technology. (Continued from Power for Prairie Plows, *1971.)*

An Alberta farmer taking delivery of a 1970-model tractor was heard to remark that he would now command "more field power, more working comfort and convenience and more debt" than at any time in his farming career. The new and sophisticated thing, rated at 135 horsepower, would pull up to eight plows and was described as a turbocharged diesel. It had eight forward speeds ranging to eighteen miles per hour, and two reverse speeds. It had a six-cylinder high-compression motor, power steering, dual headlights, a twelve-position adjustable seat for the driver, and a cab offering "living room comfort with sundeck view." For what more could a power farmer ask, unless it were a price which would be somewhat less than the equivalent of a quarter section of wheat land?

It was a bigger tractor than most of those seen on farms, but the fact was that the popular fancy in tractor size was changing again. Older farmers remembered when all tractors were massive, awkward, and slow. But the big ones lost favor and demand was for small ones. After more years, farmers were asking for bigger tractors to match their bigger farms, and the popular unit came to have the appearance of a tractor of medium size and the power of a big one. The sixty-five tractors tested in the University of Nebraska Tractor Testing Lab in 1920 averaged 33½ in horsepower; and the thirty-two tractors tested in 1968 averaged over 70 horsepower.

When the Canadian Western Farm and Ranch Show was held at Edmonton in March, 1970, each manufacturer had an opportunity to display one unit from its line of tractors. Except for a few garden-type tractors, almost all the models elected for display carried ratings of 100 horsepower or over. One giant machine, with four-wheel drive and a rating of 169 horsepower, would have had no place on any but a very big farm. But western farms were becoming bigger, and their operators, quite obviously, wanted bigger tractors.

Tractor change was so great that even the most popular designs of 1926 appeared as antiques in 1966. Thanks to testing programs and the growing responsibility of manufacturers eager to gain the image of reliability, most changes were along sound and progressive lines. Farmers bought even the newest types with confidence such as they could not have found in earlier years. Some of that confidence was attributable to assurances coming from tractor-testing services conducted at Nebraska from 1919. A Waterloo Boy carried the tag of "Test Number One," and on December 2, 1968, Nebraska "Test Number 1,000" was conducted on a very modern diesel. In the intervening years, other states and provinces heard proposals for the establishment of local tractor-testing facilities, but as pointed out on various occasions by Prof. J. MacGregor Smith of the University of Saskatchewan and the University of Alberta, there was no particular advantage in duplicating what was being done — and done well — at Nebraska.

Some of the changes and improvements making farm tractors more efficient and more convenient — as well as more costly — should be noted. Self-starters, demonstrated about 1920, were adopted in the 1930's, sparing operators the tiring necessity of cranking by hand and the arm-breaking consequence of backfiring.

The newest feature of 1926 was the power take-off, allowing power from the motor to be transmitted to binder or mower or other equipment without the necessity of keeping the tractor in motion. As is the case of front-end and rear-end mounted implements, the effect was to extend tractor usefulness.

One of the most notable changes came with the almost universal adoption of pneumatic tires for wheel-drive tractors. Allis-Chalmers placed those rubber tires on tractors in 1932, and in a surprisingly short time, other companies followed and the old steel-mounted machines with heavy angle-iron cleats disappeared. With benefit of rubber, tractors could find added traction and be driven at much higher road speeds. The two-mile-an-hour speed of the heavy tractors in pioneer years would seem like monotony alongside a modern mounted-on-rubber model moving fast enough to break the village speed limit.

Many of the changes were to make the operator's work load lighter and his entire effort more effective, as in the mechanical aids in handling tractor machinery. When plowing with a heavy tractor in 1915, plows were raised and lowered individually by means of levers and every gang of tractor plows required the attention of a full-time attendant. But with the coming of small tractors, mechanical lifts replaced hand levers and then hydraulic lifts were adopted. The tractor operator's control board became more sophisticated, just as his cab became more attractive and his tractor seat more comfortable.

It was natural that the new tractor with a wider range of capabilities would be found performing an ever-greater number of farm tasks and chores. Whereas the early types were largely restricted to plowing and heavy belt work, the new ones were used for all kinds of field work, all jobs in the hayfields, clearing of brushland, building roads, pulling and topping sugar beets, lifting and hauling manure, moving snow, digging postholes, and even for stretching fence wire. Versatility was the new characteristic in farming communities from which draft horses had virtually disappeared.

That mechanization of agriculture advanced faster and farther in the prairie region than in any other part of Canada did not surprise anybody. The farms there were bigger, and the manner of farming invited heavier equipment and bigger risks.

If there was such a thing as an average census farm in Manitoba, Saskatchewan, and Alberta in 1966, it was one comprising 685 acres, 437 acres of which were "improved," meaning that they were producing domestic crops or in summerfallow. At the time of the official count, June 1, that farm had 36 head of cattle, 11 pigs, 2 sheep, 118 poultry and 1 horse which, it might be assumed, conformed to saddle type more than to draft. Compared with an average census farm in the six eastern provinces, the western unit was four times as large in acreage, carried twice as many cattle, had fewer pigs and poultry and had a much bigger investment in tractors and other machinery. (Compiled from *Canada Year Book* data.)

Many western farmers admitted that power machinery had become an obsession. Across their three provinces there were 160 tractors for every 100 farms, 115 motor trucks per 100 farms, and 69 grain combines per 100 farms. The capital investment in machinery and equipment averaged $11,219, over 20 per cent of the total capital investment of $55,862. The eastern farm had become mechanized also, and considered on the basis of tractors per 100-acre or more farms rather than per 100 farms, it was highly mechanized. The 1966 census figures for those eastern provinces showed 122 tractors per 100 farms, 49 motor trucks, and 16 grain combines, while the average capital investment in machinery and equipment per census farm was $5,738 or about 17 per cent of the total. Clearly, the Canadian farmer had become an esteemed customer of the machine companies and the western farmer, with bigger holdings, an especially esteemed customer whose fortunes in the marketing of produce was a prime factor in determining company dividends.

Farm tractor replacement averaged about 10 per cent per year, but when crops or markets failed, farmers bought more repairs and fewer new tractors and manufacturers prepared for reduced sales and reduced profits. Company officials followed the movement of wheat, knowing it was likely to be the biggest single factor in determining volume of business for them. When Canada's grain exports were falling in recent years, makers and dealers in machinery knew what to expect: Sales of all farm implements and repairs dropped from $494,298,000 in 1967 to $406,646,000 in 1969.

The whole Canadian economy felt the impact from new tractors in large numbers, but the most massive impact was upon the shape and character of agriculture itself. Farms increased in size and a greater number of farm homes stood abandoned. With the new mechanical power, fewer operators and workers were needed and rural population declined. One man with the newest power machinery could work several times as much land as could his father or his grandfather using the equipment available to them.

George Lane of the Bar U Ranch, in 1908, had eighty horses and twenty-eight hired men to farm the land which Senator Harry Hays ultimately worked with three men and the best modern tractor power. And, according to the Senator, "we now produce about twice as much on the same ground." While a farm worker in the World War II period produced roughly enough food for himself and ten other human consumers, his modern counterpart, employing the most up-to-date machinery aids (1971), can produce enough for himself and about twenty others.

Farmers argued that the tractors they wanted should not cost them as much as they were required to pay, and a government-appointed commission agreed. But they bought just the same, and there was no doubt about the new machines increasing the effectiveness and output of each worker and making it possible for rural people to enjoy more of the rewards of leisure. Because production costs were beaten to near-minimum and farms were made more productive, standards of living were raised appreciably. The gap between rural and urban living was made more narrow. It would have been difficult for even an old and loyal horseman to deny the gains.

Crowfoot
Man of Wisdom

This excerpt shows MacEwan at his best, dealing with a strong personality and a leader who held the future of the West in his hand at one important juncture. Crowfoot was a man of great stature and will be remembered as such in future, at least partly because MacEwan wrote about him in his own inimitable way. (From Portraits from the Plains, *Toronto: McGraw-Hill Ryerson, 1971. Reprinted by permission of McGraw-Hill Ryerson Limited.)*

On at least four occasions, Crowfoot's statesman-like decisions were crucial in shaping Western Canadian destiny. The first was when the noble Blackfoot stood before Assistant Commissioner James Macleod and voiced acceptance of the Mounted Police, thereby making the work of the force much easier and more likely to succeed. The second history-making decision was his approval of Indian Treaty Number Seven. Next was his rejection of overtures from Sitting Bull to cooperate in the Sioux war against the incoming whites and the fourth decision of very far-reaching importance was in the great leader's refusal to join Louis Riel and Gabriel Dumont in their attempted overthrow of the new authority. The decisions were not easy ones to make but if any one of them had been reversed, the cost in human lives and retarded progress could have been very high.

Crowfoot commanded the respect of his tribesmen and their neighbours for many moons but it was at the signing of the Treaty that he seemed to rise to his greatest stature. There he stood out conspicuously, holding the outcome of negotiations in his hand. Other Indians waited for his approval or disapproval before venturing to form their own opinions. Finally, after weighing the conditions of the Treaty carefully, the leader was satisfied and made his famous pronouncement: "I will be the first to sign: I will be the last to break the Treaty."

Always, his speech was picturesque, like poetry. Few men of any race could have surpassed him in oratory. True, he had the benefit of an educated friend and confidant who acted as his interpreter, Jean L'Heureux, an Old Country Frenchman who found Blackfoot company preferable to that of white men. Be that as it may, many of Crowfoot's pronouncements were gems of wisdom and beauty, with a Churchillian quality about them.

He sounded very much like Sir Winston Churchill when he proclaimed: "Though our enemies be as strong as the sun, as numerous as the stars, we will defend our lodges." And what thoughtful scholar would not find pride in being remembered for saying: "Our land is more valuable than your money. It will last forever. It will not perish as long as the sun shines and the water flows, and through all the years it will give life to men and beasts. It was put there by the Great Spirit and we cannot sell it because it does not belong to us."

In the opinion of Chief Walking Buffalo, patriarch of the Stonies who died late in 1967, Crowfoot of the Blackfoot Tribe was "the greatest of them all." The old Stoney remembered Crowfoot as a man of striking appearance, with penetrating eyes, chiselled features and long and unbraided hair. With different clothing and an appropriate cut to his hair, he might have played the role of a Roman centurion.

Nobody could say exactly where or when Crowfoot was born. Indians did not bother with vital statistics. What did it matter about the particular moon under which a person was born or where the event took place? The main thing was to survive to hunt and fight and steal horses. But Crowfoot supposed he was 69 years of age when consulted just prior to his death in 1890, which would make his birth coincide with the amalgamation of the Hudson's Bay Company and the North West Company. As for place of birth, all he knew was that it was somewhere south of the Red Deer River.

Leadership seemed to run in the family. The father was a Blackfoot Chief and the eldest brother, Isapo-Muksiko — meaning Crow Big Foot — gave promise of becoming a tribal leader. But that brother met with tragedy. While visiting a Snake Indian encampment in the South his peaceful intentions were misunderstood and he was attacked and murdered. The Blackfoot tribesmen were furious and the murdered man's younger brother led a war party which inflicted severe revenge. As a result, followers bestowed the dead man's name, Crow Big Foot, upon the victorious brother. Some pioneers believed that Police Scout Jerry Potts was responsible for shortening the name to Crowfoot.

In any case, the young man came to maturity with a reputation for courage and success in battle. For the edification of campfire audiences, he could relate a hundred warpath adventures, most of them victories.

And the fact that he always rode a good horse — either white or spotted — testified to his skill at horse stealing.

The Blackfoot were the first of the Canadian Indians to have horses and they became equestrian experts, good riders and conscious of quality in the stock they filched from their neighbours. A fast horse offered practical advantages on the warpath and in the hunt and there was satisfaction in owning a mount capable of outrunning every other steed in the camp. From horse stealing expeditions the young Crowfoot always returned with the best horses, and in a run for a buffalo he was in the best position to make the kill. On occasion, the horse stealing adventures took the Blackfoot braves far into the Southwest where Nez Percé Indians were practicing selective breeding and raising spotted-coated animals of superior speed and stamina.

Standing out in the memory of one of the Blackfoot elders — a boy when Crowfoot was at the peak of his influence — was the Chief's beloved umbrella which he carried for protection from sun, rain, and even snow as he rode across the plains. Not all of the white man's inventions were good but here was one for which the Chief found purpose and felt attachment. Crowfoot fancied clothes with bright colors, and the appearance of a well-dressed Chief carrying umbrella and riding a white or spotted horse was enough to enliven any prairie scene.

Rev. John McDougall had been commissioned to inform the Indians in the region that the Mounted Police were coming and that their intentions were good. Thus, when the force arrived at Oldman River on October 13, 1874, after the long and exhausting trek from Southern Manitoba, the native people were not totally surprised. They were curious but still sceptical and certainly in no hurry about embracing or even accepting these newcomers with bright uniforms and polished guns. Crowfoot wanted to know more about the police before forming any conclusions and on the first day of December, while the fort was still under construction, the great Chief came and stood boldly — almost defiantly — before Assistant Commissioner Macleod. He wanted it clearly understood that he was there without either friendliness or hostility. He was there with an open mind, wanting to hear about police intentions and methods.

Col. Macleod, with Jerry Potts to interpret, explained the Government determination to end whiskey trading and punish anybody, white man or Indian, who refused to obey good laws. Crowfoot listened in silence. The idea of a police force was not easy for a native to grasp and for some time the Chief gave no indication of how he felt about it. It was a crucial moment in Western Canadian history because police success in making the plains safe for settlement depended very largely upon acceptance by the most influencial Indian in the Southwest. But

Crowfoot's reaction was favourable and he replied with a speech which removed all doubt:

> My brother, your words make me glad. I listened to them not only with my ears but with my heart also. In the coming of the Long Knives, with their firewater and quick-shooting guns, we are weak and our people have been woefully slain and impoverished. You say this will be stopped. We are glad to have it stopped. We want peace. What you tell us about this strong power which will govern good law and treat the Indian the same as the white man, makes us glad to hear. My brother, I believe you, and am thankful.

A short time later, when a member of the Blackfoot Tribe faced a criminal charge, the Chief attended the trial. After following proceedings carefully, he nodded approval, saying: "There is no forked tongue here; when my people do wrong, I will send them here to be tried."

In refusing to join the Sioux Indians, Crowfoot's service to settlers on both sides of the International Boundary was of the highest order. Sitting Bull's Sioux were being hard pressed by United States troops and both before and after the Custer Massacre at Little Big Horn, Montana, in 1876, the Sioux Chief sent runners, inviting Crowfoot to smoke his tobacco and, in so doing, declare his readiness to join in a campaign of extermination against the white intruders. Prior to the Custer Massacre, Sitting Bull's plan called for a joint effort against the American forces before turning to the Canadian side. After the fugitive Sioux fled into Canada, the Chief reversed the order of proposed attacks and suggested combined operations directed against the Canadian white population, after which the Sioux and Blackfoot warriors would move together to United States territory to continue the onslaught. There would be reward for the Blackfoot, of course — horses, captured white women and the restoration of Indian lands. It was an inviting prospect and many of the younger Blackfoot men were eager to accept the Sioux invitation. But Crowfoot, thoughtful and resolute, rejected the Sioux tobacco and with it rejected the idea of rebellion.

The angry Sioux replied to Crowfoot's rejection with a threat against the Blackfoot Tribe. Crowfoot shared the information about the threat with the Mounted Police and was assured by the officers that the Canadian strength would be brought to the defense of all Canadian Indians who might be under attack from outside the country. Crowfoot then told the law enforcement men that cooperation should work both ways and if the police needed help in keeping the Sioux under control he would furnish an army of Blackfoot warriors eager to fight.

"Tell the Great White Mother," he said, "that we are loyal and we hope she will not let her children starve."

Many times he found himself occupying a position somewhere between his own people and the police, as in 1883 when young members of the tribe displayed their anti-railroad feeling by tearing up the first rails on the new Canadian Pacific Railway grade where it penetrated the Reserve. The Government had been lax in failing to consult the Indians or offer compensation for lands taken. To further incense the aggrieved Indians, a spell of illness suffered by Crowfoot about that time was attributed to smoke poisoning from a construction locomotive and the young men were mad enough to start demolishing the Canadian Pacific Railway. But at the request of railway and Government officials, Father Lacombe intervened and promised land compensation. Satisfied with the assurance of a fair adjustment Crowfoot ordered a halt to the sabotage.

Yes, Crowfoot's proudest moments came at the signing of Blackfoot Treaty Number Seven. Throughout the negotiations, the Chief was the unchallenged "man of the hour," with several thousands of Indians from five tribes ready to accept his guidance and echo his conclusions. Even before the Indians assembled, the Crowfoot power was apparent. Authorities announced that the meeting place would be close to Fort Macleod but they had forgotten to consult the Chief of Chiefs and when he heard about the plan he announced calmly but firmly that the meeting would be held at Blackfoot Crossing, on the Bow River, and no other place. Wisely, the police and others in authority agreed, and to that picturesque location in the river valley came missionaries, a few legitimate traders, members of F. Troop of Mounted Police from Fort Calgary, between 4,000 and 5,000 Indians and the two Government-appointed negotiators, Lieutenant-Governor David Laird and Colonel James Macleod. Indian ponies and Indian dogs were there in thousands; drums beat loudly with no particular rhythm; squaws carried firewood from nearby groves of poplar, and a heavy scent of campfire smoke permeated the valley atmosphere.

To be present for the discussions, Lieutenant-Governor Laird left the Territorial Capital at Fort Livingstone on Swan River on August 11 and arrived at Fort Macleod 24 days later. Monday, September 17, was the date set for negotiations between Indians and the Commissioners but Bloods and Piegans, with Indian scorn for the white man's slavish devotion to clocks and calendars, had not arrived and the meetings were postponed for a couple of days. But most of the Blackfoot, Stonies and Sarcees present had no objection to delay, certainly not as long as Government rations of beer, flour, sugar and tea were being furnished. Most Indians accepted the handouts readily, but not Crowfoot. This man of principle could never be bribed and he would have no part in anything carrying even an appearance of bribery. He would accept no Government gifts until all matters relating to the Treaty had been resolved.

Bloods and Pigeans arrived in time for discussions on the Wednesday, September 19, and negotiations got under way. The day was not without some wild demonstrations, the wildest occurring when a few hundred youthful Blackfoot warriors, mounted and painted, broke from a nearby valley and charged toward the meeting ground, shrieking war cries and firing guns in the air. Whites, wondering what would happen next, tried to hide their fears. It was, indeed, a protest against the general trend of events but nobody was injured.

The Lieutenant-Governor explained the Government wish for a complete understanding. The buffalo herds were disappearing but the country was big and there was room for everybody, the speaker took pains to point out. To the Blackfoot and members of the other tribes represented, the Government would offer reserves and assistance in any Indian attempts to farm or ranch, also the same money payments as those accepted by the Crees.

There were pauses for discussions among the Indians. A few spoke as individuals but all eyes were upon Crowfoot. Most Indians would accept his judgment because they had learned to have confidence in him. Finally, on September 22, the Great Chief spoke. As he hesitated, to get full attention, silence came to the valley.

While I speak, be kind and patient. I have to speak for my people who are numerous and who rely upon me to follow the course which in the future will tend to their good. The plains are large and wide. We are the children of the plains. It is our home and the buffalo has been our food, always. I hope you will look upon the Blackfoot, Bloods, Piegans and Sarcees as your children now and that you will be considerate and charitable to them. They all expect me to speak for them, and I trust the Great Spirit will put into their breasts to be good people, also into the minds of all men, women and children of future generations. The advice given to me and my people has proven good. If the police had not come to this country, where would we all be now? Bad men and whiskey were killing us so fast that very few of us would have been alive today. The Mounted Police have protected us as the feathers of the bird protect it from the frosts of winter. I wish all my people good and trust that all our hearts will increase in goodness from this time forward. I am satisfied. I will sign the Treaty.

The Commissioners breathed sighs of relief, knowing that Crowfoot's announced intention to sign would ensure similar intent from all the other Chiefs. Red Crow of the Bloods declared his willingness to sign, then Eagle Tail of the Piegans, Bearspaw of the Stonies and Bull Head of the Sarcees. Crowfoot was the first to sign and other Chiefs followed, each one inscribing his mark in the form of an "X."

The cannon brought by the Mounted Police boomed to signal a successful completion and payments of Treaty Money followed: $12 for every man, woman and child, $25 for each Chief and $15 for each Councillor. In addition, each Chief qualified for a suit of clothes, a flag and a medal.

Perhaps the greatest risks for settlers on the frontier came during the period of the so called North West Rebellion, in 1885. Louis Riel who led the disgruntled Métis in the Red River insurrection of 1869-70 had retired to the life of a school teacher in Montana but did not forget the dream of helping halfbreed friends to gain what he believed to be their dues. The Government of Canada forgot all too quickly the lessons from the insurrection and the embers of rebellion smouldered in Métis communities such as those on the South Saskatchewan River, south of Prince Albert.

Riel was well known to the Indians and he did not overlook the possibility of winning the Sioux and Blackfoot to his cause. There is reason to believe that he travelled from Montana to pay a personal visit to Crowfoot for the purpose of assessing the chance of gaining the Chief's support. In any case, Riel messages reached Crowfoot while the Sioux refugees were camping on Canadian ground and the Blackfoot Indians were on the very verge of starvation. But the Chief remained steadfast in his loyalty to the Queen and the Treaty.

It was an anxious time for the Mounted Police. There was some cattle killing by hungry Indians but, in the light of a situation made grave by the serious food shortages, the acts of violence were not surprisingly numerous. Probably nobody but Crowfoot could have prevented a more serious rash of raiding and killing at that time.

But then came the March outbreak at Duck Lake, to be followed by massacre at Frog Lake and open warfare at Fish Creek and Batoche. Riel's need was very great; to succeed in his plan he required Crees, Blackfoot, Assiniboines and other tribesmen as allies. Again and again, the Riel emissaries travelled to Crowfoot's camp, pleading for help and promising to rid the Indians of the yoke placed upon them by the intruding whites. But Crowfoot's decision was to remain at peace. His young men were keen enough to join Riel and begin by moving against nearby settlements like Calgary and Fort Macleod. General Strange considered keeping his Alberta Field Force at Calgary in case of attack but he knew that military strength was needed in the North. He also knew Crowfoot and, bluntly, he placed the problem of a decision before the Chief, saying: "If you are unable to control your young warriors, I will hold my force here to help you; otherwise I will take troops to the North." Crowfoot replied: "Go North."

"To rise there must be an object," said the Blackfoot man of reason. "To rebel there must be a wrong done. To do either, we should know how it would benefit us. Why should we kill? Let the Government know we favour peace."

They were the words of a warrior who had never been known to shrink from a fight when the cause and circumstances made it right and sensible. He could see no point in becoming involved in the hostilities of 1885 and made his position very clear in a message dated: "Blackfoot Crossing, April 11, 1885." It was to Prime Minister, Sir John A. Macdonald: "On behalf of my people, I wish to send through you to the Great Mother the words I have given to the Governor at a Council at which my minor chiefs and young men were present. We are agreed and determined to remain loyal to the Queen. Our young men will go to work on the reserve and will raise all the crops they can and we hope the Government will help us to sell what we cannot use.

"Continued reports are brought to us and we do not know what to believe but we know we have seen the Governor and heard him speak; we will shut our ears and only listen to and believe what is told us through the Governor. Should any Indians come to our reserve and ask us to join them in war, we will send them away. I have sent messengers to the Bloods and Piegans who belong to our Treaty to tell them what we are doing and what we intend to do about the trouble. . . . The words I sent to Father Lacombe I again send: We will be loyal to the Queen, whatever happens."

Understandably, the message was received most gratefully at Ottawa and the Prime Minister, without delay, replied to express his thanks: "I have received your good and loyal message by telegraph and I have shown it to the Governor General who is our Great Chief under the Queen. He desires me to thank you for the promise to be a faithful friend of our Great Mother, and is sure your words are true. . . . What Governor Dewdney has promised shall be performed. We will help you to sell what you cannot use of your crop and shall not forget the good conduct of yourself, your minor chiefs and warriors."

After the Rebellion the Government of Canada made Crowfoot a gift in the sum of $50. But that was not all. Sir William Van Horne presented the Chief with a lifetime pass on the Canadian Pacific rail lines. It was not used extensively but the Chief was proud of his "key" to the railway.

As a further expression of gratitude, the Government of Canada treated Crowfoot, Red Crow, One Spot, North Axe and Three Bulls to a trip to Ottawa. Father Lacombe accompanied to help make the Indians feel more at ease. The trip filled the native leaders with amazement and served to demonstrate the white man's growing might. Crowfoot returned convinced of the practical folly of any attempts at revolt. "The whites are as thick as flies in summertime," he told his people.

Death came to the old warrior in the spring of 1890. It was difficult for anybody who had known him to imagine the Blackfoot Nation without his guiding hand. He was ill for a few weeks and when his condition deteriorated alarmingly, Dr. Henry George was instructed by Lieutenant-Governor Royal to proceed from Calgary to the Reserve and give his full attention to the Chief until there was recovery or no hope of recovery. Dr. George related the weird demonstrations of tribal grief which confronted him. The beat of the Indian tom-toms was slow and muffled. A warsong of the Chief's own composition was being chanted continuously. Women mourned loudly. Crowfoot's three wives sobbed incessantly. Armed braves with more of warpaint than clothing, stood on guard around their Chief and Medicine Men performed strange incantations over him.

Presumably the Chief was, by this time, suffering from advanced pneumonia and the doctor prescribed mustard poultice and a slug of brandy. The poultice was quite acceptable but not the brandy. Even on his deathbed, the Chief, ever opposed to liquor, was not prepared to compromise with his convictions.

The Indians about him knew he was dying but there was misjudgement about the time of actual death. Believing their Chief had breathed his last, friends shot his best horse so he would be sure of something to ride when he reached the "Sandhills" and, at the same time, they set out his saddle and rifle to be taken to the grave with the body. Each of his wives cut off a finger and the wailing grew louder. But Crowfoot was not dead; he regained consciousness and lived until the next day. In the meantime, the old orator made another of his philosophical speeches: "A little while and I will be gone from among you," he said. "Whither, I cannot tell. From nowhere we came; into nowhere we go. What is life? It is the flash of a firefly in the night. It is the breath of a buffalo in the winter time. It is as the little shadow that runs across the grass and loses itself in the sunset."

His last request was to his people, to be good and remain on friendly terms with the whites.

After his death was confirmed, the drumming and mourning and chanting grew louder and the body, adorned by the finest buckskin suit, feathered headpiece topped with a stuffed crow, and a well-seasoned stone pipe, was carried solemnly to a burial site overlooking Blackfoot Crossing where Treaty Number Seven was negotiated and signed. It was a place ever close to the old Chief's heart.

Disposal of the Chief's chattels had not been overlooked and, according to the *Lethbridge News* of May 7, 1890, a will had been drawn up for Crowfoot's approval. His house and the treasured Treaty medal from 1877 were for his "favourite" wife. The Medicine Men were to receive 15 horses as their fee for services rendered during the last days and other horses and medals were to go to his brother, Three Bulls, who, at Crowfoot's request, was to succeed him as Chief.

A bronze marker was erected at the grave. On one side were the words: "Crowfoot, Age 69, Died April 25, 1890"; on the other side was the simple statement: "Father Of His People." And there, 58 years later, a stone cairn was erected to the memory of the Chief of Chiefs, the man who remained firm in the religion of his forefathers, the man of courage, oratory and wisdom.

Bull Faces the Commission

The writer complains in this selection that journalists who observed the dramatic confrontation between a United States Commission and Sitting Bull on Canadian soil carried no cameras to capture the colorful scene. The reader is fortunate that MacEwan dealt with it in his own way, substituting a few well chosen words for photographs to convey some of the tension that fairly hummed in the air on that historic occasion. (From Sitting Bull: The Years in Canada, *Edmonton: Hurtig, 1972. Reprinted by permission of Hurtig Publishers Ltd.)*

Snow blanketed the Cypress Hills when Commissioner James Macleod and thirty members of the Force, including Jerry Potts as guide, rode in from Blackfoot Crossing on the first day of October, 1877. But warm weather followed and by the time Major Walsh arrived with Sitting Bull and his party, Indian summer in all its glory had come to the Hills. There was a stir of excitement about the Fort as preparations were being made for the visit from the high-ranking United States officials. Nothing like it had happened before and there was enough uncertainty about the outcome to furnish an air of suspense.

Colonel Macleod paused to write a short letter to his wife whom he had not seen for weeks.

My dearest Mary,
 I have just got to this place [Fort Walsh] with Sitting Bull and a lot of his Chiefs. It was quite a job getting them this far, they are so very suspicious. However, here they are, safe within the fort, about 25 of them. I expect General Terry at the Boundary on Sunday and am going to meet him myself. I hope to get thro with them on Tuesday or Wednesday and then, if possible, I shall start for home. How I do look forward to getting there, day and night. Winder writes by Mr. Powers that you were not well. I sincerely hope it was only that cold you spoke about.

Perhaps you will see me before you see this. The messenger is waiting for my dispatches so good-bye my own darling.

I am, as ever, you own, Jim[1]

The proposed meeting between the Sioux leaders and United States representatives had been a Canadian idea and it was now up to the Police to make it a success. Observers in Ottawa and Washington were confident. Major Walsh who had been assigned the task of bringing the Sioux chiefs to the Fort in the Hills and the only man who could have accomplished it was not optimistic. Sitting Bull was recalcitrant and while General Terry had the reputation, in non-Indian circles at least, of a gentleman, Walsh knew that his role in the recent Indian wars made him not the best choice to head a mission intended to convince the tribesmen of United States willingness to show compassion.

Members of the United States Commission left St. Paul, Minnesota, on September 14 and reached the International Boundary, south of Fort Walsh, a month and a day later. Commissioner Macleod, having received a letter from General Terry reporting his hope to be at the border by October 14, ordered a twenty-five man escort and rode south to meet him. But for those who left Fort Benton on October 10, there was further delay and the two groups finally met late on October 15. As though rehearsed for the stage, the two leaders on horseback came face to face, saluted, dismounted, took one step forward and greeted each other with a handclasp.

General Terry, a big and affable fellow, six feet six inches tall, and dignified by a sharply trimmed Vandyke beard, introduced the members of his group: Commissioner A. G. Lawrence; Commission Secretary Captain H. C. Corbin; Aide to the General, Captain E. W. Smith, and newspaper correspondents, Jerome B. Stillson of the *New York Herald*, and Charles Dehill of the *Chicago Times*. The American escort consisted, according to J. P. Turner, of an infantry company and "three companies of the 2nd Cavalry that participated in the battle against Chief Joseph at the Bear Paw Mountains."[2] The General did not hide his surprise at the small size of the Police escort. But he was impressed by the smart appearance of the twenty-five mounted men in red coats and pillbox caps carrying long lances.

It was late in the day and General Terry did not expect to march toward Fort Walsh at once. In making the suggestion, Colonel Macleod was thinking of the extreme difficulty Major Walsh had experienced in bringing the Sioux chiefs to the Fort and in holding them there. It would have been humiliating to the Police if, after escorting the visiting Commissioners to Fort Walsh, it was discovered that the Sioux contingent had disappeared. General Terry, although tired from long hours in the saddle, indicated willingness to proceed without further delay but there remained a point concerning the escort to be settled. He understood enough about international protocol to know that armed forces are not permitted upon foreign soil except by permission or under circumstances of extreme provocation and he issued instructions for the cavalry units to make camp on the south side and to employ themselves enjoying the prairie landscape and the view of the Sweet Grass Hills until his return a few days hence. Because of the small size of the Police escort and his personal unpopularity with certain Indian tribes, he felt he would be more comfortable if his infantrymen were to accompany him. Commissioner Macleod may have had some misgivings, but he would have found it difficult to refuse the General's request. He permitted the United States infantrymen to ride in wagons as personal attendants.

The little cavalcade was on its way with General Terry and Commissioner Macleod chatting as they jogged stirrup to stirrup. When a halt was called at sundown still forty miles from the Fort, the Police looked with envy upon the American soldiers preparing their night camp with the luxury of stoves to warm their tents. By making full use of daylight hours, the travellers reached their destination the following evening. Officers moved inside the stockade while the infantrymen set up their tents within view of the Sioux tepees.

Major Walsh, relieved that the Sioux chief and United States Commissioners were within speaking distance or at least shouting distance of each other, paid a visit to Sitting Bull's tepee. Sitting Bull repeated in emphatic terms that he had no intention of being talked into returning to the United States. The Commissioners could make fine promises and offer gifts but he would not yield in his determination. The Treaty of 1868 was broken; promises were not honoured; he did not trust these people and would not give them another chance. His Indians might experience hardships in finding sufficient food in this country where buffalo herds were shrinking but for the first time in years they were sleeping at night and living without fear of bloodshed. Walsh reiterated that Sitting Bull's people would be better off if they accepted the Commission's proposals and returned to the United States but, as long as they behaved themselves, they would not be forced to leave Canada.

The Fort Walsh mess hall, the biggest room at the post, was chosen for the meeting which got under way in the midafternoon of October 17. The American Commissioners and reporters were the first to enter. Sitting Bull, with a wolfskin hat on his head, an old shawl draped about his shoulders, a pair of beautifully beaded moccasins on his feet and an angry scowl on his face, swept into the hall. If he saw the American Commissioners, he ignored them completely, but recognizing Colonel Macleod, shuffled directly toward him and shook his hand amiably.

Then, passing the visitors with disdain, he squatted on a buffalo robe spread on the floor. Shifting so that his back was unmistakably toward the visitors, he prepared his pipe for a relaxed smoke.

Spotted Eagle, a younger man than Sitting Bull, taller, handsome, and naked to the waist, sat down close to him. Other chiefs followed; Bear's Cap, Flying Bird, Whirlwind Bear, Medicine Twinround, Iron Dog, Bear-That-Scatters, The Crow, Little Knife, Yellow Dog, and about a dozen minor chiefs, all took squatting positions on the robe. Finally a lone squaw, wife of Bear-That-Scatters, entered and sat on the bare floor. That a squaw should attend a tribal council meeting was unthinkable and the lady's presence was intended as nothing less than a premeditated insult to the Americans.

In the cramped and somewhat polluted atmosphere of the mess hall, casual spectators could not be accommodated and only a few people were to enjoy this notable scene in western history. And regrettably, representatives of the press at that period were not equipped with cameras. No photographic record was made.

The main dialogue was between General Terry and the Indians. Colonel Macleod made his own summary of the discussions and later shared his notes with the American Commissioners. General Terry was the first to speak. The General's interpreter, Constant Provost — better known as Old Provo — stood in readiness between the Indians and Commissioners. Rising to his full height and standing with an exaggerated straightness, the General read the official message, pausing after each sentence to allow the interpreter all the time he needed. The statement, as recorded by the Mounted Police, was in clear and simple terms:

> We are sent to you as a Commission by the President of the United States, at the request of the Government of the Dominion of Canada, to meet you here today. The President has instructed us to say to you that he desires to make a lasting peace with you and your people. He desires that all hostilities shall cease, and that all shall live together in harmony. He wishes this not only for the sake of the Whites alone but for your sakes too. He has instructed us to say that if you return to your country and refrain from further hostilities, a full pardon will be granted to you and your people for all acts committed in the past, and that, no matter what these acts have been, no attempt will be made to punish you or any of your people; what is past shall be forgotten and you will be received in as friendly terms as other Indians have been received. We will explain to you what the President intends to say when he says you will be treated the same as other

Indians who have surrendered. Of all the bands who were hostile to the United States your band is the only one not surrendered, every other band has come into their Agencies. Of these bands that have come in not a single man has been punished, every man, woman and child has been received as a friend, and all have received the food and clothing supplied for their use. Every one of you will be treated in the same manner. It is true that these Indians have been required to give up their horses and arms, but part of these have been sold and whatever money has been received from them will be expended for their benefit. Already 650 cows have been purchased for the use of the Indians on the Missouri River. If you abandon your present mode of life the same terms are offered to you.

The President cannot nor will not consent to your returning to your country prepared for war. He cannot consent to your returning prepared to inflict the injuries you have done in the past. He invites you to come to the boundary of this country and give up your arms and ammunition and go to the Agencies assigned for you, and give up your horses except those required for peaceful purposes.[3]

The Indians sat in silence as the message was read. Old Provo tried to transmit it accurately. The General was most anxious to convey the impression of sincerity without adding to the already long list of promises that could not be carried out. But the Indians were not receptive. Their angry frowns showed their determination to place no reliance on further promises from these people. Sitting Bull waved his contempt as he would wave a tomahawk, refusing to look directly at the Commissioners.

Sitting Bull knew he was expected to reply. He exchanged words with Spotted Eagle and took time to tie his moccasin and brush some dirt from the robe on which he was sitting. Then he rose slowly to his feet and inclined slightly toward the Commissioners but did not face them. Suddenly, the man who had been languishing in indifference became a showman. He paused as if waiting for inspiration from the Great Spirit and then waved his arms and began. His voice rose and fell; he gesticulated with his hands; his face beamed; he was aroused. The Mounted Police records are not quite the same as those reproduced in the eastern papers but there could be no question about the intent:

For 64 years, you have kept and treated my people bad; what have we done that caused us to depart from our country? We could go nowhere, so we have taken refuge here. On this side of the line I first learned to shoot; for that reason I come again; I kept going round and was compelled to leave and come here. I was raised with the Red River Half-breeds, and for that reason I shake hands with these people [Colonel Macleod and Major Walsh]. In this way I was raised. We did not give you our country; you took it from us; see how I live with these people [the Police]; look at these eyes and ears; you think me a fool; but you are a greater fool than I am; this is a Medicine House; you come to tell us stories, and we do not want to hear them; I will not say any more. I shake hands with these people; that part of the country we came from belonged to us, now we live here.[4]

Other chiefs spoke briefly. Runs-The-Roe repeated some of Sitting Bull's expressions: "For 64 years you treated us bad; don't like you at all; you came here to tell us lies; I shake hands with the police in peace. . . . We did not give our country to you; you stole it away from us; you come here to tell us lies; when you go home take them with you."

Then the squaw made a statement. She complained that the United States forces kept her people on the run to such an extent that she did not find time to raise children. The General failed at first to catch the significance of her remarks and asked the interpreter to explain further. Bringing a new inflection to the woman's comment, the interpreter replied: "She say you never gave her time to breed." Whatever she said, her meaning was fairly clear, that she would stay on the Canadian side and raise children in peace.

General Terry sensed the futility of his endeavors. Although deeply disappointed, he tried to smile as he asked a concluding question: "Are we to say to the President that you all refuse the offers made to you?"

Sitting Bull answered: "I have told you all I have to tell. This part of the country does not belong to you; all on this side belongs to these people." The Chief shook the hands of Colonel Macleod and Major Walsh and by-passed the Americans. Then the other Sioux, including The Crow, embraced the Police officers and similarly displayed their disdain for the visitors from the south.

General Terry thanked Colonel Macleod and Major Walsh for making the meeting possible. Perhaps it was a failure, the General conceded, but the effort was one which had to be made.

Colonel Macleod and Inspector Walsh, who took no part in the proceedings, followed the chiefs back to their lodges. Accompanying them were the interpreter and Sub-Inspector Dalrymple-Clark, the latter carrying pencil and paper for notes.

The Police officers had several reasons for seeking out the Indian company so soon. Walsh knew that Sitting Bull's refusal was final but the American Commissioner and Colonel Macleod wondered if the relaxed atmosphere of the tepees might produce some hint of a compromise. If anything of value were to be accomplished, it had to be at once because Terry and Lawrence were planning to leave Fort Walsh on the following morning. And if Sitting Bull's announced determination to remain in Canada was the last word on the subject, the Police Commissioner could take this opportunity to offer some further instruction about the conduct Canadian law would demand from the Sioux.

With the chiefs squatting around him, Macleod told them bluntly that they would always be recognized as American Indians. "The answer you have given the United States Commissioners today prevents your ever going back to the United States with arms and ammunition in your possession. It is our duty to prevent you from doing this. I wish to tell you that if any of you or your young men cross the line with arms in your hands that then we become your enemies as well as the Americans. . . . As long as you behave yourselves the Queen's Government will not drive you out. You must remember that you will have to live by the buffalo on this side of the line, and that the buffalo will not last forever. In a very few years they will all be killed. I hope you have thought well on the decision you have given today, not only for yourselves but for your women and children."

The chiefs listened but showed no indication of changing their decision. Sitting Bull admitted that it was only his respect for the Police and the desire to abide by Police wishes that he and his fellow chiefs had condescended to listen to the Americans. "Today," said The Bull, "you heard the sweet talk of the Americans; they would give me flour and cattle and when they got me across the line, they would fight me. I hope they will not come here a second time . . . the Americans robbed, cheated and laughed at us. . . . I would never live over there again."

Colonel Macleod reported to the Americans that the Indians were unyielding. At the same time, he delivered a letter which was a summary of the instructions he had given.

North-West Mounted Police
Fort Walsh, Oct. 17, 1877

Gentlemen:

In answer to your note, I beg to inform you that after the interview of the Commissioners with the Indians, I had a "talk" with the latter.

I endeavoured to press upon them the importance of the answer they had just made; that although some of the speakers to the Commissioners had claimed to be British Indians, we denied the claim, and that the Queen's Government looked upon them all as American Indians who had taken refuge in our country from their crimes.

I pointed out to them that their only hope was the buffalo, that it would not be many years before that source of supply would cease, and that they could expect nothing whatever from the Queen's Government except protection as long as they behaved themselves.

I warned them that their decision affected not only themselves but their children, and they should think well before it was too late. I told them they must not cross the line with a hostile intent, that if they did they would not only have the Americans for their enemies, but also the Police and the British Government, and urged upon them to carry my words to their camps and tell all the young men what I had said and warn them of the consequence of disobedience, pointing out to them that a few indiscreet young warriors might involve all in the most serious trouble.

They unanimously adhered to the answer they had given to the Commission, and promised to obey what I had told them.

I do not think there need be the least anxiety about any of these Indians crossing the line, at any rate not for some time to come.

In haste, Most respectfully yours,
James F. Macleod
Commissioner[5]

General A. F. Terry,
General A. G. Lawrence,
Sitting Bull Commission,
Fort Walsh

The Commissioners had their answer, and the American people were waiting for news of the outcome. It was a challenge for the journalists at Fort Walsh to find ways of reaching telegraphic facilities. When the *New York Herald* carried the story three days later, many people wondered how it had been accomplished. The explanation lay in a remarkable ride by Johnny Healy of Fort Benton, who, according to the story, came to the meeting place with the avowed intention of shooting Sitting Bull if the Chief refused to accept the proposed terms for his return. When warned that hanging could be the punishment, he was supposed to have replied: "Give me ten minutes start and all the Mounted Police in Canada won't catch me." He was diverted from his plan by the challenge to carry the dispatch for the *New York Herald* to the nearest telegraph office at Helena, about three hundred and forty miles from Fort Walsh. He boasted that he would deliver the papers in forty-eight hours. General Terry laughed, saying it couldn't be done. "I'll do it and maybe carry the news about Sitting Bull's death too," Healy replied. According to the Saskatchewan historian, George Shepherd,[6] he rode all night, covering the first hundred miles before changing horses at Milk River. The second stage of the relay brought him to Fort Benton twenty-four hours after leaving Fort Walsh. Changing horses there and twice more en route, he reached Helena forty-three hours after he set out.

Early on the morning of October 18, the day after the meeting, the American officials said their farewells to Colonel Macleod, thanked him again for his co-operation and conceded that the Police had done all possible to facilitate the Commission's purpose. Then, with Major Walsh heading the Police escort and General Terry riding close to him, the mule teams carrying United States infantrymen fell in line and marched away toward the Boundary. Two days later, Walsh was back at the Fort to keep his promise to Sitting Bull that he would accompany the chiefs when they returned to Wood Mountain.

The outcome was not a surprise to Walsh who had come to understand the Sioux temperament. "These Indians," he said, "are going to be guided by their own good judgement and their own good conscience. They are generally very sound. Don't under-rate them."

I. AND C. 186

DAILY NON-IMMIGRANT REPORT

Churchill Man. Aug. 29, 1932

(A)	CANADIAN CITIZENS BY BIRTH	1 Mr. J. W. G. MacEwan
(B)	BRITISH SUBJECTS WITH DOMICILE	
(C)	CANADIANS NATURALIZED WITH DOMICILE	
(D)	ALIENS WITH DOMICILE	
(E)	PERSONS RETURNING	

Readmitted

National Revenue Canada
Customs and Excise
AUG 29 1932
CHURCHILL, MAN.

(F) TOURISTS, ETC.

First Person to be admitted to Canada, by Customs and Immigration Via Churchill.

S.S. Ucksworth

_____ Inspector

_____ INSPECTOR

The author was the first person to be admitted to Canada by Customs and Immigration via Churchill, August 29, 1932.

The Diary
of a 1932 Passenger

*This excerpt shows MacEwan's reaction to days of enforced "idleness"
on board ship between Britain and Canada via the Hudson Bay route. Not
much of a diarist in ordinary life, he became one within the confines of the
S.S. Silksworth. He not only unearths an astounding volume of interesting
fact about the ship and the route but also unintentionally provides the reader
with a portrait of a most industrious observer at work. (From* Battle for the
Bay, Saskatoon: Western Producer Prairie Books, 1975.*)*

The official certificate in the author's files declares "J. W. G.
MacEwan readmitted to Canada, August 29, 1932." Dated at Churchill,
it bears the notation: "First person to be admitted to Canada by Customs
and Immigration via Churchill," and is signed by Federal Inspectors T.
R. Moulton and Hubert Legg. The following notes are from the
"passenger's" diary:

August 11, 1932 — My first trip overseas has not been marked by
luxury but it has been a great experience. It is fashionable for my
academic friends at the University of Saskatchewan to travel overseas on
scholarships; I came on a cattleship and the company of our cattle on the
nine-day crossing from Montreal to Manchester was moderately
congenial. After seeing 112 head of our experimental animals marketed
at Birkenhead and Smithfield, I set out to see as much as possible of the
Old World. I enjoyed England, loved Scotland and was captivated by the
Channel Islands. My only disappointment is the necessity of having to
return home to Saskatoon by way of Montreal — the way I came over —
when I had hoped so much to obtain passage back by Hudson Bay and
Churchill in order to make a study first hand of the new northern
shipping route. But the last message to reach me from the office of the
Canadian High Commissioner in London, reported tersely: "Hudson
Bay appears to have dried up. No more ships expected to go there this
year."

It leaves me with no choice; I will sail tomorrow for Montreal on a Manchester ship.

August 12 — I celebrated my 30th birthday by boarding the S.S. Manchester Citizen at Manchester. The ship was due to leave at 12 o'clock noon. At 12.15, as I sat at the lunch table on the ship — 15 minutes after the scheduled time for leaving — I was handed a telegram from W. A. Wilson, Agricultural Agent for Canada, Canada House, London, advising that if I could get to Newcastle-On-Tyne sometime tomorrow, I would be permitted to go with the S.S. Silksworth, sailing for Churchill for a cargo of wheat. Excitedly, I repacked my travelling bag and dashed from the ship as though it were burning, reaching the dock just as the signal was given to lift the gangplank. The officer on the dock looked in surprise and gasped: "W'at the bloody 'ell's the matter with you?"

Trying to recover my breath, I explained that I had a chance to sail to Churchill instead of Montreal, and he grunted: "Bloody fool! You'll wish you hadn't. But Blimey, if a man wants to drown in iceberg water, I wouldn't stop 'im. Go right ahead."

The Manchester Citizen pulled away and I made my retreat to the nearest bus depot, prepared to travel all day and all night in order to cross England and be at Newcastle-On-Tyne in plenty of time for the sailing I dearly wanted to make.

August 13 — The bus on which I left Liverpool yesterday continued on what seemed like an unsteady course and schedule until shortly after midnight when the driver announced: "We're at Darlington and this is as far as we go tonight." I stepped out into the darkness and looked about for some sign of a hotel. Seeing none, I asked the driver if there was one nearby and he replied: "No, and if there was one it wouldn't be open at this late hour." There was a moment of silence and he asked: "Where are you from?" I answered: "Canada." "Well," he said, while locking the door of his bus, "you'll have trouble finding a place to sleep unless you've made a reservation somewhere, but if you'll come with me I think I can find something for you."

Obediently, I followed on foot and then discovered to my surprise that he was taking me to his home and directing me to the spare bedroom kept for visiting relatives. I slept well. This morning there was a pot of tea at my door and I used it but not for drinking. Because I do not care for tea and find that hot water for shaving is almost unknown over here, I used the hot tea for shaving, just as I have been doing rather often in England, often enough to give my face a distinct smoked-ham complexion which I do not need or want. I tried to pay my host for the room and his kindness but he would take nothing and I left muttering: "I was a stranger and ye took me in." I shall not forget the genuine generosity of U. W. Key, 86 Geneva Road East, Darlington.

August 15 — I spent part of this forenoon and the lunch hour with Robert Dalgliesh, President of the Dalgliesh Shipping Company and former Lord Mayor of Newcastle-On-Tyne and found him excellent company and quite sympathetic to Churchill shipping. The two boats taking wheat from Churchill last year belonged to his company, likewise the Pennyworth which sailed to Churchill about two weeks ago and the Silksworth on which I will now return to Canada. He believes the practical season for shipping through the Straits will be from August 1 to October 15. This year the underwriters specified that an insured ship must not pass Cape Chidley before August 10th. The Dalgliesh ship, Pennyworth, left Newcastle two weeks ago to reach Chidley on the very first permitted day for entrance to the Straits. Mr. Dalgliesh explained that British Board of Trade regulations prevent him from carrying passengers on the Silksworth, sailing this afternoon for Churchill, but I can sign on as member of the crew.

But that's all right with me. I'm travelling to observe. I will pay for my cabin and my food and will receive no wages but I should be able to learn much about the new route and I was happy to accept the plan as he presented it. After meeting Captain G. Blacklock of the Silksworth, I signed on and moved into a very comfortable cabin which will likely be my home for the next 10 days or two weeks. At 3 o'clock, the good ship left its moorings and steamed away for Churchill.

August 16 — A splendid day but we struck some rough seas on the north of Scotland, Pentland Firth way.

August 17 — Cool and windy. I'm getting acquainted with the ship and sailors. The S.S. Silksworth appears to have had good care even in this time of depression when many ships have been neglected, and the members of crew impress me more than the sailors I met on the Manchester Division.

August 18 — Cool and windy.

August 19 — Cool and not so windy.

August 20 — Fog and rain.

August 21 — Fog and a harsh warning of danger. At midmorning there was a mild impact and the signal was given to cut the power. The ship had struck a "growler" or small piece of ice. It did no perceptible damage but was a frightening warning of the folly of proceeding with less than perfect visibility, especially in these waters off the southern point of Greenland. When the fog lifted, momentarily, we could see a dozen mountainous icebergs uncomfortably close to us, which explained the penetrating damp cold.

Captain Blacklock admitted that advice from Ottawa was to stay away from the point of Greenland by 100 miles to avoid most of the bergs moving down from the Arctic, skirting the Greenland coast. The Gulf Stream, it appears, strikes the Arctic and rebounds southward along the east coast of Greenland, bringing the giant bergs with it. As it is, we are right on the path of the bergs. In the light of the warning we've just had, we'll probably not turn a propeller until we can see exactly where we're going. We'll just drift with the current and hope we drift with the bergs rather than into them. Blacklock is a good head and I'm enjoying his company but he has the Englishman's irritating opinion of his own judgement.

August 22 — No progress today. Fog continues and the proximity to bergs gives an Arctic feeling to the air. With much time to spare, I have been doing a lot of writing. When I ran out of writing paper, I resorted to English toilet paper which is thicker than Canadian. When I became tired of writing, I tried my hand at fishing. I borrowed a thousand feet of line from the steward, also a few sausages for bait, then let my baited hook over the edge of the ship and unrolled the line full distance. The sailors told me I might get a halibut there. As it turned out, I caught no halibuts, didn't even get a nibble from a deep sea fish, and lost my sausages. At least, I can boast of having done deep-sea fishing.

August 23 — Fog lifted sufficiently to let us get a view of the southern tip of Greenland and be on our way at 9 a.m. It's still cold enough to be Greenland's icy mountains.

August 24 — Better day but still very chilly.

August 25 — We passed Cape Chidley and entered Hudson Straits at 9 a.m. For most of this day we could see ice floes and occasionally a berg. There was a two-hour stop this morning on account of fog and the dangers it might be hiding. But Captain Blacklock said again that he would prefer coming over this route than going to Montreal. Here there are more ice hazards but no shoals, not more than a slight current and no narrow channel about which to worry. And as he points out, the best insurance against icebergs is in the fact of knowing they are there and refusing to travel blind. If a ship is stopped when the fog limits visibility, there is not much risk of accident. Ice floes, of course, are quite another matter.

August 26 — Still a few bergs but we have visibility and are making fair progress. Today I had a lesson about compass aids. Early on this season's trip I learned from a Manchester sailor that the Hudson Bay Route would never be a success because the magnetic compass is unreliable in the northern waters. It sounded serious. The sailor was partly right; due to northern mineral deposits or proximity to the magnetic North Pole, the magnetic or conventional type of compass is definitely unreliable. But apparently my informant did not know about the use of the gyro compass which does not depend upon magnetism at all. In principle, the gyro is a high-speed spindle making something like 15,000 revolutions per minute. At such high speed, the gyro axis assumes the same direction as the axis of the earth. And the Silksworth has both compass types, magnetic and gyro, side by side, on the bridge. With the Captain's cooperation, I have been able to study them and make comparisons. The gyro compass is costly but it is available, very reliable and ships so equipped can qualify for lower rates of insurance.

August 27 — We entered Hudson Bay last night about midnight. No ice, no fog, and water as still as that of pond.

August 28 — A perfectly delightful day on the broad Bay. Hardly a ripple on the water. I believe we have changed courses only twice since entering the Straits.

Near sundown, we came within sight of Churchill, at least within sight of the big elevator which can be seen for many miles across the water. Breaking the horizon like a skyscraper, that elevator can be misleading, too. One of the sailors standing beside me rejected my warning that this was not a big city centre likely to afford all the shore-leave pastimes in which sailors like to indulge, and exclaimed as he gazed at the elevator tower and the flat rocks looking slightly like buildings: "What you trying to tell me? That place is as big as Newcastle." Poor fellow, he was due for some disappointment.

August 29 — We anchored outside the harbour last night, entered first thing this morning and docked at 9:30 a.m. It is a grand sensation to set foot once again on my own Canadian soil — indeed, any soil after two long weeks on the ocean.

Our first operation after tying up at the dock was to unload the water ballast. It seems incredible but there it was, the spectacle of pumping out the 3,000 tons of Atlantic water the S.S. Silksworth had carried across the ocean — for ballast. Surely there was something we could have brought to better advantage. As Robert Dalgliesh reminded me, the northern route will be severely handicapped until it is assured of two-way freight movement. It is all very well to be taking wheat from this Manitoba seaport but wheat should not have to carry the cost of operating the ships in both directions. The charges against our wheat will be substantially reduced when incoming ships carry valid cargo instead of the thousands of tons of water pumped in at a British port and pumped out at the Churchill end.

It doesn't take long to see the town; a fine 2½-million-bushel elevator and not much else. It takes longer to inspect the relics of history, mainly across the harbour. This afternoon I began exploration beyond the harbour and was intrigued by Fort Prince of Wales which dates to 1733 and took 40 years to bring to completion. It is one of the rarest treasures in all of North American history and even today it shows only a slight trace of the erosion of time. A few stones have fallen from the walls and most of the big guns have come to rest in the soil but the main structure stands four-square and solid, 300 feet long, 300 feet wide and about 16 feet in height of walls. Three of the walls are approximately 25 feet in thickness and the fourth wall which was to carry the cannons, is just about 40 feet thick.

One can only imagine the toil involved in transporting and shaping those huge boulders and building them into walls. Some of the partition walls have developed fractures but the outer ones have the character of timelessness. On the Churchill side of the harbour are an ancient powder magazine and a lime kiln used no doubt by those early men of the Hudson's Bay Company.

I made my way along the shore line on the fort side of the harbour to inspect Sloop's Cove where rocks bear the etchings of familiar names, including that of Samuel Hearne for whom spells of inactivity must have inspired the desire to imprint his signature on the register of the immortal rocks. One of the nearby sketches depicts a John Kelly from the Isle of Wight, hanging from a scaffold, paying dearly for the sin of stealing a goose.

At various times today we watched the white whales performing playfully in the harbour. There they were in quite big schools, running the risk of being hunted by the native people for dog feed or for sale to the whale-oil rendering plant. Whale hunting is a popular pastime and I am sorry I have not seen these Indian and Eskimo "cowboys" — or "whaleboys" — riding bareback on the belugas. The hunters, I was told, pursue the whales with motor boats and when alongside, a man with nothing more than a sharp knife will spring from the speeding boat to land on the whale and ride it and knife it until it gives up or succumbs. It is then a simple matter to tow the body to shore.

This evening I walked out into the tundra to inspect the sparse sub-Arctic flora. Although the vegetation is predominantly mosses and lichens, there are many beautiful northern flowers blooming at present. They do well growing less than 16 inches above the permafrost.

A cairn has been erected here, the plaque of which bears the following: "Port Churchill. Discovered in 1619 by the ill-fated Danish expedition under Jens Munck. In 1689 the Hudson's Bay Co. built the first Fort Churchill which in the same year was destroyed by fire. In 1717 the Company rebuilt Churchill, for nearly 200 years its most northerly post on the Bay, and starting point for many Arctic explorations. The Hudson Bay Railway was completed to this point on 1st April, 1929."

August 30 — I will be unable to remain to see the Silksworth fully loaded and sailing but this morning I saw the great streams of prairie wheat pouring into the ship from a four-belt conveyor system. The gallery along the dock is 1,400 feet long which will allow three grainboats to berth under the gallery spouts at one time. Four streams of grain can be discharged at the rate of 20,000 bushels per hour for each stream.

Before boarding the "Muskeg Special" for the 510-mile rail journey to the Pas, I accepted my "honorable discharge" from the Silksworth, on a British Board of Trade form. Until today I did not know my official rank with the ship's crew but now, from the discharge certificate I discover that my post bearing recognition of the British Merchant Marine was that of Assistant Purser. Perhaps it should be added that I was the Assistant Purser on a ship which had no Purser and nothing to purse. But I shall be ever grateful for the opportunity of travelling over the new route. After saying "farewell" to Captain Blacklock and other members of the congenial crew, I boarded the southbound train, known in these parts as the "Muskeg Special." The train's passengers are a cosmopolitan lot, a couple of Eskimo men, a few Indians, the vice-president of the Canadian National Railways and Bishop Arsene Turquetil, Bishop of the Arctic, who has been serving the Roman Catholic Church there since 1900 and probably knows the Eskimo people better than any other living white man.

The roadbed consisting of gravel and a cushion of moss and base of ice feels surprisingly good and we travel along at 30 miles an hour. The countryside is strange and a little terrifying, mile after mile without a railway crossing, a road or sign of human habitation. The Churchill end, of course, is treeless tundra with water in abundance, then the "land of little sticks" and ultimately forests and park country. It is vast and lovely and lonely. Nature has found uses for it. How much use man will find for it remains to be seen.

Noting the names of stations and sidings on this new line is like a lesson in Canadian history. I'm glad to see names with a Canadian ring about them instead of those we have so commonly imported. That is not to quarrel with Old World names and heroes; it's just time we recognized our own. The second station south of Churchill, at Mile 493, is Digges, a name which recalls Sir Dudley Digges who helped equip the ship Discovery for Henry Hudson in 1610 and in whose honor, also, Digges Island at the mouth of the Bay was named.

The next station is Bylot, Mile 485, with its name taken from that of Robert Bylot who was Henry Hudson's first mate on the Discovery. Then there is Lamprey, Mile 477, commemorating one of Jens Munck's ships with which he entered the harbour at Churchill in the autumn of 1619. Farther south on the line is Back, Mile 434, carrying the name of Captain George Back, a member of the Sir John Franklin expedition of 1819.

We come to Gillam at Mile 326 and then Nonsuch at Mile 295,

taking their names from Captain Zachary Gillam and the ship Nonsuch which sailed from Gravesend to Hudson Bay in 1668 and carried out much of the experimental work upon which the Hudson's Bay Company was founded. The railway point of Munck, Mile 269, is of course, named to honor Jens Munck who, sailing under the Danish flag, wintered and suffered at the mouth of the Churchill River in 1619-20. Stitt, at Mile 243, bears the name of a prominent figure at early Red River, and the Bridgar name encountered at Mile 218, is in recognition of John Bridgar, one of the very early Masters at Albany House.

La Pérouse who sailed into the Bay and captured Fort Prince of Wales in 1782, gave his name to the siding at Mile 171 and William Lyddal, an early Governor of the Hudson's Bay Company did the same for the siding at Mile 148. Then there is Wabowden at Mile 136, named for W. A. Bowden, a Chief Engineer in the Department of Railways and Canals. There are Button and Tyrrell stations at Miles 114 and 101 respectively, reminding travellers of famous northern personalities, and Turnbull at Mile 93 named for Thomas Turnbull, another engineer on the line during the years of construction. Rawebb at Mile 54 is for Ralph Webb, former Mayor of Winnipeg and always a vigorous supporter of the Hudson Bay Railway. It's time Canadians acknowledged that they have some history.

August 31 — I arrived at The Pas, Mile 0, almost 24 hours after leaving Churchill. There is more history here and the community retains the marks of the frontier. The Pas, like other settled areas, did not escape the painful pinch of depression and I could have bought a polar bear skin, nicely tanned, for $10. The trouble was that I did not have that much money for investment in non-essential wares at this time on my journey. The people here are intensely enthusiastic about the Hudson Bay Railway, and they should be. It could do much for this town with its roots penetrating deeply into the fur trade era.

It was here at the confluence of the Saskatchewan and Pasqua Rivers that the La Vérendryes — Pierre and Louis Joseph — built a trading post in 1751 and called it Fort Paskoyac. It became an important landmark for explorers and travellers and freighters. Henry Kelsey passed that way on his historic trip in 1691 and Anthony Henday stopped to fraternize and drink a little French wine when making his famous cross-country journey in 1754 and '55. And there on September 10, 1910, the Hon. G. P. Graham, Minister of Railways and Canals, turned the first sod for the Hudson Bay Railway.

From here I take train to Melfort for a short visit with parents and then to Saskatoon and my employer, the University of Saskatchewan.

A Name Is Chosen

Grant MacEwan is at his most persistent in this excerpt. He has researched everything ever written about the name of Calgary. Referring to notes taken in the 1920s during conversations with pioneers who were close to the scene at the time, in a few words he has saved an incident in our history that might well have otherwise been lost. (From Calgary Cavalcade: From Fort to Fortune, *Edmonton: Institute of Applied Art, 1959. Reprinted, with additions, by Western Producer Prairie Books, 1975.)*

From its beginning as a Mounted Police outpost, Calgary distinctiveness took many forms. Even in the soft, Gaelic name there was romance — and some mystery.

About the meaning of the word "Calgary," there was wide difference of opinion. The earliest definition was "clear running water," appropriate, of course. But other interpretations advanced at one time or another by people who professed a knowledge of the lovely Gaelic tongue added confusion. "A Hut In The Thicket," said one authority; and according to others with self-proclaimed qualifications to render judgment, the word could mean "The Willows Beyond The Boundary"; "A Harbor Of The Sea"; "Cabbage Garden"; "Laughing Waves"; "Den Of The Rough." There is still another theory — that Calgary's name was Scandinavian in its origin and might have been taken to mean "Bay Of Laughing Waters."

But when scholarly opinion differs, Calgarians could ask with Pope: "Who shall decide when doctors disagree?" On one point, however, there was no lack of agreement — that the name was attractive and that the events leading to its choice held more of interest than its derivation.

It was November [1875] when the Baker men completed the new fort and the place was still nameless — nameless except that people at Fort Macleod referred to it quite commonly as "The Mouth."

Only Brisebois, it seems, was giving any special thought to the question of a proper name. In this humble post on a magnificent site, he had more secret pride than he was admitting. One police fort, he knew very well, had been named to honor Assistant Commissioner Macleod and another would bear the name of Superintendent Walsh. Why should this new fort beside the Elbow not be given the good French name of Brisebois, especially when it was built over the ruins of what the Inspector still chose to believe were those of the French post La Jonquiére?

That was the way this man with justifiable sentiment for race and name wanted it, and when the Mounties were celebrating Christmas dinner with roast buffalo hump, prairie chicken and Toronto-made plum pudding brought from Fort Benton by ox-powered freight, the effusive inspector proposed a toast to "Fort Brisebois."

Nobody challenged the proposal until senior officers came that way and displayed some high-ranking displeasure. Two weeks later, when back at Fort Macleod, Major A. G. Irvine, still annoyed about the unauthorized naming of the new fort, penned a Leap Year Day letter to the Deputy Minister of Justice at Ottawa. It was dated, February 29, 1876.

> Sir: As we have now a post or fort at Bow River, it would be well if it was known by some name. I visited the post about a fortnight ago with Col. Macleod and when we were there Inspector Brisebois issued an order without consulting either Col. Macleod or myself stating that all public documents sent out from this fort were to be headed "Fort Brisebois." I, of course, cancelled the order at once, as in the first place Inspector Brisebois had no authority to issue such an order, and in the second place the fort was not built by Inspector Brisebois' troop, and neither the troop or the people about there wish the place called Brisebois.
>
> Col. Macleod has suggested the name Calgary, which I believe, in Scotch means "clear running water," a very appropriate name I think.
>
> Should the minister be pleased to approve of this name, I will issue an order to that effect.
>
> I have the honor to be, sir,
> Your obedient servant,
> (Signed) A. G. Irvine, Asst. Commr.

The Ottawa people were in agreement with Irvine's suggestion and from Minister of Justice Edward Blake went a memo to his deputy: "Do not interfere with Assistant Commissioner's discretion in choosing the name he mentions. E. B."

And so, in the spring of 1876, the name became "Calgarry," written with two "r's." But why did Macleod choose that particular name? Was it because of "Calligarry" on the Isle of Skye, five miles from which his grandfather had a farm? Or was it from memory of Calgarry House on the Isle of Mull? The Assistant Commissioner had ancestral connections on both of those "Misty Islands" and islanders from both places have tried to claim the honor of furnishing the name for a Canadian city.

Skye was the ancestral home of the Macleods and Macdonalds, and Mull the home of Colonel Macleod's mother's people, the Mackenzies. Prior to the formation of the Mounted Police, Macleod visited his uncle, John Hugh Munro Mackenzie, who occupied Calgary House, a castlelike place overlooking Calgarry Bay on the west coast of Mull — and loved what he saw. Probably it was the impression from that visit which led him to suggest the name for the fort destined to beget a city.

But as though the nice, Gaelic name were not enough, the city acquired descriptive terms of various sorts — mostly complimentary. In 1895 the place was described as "the western edge of civilization"; in 1903 it was the "Sandstone City," and in 1912 "The coming Chicago of Canada." Still later it was dubbed "Sunshine City," and "Stampede City," and "Oil Capital," but not because of any failure to appreciate the attractiveness of the real name.

Any way one looks at it, the community received a good name, one that appealed to songwriters and poets as well as to those who knew something of its origin. And citizens who wrote the word many times a day should have been perfectly satisfied that it was not spelled the way some Gaelic scholars would have done it: "Calgearraidh."

Caroline "Mother" Fulham: The Lady Kept Pigs

Here is one of those stories MacEwan delights in relating: a simple tale about a humble character who occupied, nonetheless, an important place in the community. It is a MacEwan trademark — a story about a person few would expect a writer to take seriously. (From And Mighty Women Too, *Saskatoon: Western Producer Prairie Books, 1975.)*

When Mrs. Caroline Fulham — better known as Mother Fulham — left Calgary in 1904, members of the police department breathed sighs of relief and prepared to celebrate the great day. Most other citizens were secretly sorry to see her go because she was, in those years before radio, television and movies, the best source of local amusement. As the leading entertainer on Stephen Avenue, she needed no make-up, required no rehearsal and followed no script. Her charm was in being herself, rough as it might be.

With a sharp Irish tongue and a loud voice, she had the last word in almost every argument and when more was needed, she could draw upon the persuasiveness of two ready fists. Plump and powerful, she was a fair match for the best policeman on the beat. For one reason or another, the police officers saw much of her and knew that to escort her to a cell was normally a task requiring the chief and two constables — the entire Calgary force for some years.

The lady could neither read nor write but such circumstances were not to restrict her in gaining publicity. Between visits to the police court and her daily appearances guiding her horse-drawn democrat on Calgary streets, she became one of the best-known personalities in the community. And while police officers did their best to spare her from trouble, men and boys seeking fun delighted to tease and annoy her, knowing they would get instant and often exciting reaction.

Nor were those fellows above playing tricks on her, as on that day when she left her horse and democrat in the lane while she visited the long bar of the Alberta Hotel. In her absence, the pranksters unhitched the horse from the vehicle and then, after drawing the democrat shafts through the woven wire fence containing the railway right of way, rehitched with horse on one side of the fence and democrat on the other. In due course, the lady emerged from the hotel, feeling good enough to forgive all her enemies or make some new ones. Unsteadily, she walked to her democrat, mounted and clucked to her horse to move on before realizing that something was wrong and progress would be impossible. Sensing mischief, she seized her buggy whip and dismounted to search for the miscreants, all the while muttering threats of violence.

For most of her years in Calgary, Mother Fulham lived on 6th Avenue, just a short distance west of the site on which Knox United Church was built. Her occupation was that of keeping pigs. With no bylaws restricting livestock within the town, her pig feeding operations were entirely legal, even though they drew criticism from neighbors. To feed the swine, she gathered kitchen waste from Calgary's best hotels and restaurants. Here was good and economical raw material for pork production and she chose to believe that she had a monopoly on the contents of all garbage containers behind the Alberta, Queen's, Royal and Windsor hotels, and Criterion and New Brunswick restaurants. When other feeders of pigs threatened to encroach upon her garbage preserves, she was prepared to protect her interests with force if necessary.

With regularity befitting a town's bell-ringer, she made the rounds to gather the precious pig feed. Sitting squarely in the middle of the democrat seat, with barrel in the back for the transfer of the pig feed, she employed a willow switch to urge her aging horse to something faster than a walk and slower than a trot, muttering uncomplimentary epithets in reply to rude remarks from the sidewalk spectators. When somebody would shout "Hurray for Ireland," the speaker could expect to hear the rejoinder, "Sure, you'd like to be Irish too, ye pur fool."

Sometimes the mischief-makers visited her premises at night to carry out some nefarious trick. On a certain St. Patrick's night when the lady was celebrating, visitors painted her pigs a brilliant green, and on another occasion, according to the *Calgary Herald* (September 1, 1903): "Mrs. Fulham last night was awakened by hearing some men around her yard and saw them running away. This morning she got in her buckboard and the wheels came off after the horse had gone a few yards, so she knew the men had taken the nuts. She thinks she knows who the men were."

She kept her most outlandish green clothing for St. Patrick's day and began celebrating early. Her pigs might be neglected but a thoughtful neighbor was likely to give them feed and water. On that Day of Days, she took special license to sing Irish songs from her throne on the democrat and, perchance, reach a state of intoxication long before it was time to attend the annual Firemen's Ball on that date.

Although uneducated, her wit was keen, as Dr. H. G. Mackid could testify. Meeting her on Stephen Avenue and seeing her walking with lameness, he inquired sympathetically if he could do anything for her. She replied that an ankle had been giving her trouble, to which the kindly doctor invited her to step inside Templeton's Drug Store where he could examine it. The doctor was, no doubt, aware that cleanliness was not one of the lady's obvious characteristics, but when she peeled down a stocking to expose the sore ankle, the doctor reeled at the sight of the unwashed limb and exclaimed repulsively, "By George, I'd bet a dollar there's not another leg in Calgary as dirty as that one."

Quick as a flash, the women shouted back: "Put up your money, Doctor. I'm betting ye a dollar there is another and here's my money."

Before there was time for a retraction, Mother Fulham dropped her other stocking, thereby exposing another leg, just as dirty as the first one, and held out her hand to collect the doctor's dollar. (As told to the author by Dr. Mackid, May 3, 1956.)

They were altercations with police and neighbors that brought her name into the newspaper columns most often. And when she came to court, she would have nobody but the great Irish lawyer and personality, Paddy Nolan, to plead her case. Nolan may have enjoyed the assignments, even though he was never paid, because he was fascinated by the woman with the sharp tongue and was always assured of a big courtroom audience. When it was known on the streets that Mother Fulham and Paddy Nolan would appear together, everybody in the community wanted to be present. Sometimes the woman would be evicted from the court for reasons of undisciplined remarks and sometimes spectators had reason to wonder if the police were prosecuting the Fulham woman or if she was prosecuting the police.

Generally she was the defendant but in at least two instances she was the plaintiff. In April, 1890,[1] she was charging a Chinese employee of the Alberta Hotel with assault. As Paddy Nolan explained the circumstances, Mrs. Fulham caught the man bent over a garbage barrel at the rear of the hotel and administered a good Irish rebuke, either verbal or physical, and he struck her. But the evidence was confusing and there was reason to believe that the accused, instead of stealing garbage as alleged, was simply trying to recover a dressed chicken he had earlier stolen from the hotel kitchen and hidden temporarily in the barrel. The case was dismissed.

On the other occasion when Mrs. Fulham was charging rather than defending, she accused her neighbor, the Reverend Jacques, of insulting her with improper language. J. A. Lougheed acted for the reverend gentleman and Paddy Nolan, as usual, was on Mother Fulham's side. The evidence indicated that the woman had threatened to slaughter the minister's hens if they continued to wander onto her property and he replied by calling her a "blackguard." She admitted that she did not know what the word meant but was sure it was not a compliment. Paddy Nolan tried to take the argument from there, saying that his client was too often the object of barbs and insults. It was time the authorities took a stand against what looked like "a Fulham Extermination Society." The lawyer for the defense replied that Mrs. Fulham was "a notorious nuisance" in Calgary.[2] Because of her presence and occupation, property in the neighborhood had fallen in value. To this the lady replied with some well-chosen abuse for the lawyer and was promptly ordered removed from the court. The defendant was fined one dollar and everybody present agreed that it was worth at least that much to be in attendance for the amusement.

For the next decade, she was one of the most frequent visitors at the police court, generally facing charges of disorderly conduct and generally ready to settle differences of opinion out of court by the expedient of a fight with the police. Editors knew that her story was always acceptable news and on October 21, 1901, she was reported as entering the *Herald* office and greeting the first man to face her with: "Good morning to you young man. An' it's an ill-used woman I am this day." While thus introducing the reason for her complaint, she placed a parcel on the desk, removed the wrappings and displayed a pile of dark-grey hair. Then, removing the ancient hat from her head and pointing to her uncombed locks, said, "The bastes of policemen tore that from me head."

Her complaint did not end there. A few days later, when city council met in regular session, the Fulham lady, carrying the same parcel of hair, made her way to the mayor's chair and insisted upon having the full attention of the City Fathers. Yes, she had a grievance. She'd been sitting peacefully in the kitchen of the New Brunswick Restaurant on a recent night when, according to her story, Constables Fraser and Walden entered, seized her by the hair and dragged or forced her into the police wagon and lodged her at the jail where she spent the night. In the morning she was brought to court, charged and fined the "usual fee for being arrested." She had had enough of this, especially when the police took to pulling her hair. She wanted the aldermen to fire all the city cops.

The mayor promised to look into the complaint but the lady wanted immediate action and was still talking loudly when the aldermen were considering the next item of business. "Sure an' isn't mesiff that knows the wickedness of thim both. Those policemen are bad men. Sure gintlemen, this is my hair them bastes pulled out."

But the mayor, when he investigated, heard the other side of the story. The lady had been celebrating as she did rather often and when the police were called to the restaurant, she was in a fine fighting mood. As for the hair, it was found to match the mane and tail of the lady's horse and there was reason to believe it did not come from a human head.

Then there were the memorable negotiations about the Fulham cow, Nellie, which lost its life when hit by a CPR train. The owner made complaint, saying compensation would have to be high because Nellie was a very superior bovine. A hearing was convened and the railroad officials pointed out that "No Trespassing" signs were posted prominently and neither cow nor person had any right to be on the railroad track.

But the cow's owner proceeded to nullify that point of argument, saying, "Ye pur fools, what makes ye think my pur old Nellie could read yer signs?" But failing to gain satisfaction from the company's minor officials, the lady wrote to Sir William Van Horne, president, and when he happened to be in Calgary, she forced her way into his private car and proceeded to hold him responsible for her loss. The president, with some feeling of sympathy, offered to find a replacement for the cow but that did not satisfy the woman because there was no other cow quite like Nellie. She contended it would take two cows to replace Nellie, but was obliged in the end to settle for one.

In any case, she exercised power and influence which might have brought envy to other citizens. And indirectly, she was the means of bringing a code of building restrictions to the city. Senator Lougheed, addressing the aldermen, said the time had come to bring in and enforce building regulations. "I for instance, have a number of lots in the vicinity of Mrs. Fulham's place and certainly no one would buy them when her pig ranch is taken into consideration. . . . Indeed, I had a sale balked just on that account."[3]

Calgary obtained its building restrictions at about the time the city's celebrated lady specialist in pigs was departing. The *Calgary Herald* carried the disappointing news: "Mrs. Fulham, who has been a noted character in Calgary for many years, has sold out her business and property and gone to Vancouver to live."[4]

The last news item to be found touching upon the lady was in the same paper about six months later: "Mrs. Fulham, who was without doubt the best known woman in Calgary, passed through the city on Monday night. She informed some of those at the station that she was coming back to live here in six weeks. This news will be received with mingled feelings."

Sure, she was often in trouble but deep in Calgary hearts was affection for Mother Fulham. Her spontaneity and unvarnished personality were refreshing, even on a frontier. Calgarians would have been disappointed if she did not mark St. Patrick's Day by dressing in defiant green, or the twelfth of July by hurling shouts of derision at parading Orangemen.

But only those who watched her closely knew the generosity of her Irish heart. They alone knew the families she helped regularly with gifts of needed money, and the settler, Charlie Hawkes, who lost his three horses from glanders and had no money for replacements. The Sons of England presented him with twenty-five dollars but it was not enough. He met Mother Fulham on the street and told her of his predicament. Without comment, she pulled up her dress, exposing one of the perpetually dirty knees, took a roll of bills from a stocking and pressed forty dollars into the man's hand. "That'll help ye buy a horse," she said.

In spite of the remark made on the station platform, she did not return to take up residence in Calgary, but the memory of that great, roughcast keeper of pigs on Calgary's 6th Avenue lived on. If Calgarians did not actually love the Queen of Garbage Row, at least they missed her very much when she left.

Old Bill
Faithful and True

The focus of most of MacEwan's writing is human beings and human history. This excerpt is from a book that presents the "biographies" of horses and allows the records of man's faithful friends to speak for themselves. That "Old Bill" was closely associated with the writer's youth adds importance to the following account. (From Memory Meadows, *Saskatoon: Western Producer Prairie Books, 1976.)*

Old Bill was no beauty. In fact, he was so ugly that other horses on the MacEwan farm shunned his company. Advanced age showed clearly, but that was not all. His head was too big for his body; his feet were too big for his limbs; his ears pointed in different directions and his legs were decorated with splints and spavins. On top of all that, he suffered from chronic indigestion. But no horse on the western frontier served more faithfully and none deserved a monument more than Old Bill.

The unending toil on pioneer farms was hard on horses, as protruding ribs, raw harness sores and dejected equine spirits showed so clearly. But horses were much more serviceable than oxen and every farmer wanted them. Favored, of course, were the big ones with heavy bone and powerful muscles, Clydesdales, Percherons and Belgians. Such draft horses could move heavy loads on roads or in farm fields with less hardship to themselves than would be experienced by animals of smaller stature. Obviously, a horse of 1,200 pounds sharing harness with one of 1,700 pounds had to work especially hard to keep its end of the doubletree in line.

Old Bill had that added handicap of being a lightweight, presumably of Standardbred strain although his exact breeding was unknown. In other words, he was of roadster type and ill-suited for heavy draft work. The only reason for buying him to work on that frontier farm was his availability at the price of thirty-five dollars, all the cash the MacEwans were able to raise in a particular hour of need.

Having been delivered to a farm where horsepower was needed urgently, the little bay gelding was introduced at once to heavy harness and teamed with three big horses to pull a breaking plow through tough sod and tenacious willow roots. Day after day, six days a week, Bill tugged hard on leather traces, and on Sundays, when the heavy horses enjoyed a day off, poor Old Bill was burdened with an additional assignment, one which he alone could perform with reasonable satisfaction; it fell to him to pull the family buggy to church. As he was the only horse on the premises with buggy experience and the only one of roadster weight, the weekly trip — four miles each way — was one he could not escape, even though it might have been merciful and even Godly for the humans to have remained at home in order to give one of the Creator's four-footed children a chance to rest and enjoy a day on the grass.

Bill was a tired old horse but his needs were not entirely overlooked and as soon as farm fortunes would allow it, a replacement draft horse was purchased and Bill was released from heavy harness, left with no work except that of pulling the buggy in summer months and the cutter in the winter. At once, life was less cruel and a trace of fat returned to his old ribs.

Like any other aging gentleman, Bill liked his home — liked it so well that his traveling time from the near-by town to the home was only about half of what he took in going over the same road but in the opposite direction. In returning from church or town, he did not always wait for his passengers. On a certain Sunday, when the church minister preached too long for the patience of either the people in the congregation or the horses waiting to haul buggies and churchmen home, Bill used his long incisor teeth to loosen the knot which tied him in a livery stable stall and promptly struck out for home, leaving buggy and passengers stranded in Melfort. Neighbors saw the familiar horse, harnessed but without vehicle, making his way over the four-mile road to the MacEwan farm, maintaining the jog he was known to favor on the homeward part of all trips.

With Bill's home-loving nature went an uncanny sense of direction. It did not seem to matter where he was driven, a homing pigeon kind of perception would take him home. Even in the darkest night or when blinding snow filled the air, Bill seemed to know where he would find his stall and manger filled with hay.

There was that winter trip by cutter to a community six or eight miles from the home farm, in the course of which Bill's skill was put to a severe test. Much of the land was still undeveloped and when nightfall and a snowstorm came together, the three occupants of the cutter, setting out for home, felt understandable anxiety. Visibility failed completely and the man driving, trying desperately to guide the horse, unconsciously drew the animal off the trail and into an expanse of bluffs and grassland. Once having left the track, it seemed almost impossible to find it again. In an instant, all sense of direction left the cutter's occupants. No stars were visible to help in guiding them. Realizing that they were lost and probably already driving in a senseless circle, they decided in their despair to "give Old Bill his head" and hope for the best.

The night grew colder and snowdrifts became deeper. It was increasingly difficult to be cheerful. To be lost in the open country on such a night would certainly invite serious freezing and perhaps loss of life. The three men in the cutter understood the dangers very well. They took turns in walking behind the cutter, partly to reduce the load, partly to maintain circulation of blood. The horse abandoned his customary road jog — settled into a slow but steady walk. As the snow became deeper, the animal had to work harder. He was covered with snow and it was impossible to see him, even from the seat of the cutter.

An hour passed and then two hours. The cold was more and more intense. It seemed increasingly certain that Old Bill was as hopelessly lost as the men. The situation appeared ever more terrifying. Perhaps the travelers were now farther from home than when they had started. And how long would it be until the old horse dropped from exhaustion or ran into a barbed wire fence, wrecking cutter and injuring himself?

"If we could only find a strawpile," one man remarked, "we could dig in and hope to stay alive until daylight." Nothing, however, was visible, neither bluffs, fences nor strawpiles. But Bill plodded on and, then, when human hands and feet were almost paralyzed from cold, the cutter stopped abruptly. "What now?" somebody asked. "What trouble have we hit?" The driver stumbled forward to the horse's head and to his amazement found himself within touching distance of a stable door. "We're home," he shouted. "We're at our stable. God bless you, Bill, you brought us through. We'd never have made it if we hadn't left it to you."

The old horse enjoyed an extra ration of oats that night and regularly for weeks after. He did not get the monument he and thousands of other farm horses deserved but he did get the comfortable retirement he had earned so completely. Farm fortune improved and the debt to Bill was at least partly paid, paid with the best care that could be given to an old horse which had worked hard and faithfully.

The Founding Father

Early in Grant MacEwan's writing career, he was inspired by the venerable historian Arthur Silver Morton. At the latter's urging, MacEwan started a file on the Selkirk settlers, who, in Morton's opinion, had been a neglected part of Canada's history. Cornerstone Colony *was the result (many years after Morton's death), and the following excerpt is included, reflecting the influence of Morton on MacEwan. (From* Cornerstone Colony, *Saskatoon: Western Producer Prairie Books, 1977.)*

A tall thin man wearing expensive clothes grown shabby from constant use paced nervously back and forth at the west side of Red River where a city to be known as Winnipeg would someday arise. Counting steps, he was obviously measuring ground for some purpose but he was soon interrupted. After coming into view, he was quickly surrounded by curious and anxious settlers from the log-hut homes built at intervals of about 200 yards along the river front to the north of Point Douglas.

His arrival in the settlement on June 21, 1817 — one day after his forty-sixth birthday — was an event of unusual interest because he was the one and only person the settlers could thank or blame for their presence in this new land and the one upon whom their fortunes seemed to depend.

From other years in depressed Ireland and the Scottish Highlands, these people had grown to regard noblemen and other rich and powerful men with suspicion if not with scorn. But this man with quiet and gentle mien, Thomas Douglas, 5th Earl of Selkirk, appeared to be an outright contradiction of all their preconceived notions. If he had selfish motives in bringing evicted families across the Atlantic to settle on the fresh and untried soil of Rupert's Land — not yet Western Canada — he managed to conceal them well.

"There he is," a Highlander whispered to his wife, "but ye'd no ken he was the Earl o' Selkirk."

"Aye," the woman replied. "He's got a gude face but he looks frail an' ev'n ill. He's no' long for this warld I'd be thinking."

More settlers gathered and crowded in upon him to catch his soft-spoken words and touch his woolen jacket. He talked in simple and friendly terms, quite enough to dispel many of the quaint superstitions about titled gentry. These people knew they had a debt to him. Now, almost instantly, they were finding an affection for him. The admiring Irish were wishing they could claim him as a Roman Catholic and the Scots were wishing he were Highland instead of Lowland. But it didn't really matter because his slow and clear expressions of friendliness were dissolving those differences which too often breed prejudices.

To be within chatting distance of a living Earl was something these people could not have imagined, especially this one who was already one of the most controversial figures of his time, a wealthy aristocrat with an apparent concern for less fortunate people, one who would spend his own money to assist emigration from the Old Land, one who would take on the powerful North West Company, almost single-handedly, and promise to return blow for blow. And adding to the sense of astonishment, here was the man who was described as the biggest owner of land in the world, the proprietor of the District of Assiniboia, a Rupert's Land property totaling more than twice the area of Scotland.

It was almost beyond belief. With his wealth and rank and influence, he might have been spending his years in pursuit of Old World comfort and luxury, as many high-born Britishers were doing. Instead, he had become obsessed with a North American hinterland he had never seen and a colonization scheme big enough to frighten a professional promoter. This overseas scheme in settlement was not his first; actually, it was his third — and last — also the most ambitious and costly and frustrating.

As settlers continued to press in upon him on that bright June morning in 1817, he took opportunity to reassure them of his continuing support. After glancing in all directions as if to verify his directions or catch a vision of the emergence of a thriving and prospering community, the Earl raised his voice to reach all who were nearby: "I'm sorry you had so many troubles but we will not allow the attacks on this colony to be repeated. You have my word for that. It is my highest hope that you will find security such as you deserve and for which you have longed. Before I leave, I will do all in my power to ensure for you the opportunity to gain a contented way of life in this new land. May I suggest that this Parish be called Kildonan, to preserve the memory of the district from which many of you came. And here I offer you a site of ground for your school, and over there another for your church and manse. We shall take steps at once to see that you get roads and bridges, and seeds and cattle."

Primitive and still-untested Red River Settlement was six troubled years old, each of its years more troubled than the one preceding it. Who save the possessor of great faith could believe the local fortunes would change now? It was little wonder that the man upon whom the main burden had fallen looked worn and sad. Repeatedly he had heard both friends and foes saying his scheme was an adventure in folly, assured only of failure. "Preposterous," rival fur traders had shouted every time his undertaking was mentioned. "This is fur country. What stupidity to expect settlers to succeed in this land of ice and snow! Didn't somebody warn that the country is doomed to eternal sterility? What nonsense is Selkirk dreaming up?"

Now, astonishingly, the man was assuring his people of better days ahead.

In making a prophecy of better times, Selkirk was partly right. There were better days ahead for his colonists, but not for him. Much as he might have wished to remain with these people with a childlike dependence upon him, he was under the disagreeable compulsion to return to Montreal or Toronto or Sandwich — or all three — to face the courts in a long and depressing series of trials in which he would be alternately plaintiff and defendant. It would be the cruel sequel to those warlike acts in the long strife between men who believed the good soil of the Northwest could and should support agriculture and settlement, and others who held fanatically to the idea that the country should be kept exclusively for wild furs.

There in the East where the North West Company had succeeded in creating a political climate favorable to itself, Selkirk would stand alone, or almost alone, arguing for his right to test the fur country for settlement and then fight if necessary to protect the innocent homemakers against savage attacks. Hounded almost to death in Montreal, he was the first person to stage a battle of words on behalf of the West against the Eastern interests.

He promised the colonists he would return to spend more time among them. The thought made him happy. Gladly he would have spent half of his time at the Red River Settlement, correctly called Assiniboia at that time, sharing frontier food and hardships with his people, and half in Scotland and England where his responsibilities were of a demanding kind. He had farming interests at home and political obligations in the House of Lords. But, although still in middle age, the Earl of Selkirk would never again see Red River. Only one who could peer into the future could know that the next year and a half would hold him brutally to the exigencies of the courts and his enemies; and then, after paying a high price in time and money and health, he would be going home — to die.

It is easy to understand why the settlers loved him, and why men in sections of the fur trade hated him and entertained thoughts of murder. It is not so easy to know why the Selkirk role in nation building did not receive more recognition. Granted, he made himself most unpopular in Montreal where the North West Company was powerful, and elsewhere in the East, and this might have damaged the man's lasting national image; but there was no reason for Westerners failing to honor the man of so many distinctions. There might have been serious errors in judgment or indiscretions in the seizure of Fort William and the arrest of North West Company officers in 1816, but there was provocation and there was much to offset the mistakes. The magnitude of his aid to the peasant folks who came as his settlers placed him among the leading philanthropists of his time, or all time.

Even the extent of his land holdings, embracing an ownership which has never been equaled and will probably never be equaled, should have been enough to make him memorable. Any person who could mount a claim to 116,000 square miles of fertile western land — some 74 million acres — would scarcely need to look further for distinction. And no less distinctive were the circumstances of the purchase, including price. The acquisition of this land, mainly in what was later Manitoba, on May 29, 1811, for a consideration of ten shillings and an undertaking to bring a specified number of men to the country each year for ten years, must surely qualify as the best land purchase in history. That the purpose was colonization did not make the deal any less stupendous. There was a Believe-It-Or-Not quality about it.

Fortunately, land taxes were still unknown in the country and Selkirk's vast expanse could be carried at no cost except in terms of worry. He could afford to be generous in making land gifts. When he chose to recognize a friend or a debt, he might do it by making a simple gift of a township — thirty-six square miles. In recognition of long service or special feeling of friendship, the token of appreciation could and did consist of from five to ten townships, as shown in his instructions in November, 1811: ten townships for Miles Macdonell, five for Ronald McDonald, five for Thomas Clark, and so on. A letter of November 8, 1811, preserved in the Selkirk Papers, itemized land grants totalling more than fifty townships, mainly in parcels of five townships each.

Nor was it just ordinary land; much of it was Red River Valley soil which inherited its unusual richness from the ancient Lake Agassiz and was destined to occupy an important place in western agriculture.

As viewed from the vantage point of 160 years later, the Selkirk performance which overcame powerful resistance to found the first agricultural enterprise in the Canadian West, must be seen as one of the outstanding acts of faith in the history of a nation. It had to be faith because there was no such thing as a soil survey or economic report or feasibility study — not even a good map or a clear external expression of optimism about the outcome. Indeed, most of the Earl's friends at home saw as sheer madness his dream of drawing upon evicted and displaced Britishers to start a colony on an untried frontier.

But was it madness or was the scheme backed by vision and judgment more penetrating than anybody of that period realized? True, the colony came close to complete failure on different occasions. Twice local enemies believed they had effected total destruction of the settlement; once the Red River, rampaging in flood, dealt a destroying blow; several times grasshoppers attacked voraciously and on one occasion there was a major exodus of discouraged settlers hoping to improve their fortunes in Upper Canada or back in Scotland. But instead of collapsing as the critics said it must do, the Selkirk Settlement survived and staggered on to become the very cornerstone of Western Canada's monumental agricultural industry.

Perhaps it was luck more than judgment that led the settlers for that initial farming experiment to locate on soil which ranks with the most fertile in the world. Perhaps it was more than luck; perhaps it was something in the hidden Selkirk wisdom but, in any case, the man was a leader far ahead of his time. Of course he made some serious mistakes, of which more will be said, and he paid dearly for them, but who, from his generation — or any generation, made a more crucial and courageous impact upon the destiny of the country to become Western Canada? If Canadian agriculture, through which the nation made its finest contribution to world needs, were to choose a Patron Saint or Founding Father, what candidate would have an equal claim upon the high honor? It would seem to belong to Thomas Douglas, 5th Earl of Selkirk, who started not one but three farming colonies in widely separated parts of the country and who practically stood alone in declaring faith in the soil of the fur country.

What emerged at Red River was a gigantic pilot plant or experimental farm. Indeed, the first project to carry the name of Experimental Farm between the Atlantic and Pacific oceans was the one started at Red River in 1818 at Selkirk's direction. That the undertaking known as the Hayfield Experimental Farm was not a great success is beside the point; Selkirk recognized the need and deserved full credit for the effort to meet it. Had the Earl lived longer, his experimental farm — Canada's first — no doubt would have survived.

A few years after the Hayfield Farm lost its special status, a second farm was set apart for experimental purposes, and then a third one. All were short-lived. But present-day citizens who find pride in Canada's

Experimental Farm System, started in 1886, should take notice of the fact that Selkirk's initial plan to provide the benefits of planned experimentation preceded the government program by more than sixty years.

Even before 1818, the Earl's Red River undertaking was making the entire colony appear like a testing ground. The money and the ideas came from him and many of his schemes and projects would have seemed timely half a century later.

If the agricultural colony had the character of an experimental farm, Lord Selkirk was like the director of research, and was the author of nearly every facet of the experimental program. Even before Miles Macdonell reached Red River, he had instructions from the Earl to make careful observations of the soil and study all crops grown with the idea of determining the ones possessing the greatest degree of genetic suitability. In the hope of finding products for export and sale on world markets, he urged the testing of flax and hemp; and hoping that wool might be an appropriate item for shipment overseas, he instructed that individual fleece records be kept for the Merino sheep sent in 1812. Every fleece should be marked with the identity of the particular ewe or ram from which it came and thus be submitted to the wool experts overseas in order to secure a proper assessment of individual breeding worth. The technique was enough to brand this man as a scientist as well as a pioneer colonizer.

It was Selkirk's idea that Miles Macdonell should capture buffalo calves and test the practical problems in raising them in captivity. He offered several proposals for domesticating the wild things and suggested a buffalo park for the colony. There should be a hybridizing experiment involving the buffalo and domestic cattle, he told Miles Macdonell, and he demanded reports on progress. He wanted information about the possibility of domesticating the muskox — "muskbuffalo" as he called those wild creatures of the North — and speculated about the feasibility of developing an export trade in muskox wool. Likewise, he wanted test data about the relative economy and worth of water power and windmill power for the colony, and he ordered a report on the kinds of tools and machines most needed by the people. Such questions raised prior to 1820 seem strikingly mature.

Although his residence in the West was brief — only a few summer months with a promise to return — his influence gave direction to a completely new economic and social shape for nearly half a continent. Without him and his ambitious undertaking in settlement, the country would have remained in the selfish embrace of the fur trade much longer. Western Canada would have waited additional decades before realizing a successful agriculture; and railroad construction in the West would have been delayed substantially. It does not require much imagination to identify the reasons.

The most intriguing question of all has barely been raised: Without the pioneer demonstration of agricultural settlement would the government of the new Canada have been interested in 1869 in buying the lands of the West which traders insisted were unfit for any other industry except furs? And if Canada had not acted to acquire the West at that time, would the United States, caught up in the spirit of Manifest Destiny, have succeeded in buying it from the Hudson's Bay Company, as that neighboring country had bought Alaska from Russia just two years before?

It becomes obvious that the West of Canada — or all of Canada — has a debt to Selkirk. Fittingly, the Earl's family names were perpetuated in western features — Forts Selkirk and Daer, the Manitoba town of Selkirk, the Selkirk range of mountains, and Fort Douglas and Point Douglas beside Red River. Appropriate as these names will seem, they are but minimum recognition and the debt has remained, a debt that was never paid and rarely recognized.

War Years and War Horses

MacEwan spends little time reading poetry of any sort, but there was one poet who caught his undivided attention for a period of time — Stanley Harrison. Possibly a factor contributing to his interest in Harrison's works was that they usually dealt with horses or, at least, with those who loved them. The following excerpt describes Harrison's attitude to man's best friend, an attitude that is as close to that of MacEwan as it is possible to be. (From The Rhyming Horseman of the Qu'Appelle, *Saskatoon: Western Producer Prairie Books, 1978.)*

Despite repeated invitations and urgings to live and work in more prestigious parts of the world, Stanley Harrison remained at Stockwell [Harrison's farm in the Qu'Appelle Valley] until the time of his enforced retirement — except for the years of the Great War, when he was in uniform. The farm he loved so dearly was just beginning to conform to his measure, like new shoes taking the shape of one's feet, when war clouds enveloped much of the world. With explosive suddenness, soldiers were marching, and the best-laid of human plans were being reversed and revised. The young proprietor of Stockwell, like thousands of other young farmers, was torn between the Empire's plea for greater food production and the equally urgent call for men who would not shrink from the dangers of front-line service. "Food will win the war," some public officials were proclaiming, offering salve for the collective conscience of those who sought escape from more serious involvement.

As an informed horseman, Harrison was asked to take an immediate part in selecting, assembling, and shipping western horses suitable for cavalry purposes. The prairie country was about to be combed for remounts. Here was something Harrison could do with skill, and he did it for a short time, but not without misgivings on two points of principle: it pricked his conscience to leave the more dangerous and unpleasant wartime tasks to others, and it bothered him no less to force innocent horses into wars of man's making. For most of the horses chosen for shipment overseas, war would mean certain death — and who was to say that man had the moral right to drive these good creatures into the Hell of battle? It wasn't easy, but Harrison knew he would have to compromise on this matter. He did so by reminding himself and those around him that members of these two races, humans and horses, had been partners in peace and war throughout the ages and horses would be sorely needed now to carry men and drag guns.

Horses would have to go, but he had a rebuke for people who had no compunction about sending them away to suffer and die:

> Wave the green flag and let them go!
> Only horses! Yes, I know,
> But my heart goes down the line
> With them. And their grief is mine.
> There goes timid, child-like trust,
> To the burden and the dust.
>
> High-born courage, princely grace,
> To the peril it must face.
> There goes honour, there goes faith,
> Down in the way of grime and death.
> Hidden in the cloud that clings
> To the battle-wrath of kings.
>
> May they find in those far lands
> Kindly hearts and horsemen's hands.

It was a fitting time to recognize with honour the age-old contributions made by horses in all the wars of history. The author of the Book of Job must have been thinking of war horses when he wrote so glowingly of one: "Hast thou given the horse strength? Hast thou clothed his neck with Thunder? . . . He paweth in the valley and rejoiceth in his strength; he goeth on to meet the armed men." Harrison had his favorites among the great horses of history. He used the name Brucephalus in his own stable to honour the horse that carried Alexander the Great to victory; he lost no opportunity to speak about Napoleon's gray Marengo, Oliver Cromwell's White Turk, or Lord Kitchener's former stake winner, Diplomat. Nor did he forget the million other war horses without names. Honouring all, he wrote:

THE WAR HORSE

> He shared the battle-wrath of ancient kings;
> Assailed the walls of Babylon, arrayed
> With hosts of Cyrus, scorning flame and slings

With lofty mien and spirit unafraid.
Clear through the song of history throbs the beat
Of swift and dauntless hooves in thundrous flight
To wrest some epic victory from defeat
And turn the darkness of despair to light.
His brave 'Ha, Ha,' has mocked the stricken field
Where hope forlorn had triumphed over might.
No fear of peril would his courage yield
As barrage shells screamed through flame-split night;
And when at dawn the signal trumpet blew
Death's call — he did not fail the rendezvous.

As he continued to ship horses to the front, Harrison was very conscious of the conflict of sentiment within himself. Taking a practical view of the war situation, he knew the horses were needed, and said so. He went on to prophesy that "before this business is over, the horse and particularly the blood horse, will have contributed his full share." He ventured "that not a soldier for his King will have struck a nobler battle-blow."

Conscience and reason ruled that he should not be party to sending horses or members of his own race into areas of danger where he would not go himself. With his pronounced British loyalties, he could not help hearing that louder call for active soldiers ready to give their all. Leaving Stockwell in the care of his brother Jimmy, Stanley went away to enlist with the Winnipeg Light Infantry.

Like most other people, he hated the thought of war; of course he did. For anybody who loved horses, people, and all living creatures, it could not be otherwise and he made no secret of it. But such feelings would not solve the world's problems and when he considered the awful threat to the Empire and his way of life, he knew he was answering the clear call of a motherland in trouble and alone.

INVICTUS

Out of the clutch of evil might,
   Her allied legions all o'erthrown,
Her broken sword still joined the fight,
Her challenge rang, For God and Right!
   Dauntless, she stood alone.

Each fierce assault, each foul blow dealt,
   But steeled her valiant heart to meet
What e'er befell. Alone, she felt;
But Freedom, Faith and Virtue knelt
   Uncovered at her feet.

Stanley Harrison had the courage, the conviction, and the imagination to be a good soldier. He was tested in some of the dirtiest and bloodiest campaigns of the war. Three times he was wounded; once he was thought to be dead, once buried alive in rubble dislodged by enemy artillery fire.

Back in England and during leaves, this dapper and articulate soldier from a Canadian regiment — at first a private, then Lieutenant and, finally, Captain — was both conspicuous and popular. The English girls were smitten, and ladies of high society, arrested by the same attraction, begged him to visit their homes. He did not escape the wartime flirtations and romances, some of which seemed to be leading towards matrimony. Years later, when his poem "Remember" (dated Flanders, 20 January 1918) was read aloud, a tear appeared in aging eyes and he answered, "Yes, I am afraid I disappointed her. She was a high-born girl, a duchess." There was another tear. "She came to France for a visit and the poem tells how much I loved her. After the war, she came to Canada to formally open a hospital. I could have persuaded her to become a Saskatchewan farm wife, but the adjustment would have been more difficult than any man had the right to expect." The poem speaks for itself:

Remember
  I love you —
And through that love I give
The beauty of the world,
The dearest hopes that live.
Dear heart
  I leave you —
Time flies — be true, be brave.
Take to your lonely heart
The shield of love you gave.

Through days of sunny warmth and storm and cold,
I'll feel with you the changes as of old —
Hear the bright laughter, see the tears that fall,
Thrill with strange gladness when I hear you call.

When night shall come and moonlight tip the pine,
  Be then aware
Within your heart I come to claim you mine —
  Look for me there.

By every seed that grows and tree that towers
  Above you,
By every leaf that blows, by scent of flowers —
  I love you ... know that I love you.

In the Hell heat of war and the awful uncertainties it nurtured, every soldier longed for home. Stanley Harrison's constant dream was of an end to the cruel slaughter and return to Saskatchewan. Friends and relatives were losing their lives in the holocaust, and the common question was "Who will be next?" Before his very eyes, Harrison saw young men from Fort Qu'Appelle sacrifice forever the hope of returning.

> I saw him stand where ripening grain
> Drank deep the gold of sunlit skies;
> Where he had made the virgin plain
> A simple freeman's paradise.

> I saw him next lie broken, dead,
> His shell-torn body facing west,
> And well I knew his soul had sped
> Home to the prairie's waiting breast.

It is not easy to recognize anything good in war, but at least Harrison was being driven to write more poetry than ever before. Contrary to what might have been expected, the bloodied mud of Flanders was not enough to stop his pen. Nor were the poet's lines wasted. His poem "Vimy Ridge," which he modestly described as "a thing I wrote while looking over the ground two days after the battle," inspired Canada to spend huge sums of money in following the suggestion contained in the last four lines.

> What chivalry lies sleeping at thy breast!
>   The gallant loves, brave dreams and deeds of might,
> Poured out like wine from altars of the West.
>   O Canada, these sons achieved the height
> True valour knows. From Vimy's tortured crest
>   Their souls will shine through years unborn to light
> Your loved far skies and sweet wide plains,
>   Vast mountain peaks and cities newly-grown;
> For there they died, bearing the sacred pains
>   Of sacrifice at freedom's crimsoned throne.

> Let maple trees that knew the western sun
>   Stand sentinel where heroes fell, rose-crowned
> By Death with deathless honours dearly won,
>   To guard with jealous branch this holy ground.

The effects of war are ever unpredictable. Instead of making this man forget his horses, the passage of time and his involvement with the conflict had the opposite effect, and some of his finest tributes to them came in those troubled years when he was far away. Although he was able to take his own mount to France, he still dreamed of saddling a favorite horse and riding the hills and valleys of the Qu'Appelle. As he later recalled, he had one last and unexpected chance to do so before his regiment left Canada.

"I think every man has a mental sanctuary of some thought or memory in which he may retire almost at will with a feeling of relief and rest. Hardly a day in camp but what at some time, my thoughts returned to the home pastures and in fancy I was free again of sabre and polished steel and rode the bluff-studded lawns of home, or walked with colts at my side nibbling the flaps of my pockets and the lapel of my jacket. . . . When the telegram came telling me of illness among the mares I was still within reaching distance and mention of my trouble to our colonel who was a keen horseman, got me immediate leave. . . . Delta was the loveliest mare I have ever seen. A russet chestnut of rare conformation and possessing that exquisite quality which makes a real horseman catch his breath with delight. . . . To see her in the paddock with a young foal at foot was a sight not to be forgotten, with her gliding, almost panther-like walk, her finely-wrought head upflung, her limpid eyes looking at you with a proud dignity that comes only from innate greatness . . . . And now she was dying. I felt his Dark Majesty in the stall even as I heard the mare's low whinny at sight of me. I knelt down to her, talking as I had talked on many a trail and happy care-free adventure to which her nimble hooves had carried me. How dear those days seemed now! How peaceful! For in my subconscious mind was the echo of bugles, the marching of men and the rumble of guns. . . . I scattered her ashes to the wild west wind and in fancy I saw her, imperishable, one with the dancing sunbeams."

The Harrison talents were recognized, and the Captain was soon named Adjutant to General Ketchen, who happened to be a horseman of some distinction also. The relationship, mutually agreeable, was the means of Captain Harrison remaining in uniform for some time after war's end. The General had two of his horses overseas and Harrison had one.

Harrison had a special relationship with the horse that accompanied him to France. The Captain and his mount traveled many miles together and grew to understand each other perfectly. "We were more than mere man and horse," he wrote; "we were old friends." One of the most bitter experiences of the war was having his "friend" shot from under him. Nobody reading his lines written at Passchendaele in November 1917 could doubt the intensity of the affection the Captain had for his equine companion.

"Never shall I forget the first time I saw him there in the hills at home. Head uplifted, his brilliant eye regarded me with kindly dignity. Ah, but he was superb! About him was a great shining, like a naked sword tempered in beauty and strength. Beneath his coat of rippling silk one sensed the soul of rhythm, and courage like white fire. . . .

"Nor that last hour shall I forget. Even as I caught his low whinny I knew the wings of Pegasus had touched his shoulders. There amid the rumble of guns, Death had beckoned. But there, too, was something greater than death, something shining through the long, long trailing centuries of Time.

"Beyond the cannon mist I thought I saw him again, imperishable as all true beauty, one with the wind and sun, one with the glory of life — aye, and the glory of death."

> Remember him! He helped us through
> Those sorrows whence our freedom grew,
> And by his patient agonies
> The lurid glow of angry skies
> That mirrored mankind's wrath and fears
> Changed to the peace of kindly years.
>
> Somewhere . . . somewhere in Time's Own Space
> There must be some sweet-pastured Place
> Where creeks sing on and tall trees grow,
> Some Paradise where horses go,
> For by the love that guides my pen
> I know great horses live again.

REQUIEM
(Flanders, 1 November 1917)

> Still are thy limbs — thy brave eye films
> With Death's dim, jealous veil.
> Thou hast reached too soon, with soft reluctant sigh,
> The end of Life's short trail.
>
> O mare o' mine, thy heart and mine
> Have known life's ecstasy.
> For us the shimmering gold of sunset's wealth,
> The silver of the sea.
>
> The soft snow-fall, the coyote's call,
> Haunting, wild and strong;
> The chinook winds and soft sweet twittering notes
> Of snowbirds' winter song.

The starry night — snow, cold and white,
Draping moonlit heights
And stretching away to silent icy space
Beneath the Northern Lights.

We loved the way where chipmunks play
And woodland voices speak,
Where pine and spruce rise up from tangled depths,
Laved by the murmuring creek.

Through dim-lit aisles, on scented piles
Of scarlet, gold-rimmed leaves
Thy sportive hooves have picked their dainty way.
Leaves — swirling, whispering leaves!

We knew — thou and I — the poetry
Of silence, colour, life;
We knew and loved the spirit of the wild,
Its paeans — its ceaseless strife.

The shadowed deeps, the prairie sweeps
Of undulating lawn,
The myriad mystic sounds of drowsy life
That wakes at mist-wreathed dawn.

Dawn, cool and grey, when dry reeds sway,
Rustling, mournful, sighing
In the first awakening breath of morning breeze,
When wild-fowl circle crying.

We two have seen — we two have been
Where braves once met their foes,
And teepees raise their smoke-hued poles to skies,
Soft-coloured as a rose.

And now we part — brave loyal Heart!
No more shall saddle fret thee,
While Life reflects the sights and sounds we loved
I never will forget thee.

Then, in 1919, Harrison's wartime prayer — "Please God, let me see my home again" — was answered and, shortly after his discharge, he returned to Stockwell, certain that no place else on earth could suit him so well.

The Growing Grassland Empire

Although Pat Burns is a name familiar to thousands of western Canadians, surprisingly little factual material was left by the man about his personal life, perhaps because Burns was not exactly at home with reading or writing. These tasks were suited to MacEwan, who searched for years filing away sparse notes whenever they appeared. The excerpt is a sample of the crop produced by MacEwan from pretty hard, stony, and dry land. (From Pat Burns, Cattle King, *Saskatoon: Western Producer Prairie Books, 1979.)*

When does a person have too much land? How much is too much? Some people said Burns had too much ranch land, contending that his quarter of a million acres of deeded and leased range land held at the time of the first Calgary Stampede — and more later — exceeded by far what any one person should be allowed to claim and control. It would be better, they added, if much of such a huge spread were available for the use of other and smaller ranch operators.

The critics had a point, especially if it could be shown that the demand for grazing ground exceeded the supply available, or if the reason for acquiring so much was simply to satisfy somebody's inflated ego.

Burns answered one of the questions adroitly by saying that any amount of land — whether little or much — was too much if the person owning it or responsible for it was failing to give it proper care. The greater sin was in the exploitation or abuse of land rather than in owning it. In his words and actions he was a conservationist and there was no indication that his land was ever allowed to deteriorate. Nor was there any evidence that he was ambitious to be the biggest land owner or the biggest rancher in the country. In conversation with one of his friends, he said he would rather be known as the best caretaker than as the biggest rancher. As the records showed, he was about as ready to sell ranch property as to buy it.

Nevertheless, in the years after the First World War, Burns

continued to add to his giant ranch holdings, but nobody was complaining because ranchers at that period were more interested in selling than in buying. A postwar slump brought cattle prices to distressingly low levels and many ranchers were in serious financial trouble. Almost instinctively they came to Burns requesting loans or inviting him to buy them out to forestall bankruptcy. In buying ranches he did not need, he was helping the troubled cattlemen and, admittedly, satisfying an urge lying deep within himself. He did not hesitate to express reverence for soil, the greatest of all of Canada's natural resources.

His earliest ranch holdings were on the plains, but as time passed, he was being drawn to the foothills. He was attracted by the Glengarry spread, the Rio Alto, the Flying E, and the Bar U. He wanted to own them and, of course, he did.

The Rio Alto, that excellent old ranch bordering the Highwood, about twenty-eight miles west of High River, was one which Burns had admired. History ridden, it was among the first ranches in the foothills, having been used to carry cattle belonging to O. H. Smith and Lafayette French in the early eighties. To it Dan Riley, long before he was Senator Riley, went to build the ranch house and stable. The place was sold to Ings Brothers who ranched it until the beginning of the First World War. Then, near war's end, an agreement between James Walter Ings of High River and Patrick Burns of Calgary, dated August 1, 1918, provided for the sale of Rio Alto along with "livestock, goods and chattels as herein set out" for a price of $99,840.

Clause six of the agreement held a special message for all horsemen with sentiment for their faithful animals. It also revealed something of the character and compassion of both of the signing parties. It stated:

"The bargainee agrees to permit one old sorrel saddle horse called 'Don' and two old saddle ponies called respectively 'King' and 'Prince' to run free on the ranch for as long as they live, and not permit same to be used for any purpose whatsover."[1] Inquiry proved that the old horses spent their years of retirement in perfect peace, as planned.

The Glengarry ranch, also known as the "44," west of Claresholm, was bought in 1922 and Raymond Clifford, who was assistant manager of P. Burns Ranches, Limited, under Thomas Farrell, and later manager, gave it as his opinion that as a place to go and ride and relax, Glengarry was Mr. Burns' favorite for some years at least.[2]

The Burns interest in the Glengarry place began earlier than he ever admitted. The picturesque ranch was organized and then managed by the well-known foothills personality, A. B. Macdonald, from Glengarry County in eastern Canada, and stocked initially with 1,200 cattle brought in over the trails from Montana. When it was bought a short time later by the railroad contractors, Mackenzie and Mann — friends of Burns — many people reasoned that the ranch was being acquired on Burns' behalf or on Burns' advice. The latter speculation was no doubt correct. Macdonald remained to manage it but the affluent purchasers, whatever their intentions when they bought the good ranch with excellent grass, lots of water and shelter, and spectacular mountain scenery, were not likely to become ranch residents or even remain nearby for very long, and they soon sold it.

Burns fancied it from the first time he saw it and his purchase in 1922 coincided with the postwar slump when even he was encountering some difficulty in financing. Consequently, the acquisition was the product of a deal as much as a purchase, with the seller accepting some other real estate, including the Burns Block situated at the corner of 2nd Street East and Stephen Avenue in Calgary.

Raymond Clifford recalled that after Burns became the legal owner of the Glengarry property, he, Clifford, delivered a trainload of Mackie Ranch cattle to stock it. "These cattle from the short-grass ranges of Milk River," he said, "had never seen grass like that on the Glengarry, and thought they were in Heaven." The herd grew and Burns was happy with it. The inventory taken after Senator Burns' death showed the ranch with 5,120 acres of deeded land, 24,000 acres of leased land, 845 acres of cultivated land, and 2,415 head of cattle — not one of the bigger ranches but one of the most prized.

Then, in the phenomenal train of ranch acquisitions, the next purchase was the biggest of all, the world-famous Bar U and its sister ranch, the Flying E. It was the fulfillment of a secret dream of half a lifetime.

The foothills range west of High River Crossing was Fred Stimson's choice when he was acting for the North West Cattle Company at a time when he had the whole country from which to make his selection. It was in one of the most scenic areas, back where the Rockies seemed to be just over the next hill. To the credit of Fred Stimson and George Lane and others responsible for determining the ranch policy, it was one of the few big ranches to retain solvency through good years and bad.

The first change in Bar U ownership came at the beginning of 1902 when the ranch was bought by George Lane in conjunction with the cattle droving and exporting firm of Gordon, Ironside and Fares. Eighteen thousand acres of deeded land, 8,000 cattle, 500 horses, 1,000 tons of hay in stacks, and extensive buildings were included for the payment price of almost a quarter of a million dollars, to make it, according to press reports of the time, the biggest ranch deal in the history of the Canadian Northwest.

"There is a touch of romance in the deal," a reporter noted, "inasmuch as Mr. Lane originally came to Alberta to work for this very outfit. He struck the country with exactly $100. ... By his natural shrewdness, sound horse sense and honorable dealing, he has become by his own unaided efforts, one of the most wealthy and substantial men in Alberta. From a plain cowboy he has risen to be one of the largest if not the largest ranch owner in Western Canada."[3]

The newspaper added that Lane went to Montreal to negotiate with the Allans of the Allan Shipping Company for the purchase and was given three days in which to finance the proposed deal. By the end of three days, he had secured the backing of the Gordon, Ironside and Fares firm and had the needed cash.

The George Lane story of success resembled that of Pat Burns and the two men enriched the significance by being firm and loyal friends. Both became well known but in different ways. In manner and appearance they were quite different. Burns seemed to present a better state of nutrition. He wore clothes that fitted him and walked briskly with the carriage of a businessman; Lane looked like the ranch-land character who was more at ease in a saddle than trying to guide his rather awkward legs. When Lane went to town — either High River or Calgary — his clothing for the occasion was likely to consist of a swallow-tailed coat worn over overalls; he might also be wearing his revolver belt with all the appropriate equipment.

Now with the purchase of the Bar U, Lane was bringing his ranches on the Little Bow and Willow Creek into one management. Taking George Emerson with him, he went to Mexico in the autumn of the same year and brought back 10,000 stockers which brought his Alberta herds to 18,000 cattle. By the fall of 1906, at the onset of the disastrous winter, he had 24,000, about half of which perished before the spring. The losses of that winter might have been expected to ruin George Lane but they didn't. By 1920, he was the sole owner of the big outfit.

George Lane died in 1925. Pat Burns felt the loss of a great friend and then wondered what would happen to the ranch and its herds. With thousands of his own cattle, scores of cowboys, and an estimated 500 miles of fence lines to maintain, he didn't really need any more ranches. But the Bar U captivated him and he got the idea that George Lane would have wanted him to own it. If more reason were needed, he was worried that the famous ranch would fall into hands which would not bring adequate safeguards against abuse and exploitation of soil and grass. He had seen what overgrazing under greedy management could do to ruin a pasture. It must not be allowed to happen to the Bar U.

Although it was not always recognized, this man of thrift and industry was at heart a conservationist. He had been visibly concerned about the prodigal flaring of natural gas at Turner Valley which did nothing more than illuminate the night skies for many miles. He quizzed the foresters about what they were doing by way of replanting cut-over areas, and he warned about the result of the current cropping methods that left farm soils a little poorer in fertility each year. Of course he saw range grass as another fragile resource which had suffered too often by overgrazing. He had seen thoughtless or greedy grazing policies inflicting lasting damage to good ranches. He wanted to ensure that the Bar U would be protected the way George Lane would have done it and so, he bought it.

It was a simple and straightforward deal with Burns on November 1, 1927, writing to George Lane and Company, Limited, offering to purchase all the deeded farm and ranch lands and the company rights to all lands leased in the province of Alberta. More specifically, they would be the lands "contained in what are known as the Bar U and Willow Creek Ranches, together with all cattle, horses and other livestock thereon, inclusive of this year's calves at the price of $408,001 for said lands, $50 per head for all cattle and $40 per head for all horses." Calves would be "thrown in free of charge" with the cows, and foals would go with the mares. The purchaser would, on December 1, 1927, pay cash for the cattle and horses, and pay ten percent in cash for the land with the balance in seven equal annual payments commencing at November 1, 1928. Interest would be at six percent. And if the deeded land proved to be less or more than 37,091 acres, there would be an appropriate adjustment in the purchase price, based on a rate of eleven dollars per acre.

The offer signed for P. Burns and Co., Ltd., by "P. Burns, President," was accompanied by a cheque for $10,000 being a deposit "in case of acceptance of this offer."[4]

Days later, a letter of acceptance "dated at Calgary, Alberta, this 10th day of November, A.D., 1927" was sent to Pat Burns and he had bought another ranch, the most distinguished of them all.[5]

Burns was well aware of the criticism that he had "too much ranch land" and it bothered him. He was sensitive to public opinion but he believed that he was capable of being a good custodian and he defended his position by simply repeating a principle that any person holding land to which he could not or would not extend the best custodial care, had too much, regardless of the acreage. If there was a moral issue involved — and he believed there was — it had to relate to the quality of land care more than to the size of the spread or spreads. He clung to the idea that land was a trust and if he fulfilled his duty he would deliver it up to the next owner with the least possible damage or deterioration — in other words, with as nearly as possible the same productivity as it possessed when he acquired it.

He visited his ranches often, finding his greatest pleasure in so doing. There he could throw off the cloak of responsibility which stuck with him in the office area. Here, too, his penetrating vision was at its best. He could tell at a glance if the cattle were flourishing, failing, or "holding their own." Inevitably, he was studying the grass to determine how it was standing up to grazing pressures. Just as assiduously, he was observing the saddle horses to make sure they were not being abused or neglected or overworked. The snaffle bit — the least severe of metal bits — was the rule on all the Burns ranches and both Mr. Burns and Mr. Duggan were adamant on this point. "We'll have no curb bits or severe bits used on our horses," they were known to repeat. And if saddle horses were getting thin, the boss would have something to say. His was the attitude of a person who had a great store of respect and sympathy for all of Nature's chattels; it was the sort of compassionate concern that made him ever anxious about land care.

There could be no doubt; it was always better that land be in the care of sympathetic stewards, and while one observer would speak critically of the extent of the Burns holdings, another could conclude: "It's fortunate when a resource like land receives the benefit of thoughtful care such as Pat Burns tries to provide."

The "Ugly Duckling"

In this excerpt MacEwan reminds us that while we now give recognition to the proper importance of agriculture in western Canada, it was not always so — hence the title. (From Illustrated History of Western Canadian Agriculture, *Saskatoon: Western Producer Prairie Books, 1980.)*

Agriculture has been recognized as the world's first industry but in prairie Canada it was second. It was a slow starter, having been preceded and held back by the fur trade. It was the country's "ugly duckling," the object of insults and rebuffs until the "young bird" began to acquire its "feathers" and "swanlike shape."

The fur traders, who loved the wild, free life which allowed them to make their own laws as the occasion demanded, and take and discard native wives without formality, convinced themselves that their adopted area had been consecrated by the Maker Of All Things for furs and furs alone. Many of them remembered the dull toil of thinning turnips, picking potatoes, shearing Scottish Blackface sheep, and mucking out the byres at home and were glad to be far away. The very idea of introducing such operations to Rupert's Land brought anger and, in some instances, violence. For more than a hundred years the trade in furs stood alone and unchallenged. Until the time of the 5th Earl of Selkirk, nobody on either side of the Atlantic displayed the imagination and courage to advocate a farming venture.

Prompted by the derogatory remarks from the traders, it became fashionable for others to speak scornfully about Canada in general and the Northwest in particular. Jacques Cartier started it when he referred to the country he saw beside the St. Lawrence River as "the land God gave to Cain." To Voltaire, the country which is now Canada was just "a few acres of snow." And Madame Jeanne de Pompadour, on hearing of the fall of Quebec in 1759, was said to have dismissed the matter lightly, saying: "It makes little difference. Canada is useful only to provide me with furs."

Nobody was attempting to separate the good from the inferior in the new land. It was being treated as if it were all bad. If one part of British North America was more promising than the rest, no effort was being made to define it. If some section possessed an advantage for producing cattle or wheat or peanuts, nobody was in a hurry to prove it. Instead of trying to find its worth, men of prominence seemed to be striving to surpass each other in denunciation. Without knowing what he was talking about, Sir Archibald Alison, British lawyer and historian who died in Canada's year of Confederation, would blemish an otherwise good record of judgment by proclaiming that: "Probably seven-eighths of British North America are doomed to eternal sterility from the excessive severity of the climate which yields only a scant herbage to the reindeer, the elk and the muskox."

That statement, if given credence, would certainly destroy any thought of growing wheat for trading but, as far as is known, nobody challenged the author. He, of course, did not live long enough to be embarrassed by the discovery not many years later that the western part of that land "doomed to eternal sterility" had the resources with which to become one of the leading "bread baskets" of the world. To further bedevil the gloomy pronouncement, the same area was found to possess the world's biggest deposit of oil-bearing sands, the world's largest known reserves of potash, to say nothing of wealth in coal, forests, nickel, iron ore, uranium, grazing lands, and more.

The folly of drawing conclusions before the facts are established should be obvious and the best examples can be found in utterances by men of the fur trade. Alison's hasty assessment of the country will invite less surprise than statements from people who spent years in the country and should have had a better understanding, men like George Simpson of the Hudson's Bay Company and Bishop Alexandre Taché of Red River. Simpson, as governor of the company in Rupert's Land for almost forty years, rendered notable service, but when called as an expert witness before the Select Committee of the Imperial House of Commons in 1857, he did nothing to enhance an otherwise good reputation for judgment. The committee was sitting to consider the future of the country west of Red River and Simpson was one of the first to be called. His words, some of them unworthy of the man, survive.[1]

One of the first questions put to him was: "Will you have the goodness to give to the Committee an account of your impressions of the character of the Territory of the Hudson's Bay Company in point of soil and climate, particularly with reference to its adaptation for the purposes of cultivation and colonization?"

To this, Sir George made the surprising reply: "I do not think that any part of the Hudson's Bay Company's territories is well adapted for settlement. The crops are very uncertain."

Asked if this observation would apply to Red River, the witness replied: "Yes." And then he made the statement which might have made all the other errors committed during the hearings seem trivial. His questioner asked: "Why so?" and Sir George answered in words which should have haunted him: "On account of the poverty of the soil, except on the banks of the river."

The date was ten years before Canadian Confederation, twelve years before Canada bought the West from the Hudson's Bay Company for $1,500,000 and some concessions of land. The witness was the man who, after thirty-seven years in the Northwest, traveling much of the time, should have been the highest authority on the future of the country. But the Simpson heart was in the fur business and not in colonization and agriculture and at least part of the land to which he alluded in the remark about "poverty of the soil," namely the Red River Valley, inherited its richness in soil from the immensely deep silt deposits of ancient Lake Agassiz, and was recognized a few decades later as one of the most fertile on the continent — or in the entire world. It was an area so rich that one soil expert warned against the careless application of barnyard manure because it could "dilute" the existing reserves of essential plant foods.

George Simpson's performance as the virtual ruler of Rupert's Land for nearly four decades leaves no doubt concerning his skills and leadership. How then was his expert testimony so faulty? It may be merciful to attribute it to wishful thinking or an inherent loyalty to his life's work. Although he gave dutiful support to the Selkirk Settlement — sometimes quite grudgingly — his first love was certainly for the fur trade. He would have found it difficult to believe or accept that the industrial role of furs would so soon yield to the growing might of the new giant, agriculture.

But Simpson's pessimism about agriculture and settlement in the West was not the last to be voiced. Capt. John Palliser, who came to prairie Canada as a servant of the government in London later in the same year in which Simpson was appearing before the committee, gave partial support to the gloomy view. Reporting in 1863, he spoke favorably about farming and settlement opportunities in what he termed the Fertile Belt, that crescent-shaped band which was known later as the park belt. But of the more central prairie region, what he described as "an extension of the Great American Desert," he was guarded, even pessimistic.

"In the central part of the continent there is a region, desert or semi-desert in character," he wrote, "which can never be expected to become occupied by settlers.... Although there are fertile spots throughout its extent it can never be of much advantage to us as a possession...."[2]

Palliser was correct in his favorable opinion of the so-called Fertile Belt, meaning in modern terms, Red Deer, Edmonton, Vegreville, Lloydminster, Prince Albert, Melfort, and Dauphin. The combination of precipitation, soil quality and general climate was to prove most favorable to cropping. But Palliser was only partly correct in his estimation of the prairie part. True, the prairies were to suffer from drought more often than the park belt but the same plains country was to produce wheat of the hardest and highest quality and in amounts that tended to contradict Palliser. Those prairies were to be the source of a strikingly high percentage of the entries of wheat and other grains winning world championships in the annual competitions.

More years passed without much change of sentiment for the western soil. As late as 1868 — one year after the official birth of the Dominion of Canada at Confederation and one year before Canada acquired the West by purchase from the Hudson's Bay Company — the respected Bishop Taché had something to say, confirming that the "ugly duckling" was still waiting for its coat of fine feathers. "For my own part," said the bishop, "as there are extremely great difficulties in the way of colonizing the few points in this vast territory capable of cultivation, I acknowledge frankly that I would as soon — perhaps preferably — see the country remain as it is, as see it change, if the changes are to be such as it appears to me, they would inevitably be."[3]

Although men of the fur trade rebelled at every suggestion of agriculture, the fact was that the first plantings of domestic seeds in the West were in gardens or garden-size plots at the traders' posts. It was not a case of the traders giving serious thought to cropping contrary to their principles; rather it was the expression of an instinct calling for some vegetable foods to break the tedium of a wild meat and pemmican diet. The men were thankful for that nearly indestructible blend of dried buffalo meat and melted fat — sometimes flavored with saskatoon berries — but they could not escape the longing for variety. The only tools available for cultivation consisted of spades and hoes and this fact, coupled with the absence of winter storage for vegetables like turnips, carrots, and potatoes, limited plantings to small plots.

Studies conducted by Prof. Arthur Silver Morton in the Hudson's Bay records revealed a committee minute from 1674 — just four years after the company charter was granted — stating: "Ordered that there be provided . . . a bushel of wheat and rye, barley and oats, or a barrell of each in casks, and such sorts of garden Seeds as the Governor shall advise . . . [also] a Bible and a common prayer book."

There is no indication of where these seeds were planted or if they were planted. It can be presumed, however, that if there was a planting, it would be at one of the company's posts at the bottom of James Bay.

The first cultivation and planting within the boundaries of present-day Saskatchewan may have been by the pioneer French trader, Chevalier de la Corne at his trading post on the south side of the Saskatchewan River, due north of today's town of Kinistino. The Master who built there in 1753 ordered cereal and garden seeds from France and was said to have had turnips, potatoes, peas, carrots, and cabbage from his own soil in the following year — also a small amount of wheat which he would no doubt crush between two selected stones for use in making bread or bannock. Whatever the modest amount grown, it would be enough to qualify la Corne for the distinction of being the first grower of wheat in the proud Wheat Province of Saskatchewan.

The corresponding distinction in the Alberta area is in doubt but it may properly go to the rather notorious trader, Peter Pond. There seems no doubt that he was the first of the newcomers to plant garden seeds. The only doubt is in whether he planted wheat or other grains in addition to the garden varieties.

Pond, the Connecticut Yankee who served with the British in wars against the French and then took to trading, went from the headwaters of the Churchill River over the Methye Portage, down the Clearwater River to where Fort McMurray stands today, and then north on the Athabasca River to build Pond's House for trading purposes about thirty miles from the river's outlet at Athabasca Lake. That was in 1778 and the amazing fellow, who is known as a successful trader as well as a pioneer planter, was the first white man in the area. In addition to being the first of his race in the Athabasca region where the furs were abundant and the first planter, he was the first white man to see oil seeping from the sands along the river, the first to build a place of residence with more permanence than a tepee in the area of Alberta, and the first white man in the area to be suspected of murder.

In any event, when Alexander Mackenzie came that way a few years later, he wrote in his journal that Pond's garden was as good as any he had seen in Canada. But when Pond's name was mentioned as one which might be considered in a search for a Patron Saint for the Alberta Seed Growers' Association, a historian was quick to point out that as a suspect in two murders and a participant in a couple of man-to-man duels with pistols, he would probably be the least saintly of all patron saints.

Alexander Henry the Younger harvested fifty bushels of turnips and eighty bushels of potatoes at a Saskatchewan River post in 1809 and the hens at Fort Edmonton began to lay on January 6, 1811. The traders would have refused to admit it but at more and more posts there was a faint hint of agriculture, enough to encourage those who were growing tired of pemmican.

But still, in the first decade of the nineteenth century, there was not in all the Northwest a single genuine farmer or genuine farming effort. That was soon to change but not without some major struggles and some bloodshed.

William Kennedy
History's Forgotten Hero

Here we have an excellent example of the researcher at work. Although Kennedy was a hero in his day, a performer of amazing feats of courage and daring, he was lost to us. And so it was that while much of our Canadian media was parroting the stories of American heroes, MacEwan was busy researching those of our own, admittedly remote, heroic personalities. The following excerpt is indeed subject for full treatment. (From Métis Makers *of History,* Saskatoon: Western Producer Prairie Books, 1981.)

While the rough-and-ready Jimmy Jock Bird was flaunting contempt for his father's race by deliberately choosing the lifestyle of the Piegan Indians, William Kennedy was being no less forthright in adopting the white man's world and demonstrating how a Métis boy born at a remote trading post on the lower Saskatchewan River could succeed with distinction recognized far beyond Canada's shores.

Kennedy was the first of his people to break the possessive grip of the fur country and become an international figure with a proud record in Arctic exploration and science. The story of his life and achievements should have been enough to elevate him to an All-Canadian Hall of Heroes or something of the kind. But instead of remembering him, historians, for reasons difficult to understand, almost passed him by.

In background, Kennedy and Bird were well-matched. Both were sons of chief factors employed by the Hudson's Bay Company; both had Cree mothers and both were sent overseas to attend school. But there all similarity ended. Their ways of life differed as June breezes differed from the blasts of January, proving only that Métis like others could possess the blessed gift of individuality. The Kennedy influence, however, was more effective and beneficial in both Métis and non-Métis circles.

Born in 1814 at old Cumberland House where the Hudson's Bay Company, forty years earlier, initiated a new policy by building a trading post in the Interior, William was the youngest of five children in the family of Alexander Kennedy and his Indian wife, Agatha or Aggathas. Boyhood years thereabout were much like those of other children growing up where stockade walls separated natives and whites and beaver skins seemed to rule human lives on both sides. School facilities were totally nonexistent but when the boy was eleven years old, he and his brother, George, were sent by their Scottish father to obtain elementary education on the Orkney Islands where both climate and the discipline administered by headmasters seemed slightly hostile.

After seven years in Scotland, William returned to his native land and was at once engaged as a clerk in the service of the Hudson's Bay Company. He might have expected to be posted at one of the company's western trading establishments with which he would be familiar but instead of that, he was sent to the Ottawa River district and then to distant Fort Chimo on Ungava Bay. There the young man mingled with the Labrador Indians and Eskimos and learned the harsh and useful lessons about survival in the North. One of his Labrador neighbors in the employ of the Hudson's Bay Company at that time was Donald Smith, later Lord Strathcona.

The young man performed well enough as a company servant but he was growing ever more conscious of the evil of rum as used in obtaining furs from the natives. When he rebelled against the trading practice, he was reminded that liquor in some form had become a practical necessity in obtaining furs in profitable volume. The message as Kennedy heard it was clear: he would have to follow the traditional alcoholic policies or leave the service. Kennedy left. But in departing he knew he was taking a recently discovered enthusiasm for the North with him, also some valuable discoveries about survival in that land of adversity.

For many years one of the biggest of northern challenges was to find the illusive North West Passage which would furnish the shortest possible water route between Western Europe and rich trading centers of the Far East. It was the prime inducement for Henry Hudson, Thomas Button, Jens Munck, and a score of other courageous explorers who tried to get through on North America's Arctic side. Sir John Franklin was the latest to search for the water passage between Hudson Strait and the Pacific. Having failed in his attempts in 1819 and 1825, he was embarking again in 1845, this time with two sturdy ships from the British Navy, the *Terror* and *Erebus,* and strong British backing. The navigators were carrying enough provisions to sustain them for three years but in spite of the extensive preparations, this was the expedition from which Franklin and members of his crew never returned. They were last seen by the captain of a whaler, the *Prince of Wales,* off the west coast of Greenland on July 26, 1845. Franklin's ships were said to be "moored to an iceberg, awaiting an opening in the middle ice to enable them to cross over to Lancaster Sound."[1]

A year passed and then another without further report and British people became worried. There was growing fear that disaster had overtaken the expedition. Various naval parties were organized and sent to search the Arctic islands but without success. Only in 1854 did Dr. John Rae encounter Eskimos who could tell of seeing hungry white men pulling sleighs on King William Island a few years earlier. There were reports, too, of dead bodies seen in the same area.

Lady Franklin was one of those becoming actively engaged in searching operations. She obtained a ship of medium size, the *Prince Albert,* and furnished it and sent it to the Arctic islands. Its crew was thought to have found clues of a party wintering in 1845-46 near the entrance of Wellington Channel but nothing was conclusive. Lady Franklin, clinging to the hope that her husband and crew might still be found alive, ordered that the ship be strengthened to resist the awful pressures of Arctic ice and re-equipped to sail again in 1851.

She turned to Hudson's Bay Company officials, asking them to assist her in finding a competent leader for the expedition, one who would understand the problems presented in northern travel.

It must have been obvious that William Kennedy's experience had been gained initially on the prairie land rather than on water but John McLean who had been with Kennedy at Fort Chimo said that the young Métis possessed the natural ingenuity and resourcefulness needed in a leader and, after his years on the Labrador coast, had considerable knowledge of the North. Kennedy's name was placed before Lady Franklin and she appointed him, even though his sailing experience was very limited.

Strangely enough, Kennedy had in the previous year written to offer his services in any practical way for the search for Franklin. He might have had some strong personal feelings for the eminent Britisher because of memories of Franklin's visit to Cumberland House in 1819. It was the explorer's first attempt to penetrate the North West Passage and in his search for supporting information, he came by canoe from York Factory and arrived at Cumberland House on October 23, intending to continue on his way and turn toward the Arctic. But winter was approaching and Franklin accepted Governor William's invitation to stay there for part or all of the winter.[2]

William Kennedy was a small boy at Cumberland House at the time and had some lingering memories. He recalled the distinguished visitor's concern about the lack of opportunity for the children living at the post to obtain even the most elementary schooling. Moreover, Franklin tried to do something about it and actually conducted a few beginners' classes during the few weeks he was at Cumberland House. William Kennedy could say that Sir John Franklin was his first teacher.[3]

Kennedy told that from the very moment of his appointment as leader of the expedition of 1851, he was the object of gifts and gestures from many people who simply wanted to help. His transportation over the long distance to Aberdeen, Scotland, where the ship was being made ready, cost him practically nothing. The mayor of Hamilton provided a railroad ticket to New York and at the latter place he was presented with "free passage to England in one of Cunard's steamers."[4] The response in England and Scotland was the same.

At Aberdeen, Kennedy saw the *Prince Albert* for the first time and watched the great stores of food being placed on board. Nothing, it seemed, had been overlooked as the provision of a ton and a half of pemmican — presumably brought from Rupert's Land — would indicate. There, too, Kennedy met the men who would comprise his crew of seventeen, including the young French naval officer, Lt. Joseph René Bellot, who had volunteered for the search and would serve as second-in-command. It was understood that if Kennedy were to lose his life or become incapacitated during the voyage, the Paris-born Bellot would assume the command.

The ship completed loading at Stromness in the Orkneys where Lady Franklin was present to express her wish for safety and success and then wave a tearful farewell as the ship, on June 3, headed out to sea. If anybody, including the novice Captain Kennedy, had any fears or doubts, they were not revealed.

Exactly three weeks later, members of the crew sighted Cape Farewell, the most southerly point of Greenland, and passed through a "real ice stream." They turned northward to follow the "gaunt, sterile, iron-bound shore" of Greenland's west side as far as the Danish village of Upernavik where the Captain bought six Eskimo dogs for four pounds, and a supply of sealskin boots.[5]

The ice was increasingly menacing and Bellot in his journal mentioned being in the midst of 150 icebergs. As the ice became thicker and the days became colder, there was increasing danger of depression among the men but Kennedy's inner qualities of leadership proved to be exactly what were needed to maintain morale. When Bellot spent two days in a sickbed on July 6 and 7, he wrote in his journal: "Mr. Kennedy came and read prayers to me."

With grim determination, Kennedy and his crew forced their way through the Baffin Bay ice to Lancaster Sound and then into Prince Regent Inlet. At every opportunity, members of the party were making forays over land and ice, searching for clues, anything that might bear testimony of the Franklin expedition. Often they were in danger, as they explored both coasts of the Inlet. While Captain Kennedy and four of his men were making such a side-trip on September 9, a great mass of ice shifted unexpectedly and the ship was carried thirty miles. The group of five men were at once separated and lost. The stranded fellows wondered if they would ever see their ship again. Happily, they found a food cache left by an earlier expedition and they began to build crude shelters in which they could winter if necessary.

Bellot, who remained on the drifting ship, made several attempts to locate his lost friends and it was only on October 26 — after a separation lasting more than six weeks — that he found them, still in good health.[6]

During this enforced separation, Lieutenant Bellot moored the ship at Batty Bay on the west side of Prince Regent Inlet, where it would remain for the long winter. He saw the Arctic sun sink "beneath the horizon, not to re-appear until 110 days later." By the first of December, the men were making longer sled trips with the dogs. By Kennedy's reckoning, "some of them must have travelled 2,000 miles."[7] The Captain was feeling the pain of his rheumatism or arthritis more than ever and some members of the crew were feeling the symptoms of scurvy but they did not relax and on Christmas day they played a game of soccer in the snow.

In finding Sir John Franklin and his men, these Kennedy searchers were no more successful than those of the many parties which went before, but the explorations were not wasted. Much more territory was discovered and mapped and in identifying the north tip of Boothia Peninsula, they were significantly discovering the most northerly point of the North American Continent.

Best of all, as Captain Kennedy noted when he returned the stout little ship to Aberdeen in October, 1853, he and his party had completed a seventeen-month expedition in a savagely cruel part of the world without loss of life or serious accident.

The British people were unstinting in their praise for Kennedy's Arctic operation but the best tribute came from his colleague, Lieutenant Bellot, who lived and worked with him constantly for seventeen months. In his memoirs of the great adventure, Bellot wrote: "To Captain Kennedy alone belong the praises due to the boldness and intelligence of the measures taken for the accomplishment of our mission; and that to his incredible activity and the constant care he took to secure the health and welfare of us all, we are indebted for having been able, under the protection of Providence, to do much in a little time, and to return every one of us to the embraces of our friends, without having to regret those frightful mutilations, those losses of limbs, which are often the result of cruises in the icy seas. . . ."[8]

While in England he was called frequently to lecture on his experiences in the Northern Labrador area, his search for Franklin, and his associations with Indian and Eskimo people. The English public listened.

Before returning to his native land, he married a well-educated and gifted English girl who, strangely enough, was a relative to Lady Franklin. As Mrs. Eleanor Cripps Kennedy she was to exert a valuable cultural influence in early Manitoba.

On moving to make their home in British North America, the Kennedys lived for a few years in the East, during which time the captain was drawn more and more into political discussions about the future of Rupert's Land and the entire North-West. With encouragement from George Brown, editor of the *Toronto Globe,* he was becoming bolder in his opposition to Hudson's Bay Company monopoly and rule. For the purpose of generating interest in self-government and possible union with the province of Canada, he traveled west and returned with a petition bearing the names of 575 people who favored change.

Torontonians, hoping for an extension of Upper Canada and for an active trade with the West, received the petition gleefully. They were interested at once in better communication, perhaps even a railroad. A Toronto meeting held on the last day in 1856 heard the mounting protests against the ancient Hudson's Bay Company charter which allegedly conferred the right to own and rule the huge territory known as Rupert's Land forever. Kennedy was among the speakers who contended that the boundary of Canada should be pushed westward to the Pacific.

Moreover, the large number of United States people moving northward across the border, coupled with the American dream of Manifest Destiny, possessed urgency in changing the political status of the West. On this point, George Brown was much more concerned as he was more aggressive than was his political opponent, John A. Macdonald. Brown and Kennedy were seen standing together.

The new enthusiasm demanded action. Henry Hind was appointed to conduct an appraisal of the North-West, mainly to determine if it were worth acquiring. That Hind's study would parallel and partly duplicate the John Palliser survey authorized by the Imperial Government at about the same time, did not seem to matter. Bright ideas for the salvation of the North-West were being advanced from all directions. One of the most ambitious was in support of a transportation company — the North-West Transportation, Navigation and Railway Company — to provide a railroad as far as Collingwood and steamship service to Fort William. Among the company's directors was Capt. William Kennedy. It may have been a good idea but it was premature and did not survive for long.

When the transportation plan was failing, Toronto interest shifted to an all-British mail route and service between Toronto and Fort Garry. The proposal sounded well — mail to go through twice a month each way in the summer and once a month in the winter. Kennedy was again one of the leading advocates and he gave his personal attention to the most difficult portion of the route, that lying between Lake Superior and Fort Garry. In spite of his nagging arthritis, he made a couple of test trips over it, using canoes and poor trails. Nobody criticized either the idea or the Kennedy performance but the practical obstacles were big and when the mail routed from Toronto to Fort Garry by way of Chicago was still making much better time, the all-British course was dropped, temporarily at least.

But instead of being wasted, the Kennedy labors to find the best land and water route from Lake Superior to Red River led the government of Canada a few years later to undertake the construction of the Dawson Route, giving the people of Manitoba their first direct connection with the East.[9] It was over this course that Colonel Wolseley led his small army in 1870 for the suppression of the Riel Insurrection, and over the same route that the first North West Mounted Police traveled in 1873.

Of course William Kennedy, with Métis blood boiling in his veins, would not be satisfied until he was back in the West to stay and he and Mrs. Kennedy made the move at the beginning of 1860.

It was not retirement. Kennedy at forty-six years was not thinking of retiring. He was coming west with a purpose which was close to his heart. Throughout his life he embraced a stout religious faith and the highest moral ideals and was now anxious to devote more of himself to his ideals.

Having succeeded eminently in the white man's advanced community, he could have remained in it but this godly man wanted to serve the native people of the West and was now returning with the intention of devoting the balance of his life to missionary pursuits.

Rupert's Land's first newspaper, the *Nor'-Wester,* still only a few weeks old, reported on February 28, 1860, that William Kennedy was "no longer connected with the Canadian Mail Contractors" and was being supported in his return to the West by the Canadian Foreign Missionary Society. His object was to start some Indian settlements of a new form, probably around Lake of the Woods. Within the Kennedy concept, the native people would be encouraged to settle in colonies where the children would receive a good basic education and adults would be offered useful farm training and religious education.

At the time of the interview with the editor, Kennedy was planning to visit Lake of the Woods as soon as he could arrange it in the spring, for the purpose of conferring with the tribal chiefs about the program. The funds for the project were to be provided by the Missionary Society and the Aborigines Protection Society of London.[10]

It was indeed a high purpose, worthy of the man, but it was not a success. After spending the months of April and May in the Lake of the Woods district, Kennedy was obliged to abandon the region which had been his first choice for the scheme because of failure to get the necessary support from the chiefs concerned.[11]

But he had no thought of abandoning the idea of settlements designed for Indian betterment. Having failed at the Lake of the Woods, he began looking elsewhere and fixed upon Fairford, on Lake Manitoba's east side, between Lakes Manitoba and St. Martin. There the dream came true and before long Kennedy could report a thriving farm and church community, at the center of which he and Mrs. Kennedy were very happy.

But the captain's health was deteriorating. The arthritis was becoming more severe and crippling and he felt compelled to take his family to a retirement home at Red River. He owned a good building site in the Parish of St. Andrew's, a property which belonged to his father before him, and on it ordered a handsome stone house which not only served his family but stood to become one of the architectural relics of the province.

Upon occupying the new home, Mrs. Kennedy was almost at once a leader in the community. She taught music, played the organ at St. Andrew's Church, led the choir and supported every charitable and cultural venture. She even opened a millinery store, one of the first in that part. In the late sixties when Red River crops were ravaged by grasshoppers in four successive years and settlers and residents faced famine, Mrs. Kennedy was one of the women who came forward to offer all the assistance of which she was capable. She directed international appeals for the needed aid and then became active in administering the relief.

As for the captain, his arthritic body prevented him from traveling but his great Métis mind remained clear and he continued to be Winnipeg's leading authority on Arctic Canada and Canada's native people. His support for the cause of temperance was undiminished and his enthusiasm for a railroad to Hudson Bay never failed. As one of those who helped to start the Historical and Scientific Society of Manitoba, he was the author of the first technical paper delivered, the title being "The North West Passage." Who could have done it as well?

Capt. William Kennedy died at his home on January 25, 1890, and twenty years later the Women's Canadian Club of Winnipeg authorized a memorial tablet to be hung in the old Church of the Rapids, St. Andrew's. The tablet, unveiled on May 21, 1910, by none other than Sir Ernest Shackleton, another famous explorer, bore this message:

Sacred to the Memory of
CAPT. WILLIAM KENNEDY
Son of Alex. Kennedy, Chief Factor H.B.C. Born at Cumberland House, Rupert's Land, April 14, 1814. Died at St. Andrews Manitoba, January 25, 1890. Educated in the Orkney Islands. Entered H.B. service 1833. Served at Lachine and Ungava. Commanded Expedition 1851-2 in search of Sir John Franklin. Discovered Bellot Strait and the most northern point of American Mainland which navigators had sought for three centuries. He brought the first mail to Red River in 1859. Settled at St. Andrews 1861. An earnest Christian philanthropist, a Scholar, a Loyal Friend.
"His Works Do Follow Him"
This tablet was erected in 1910 by the Women's Canadian Club, Winnipeg.

Nobody would contend that Kennedy was a typical or average Métis any more than they would call Churchill an average Englishman. The average individuals of any race are not the ones who become great leaders. But the essential point about Kennedy remained clear, that he was both Métis and great, proving something of Métis potential and Métis versatility. He had the qualities of a hero.

Thumbnail Sketches of Alberta

The following series of excerpts appear in Alberta Landscapes *and show MacEwan at his best. Meant to appear opposite to landscape photographs (by the editor) they nevertheless stand well by themselves, revealing his intimate knowledge of and respect for the countryside. (From* Alberta Landscapes *by Grant MacEwan and R. H. Macdonald, Saskatoon: Western Producer Prairie Books, 1982.)*

In the Shadow of the Rockies

Pyramid Lake, in the shadow of the Rockies, is like a rare sapphire gem held to its setting by rugged mountain clasps. There, Pauline Johnson might have found the words:

August is laughing across the sky,
Laughing while paddle, canoe and I
Drift, drift,
Where the hills uplift . . . .

In Jasper National Park, Nature's awesome grandeur seems to have been in league with history. Usable mountain passes were scarce, and the historic Yellowhead Pass brought travellers from the West. The broad valley of the Athabasca brought them from the East to that place where Jasper Hawes was operating a trading post beside Brule Lake for the North West Company from 1817. It became a landmark on that most practical route for travel between the prairies and the Pacific and was soon drawing explorers, traders, miners and settlers.

Much later it was to be the entrance for rail transportation, but the route for the C.P.R. was changed to enter the Rockies by the Kicking Horse Pass. Other rail lines — the Grand Trunk Pacific and the Canadian Northern — adopted the Athabasca Valley approach and the government of Canada in 1907 fixed upon the vast expanse of natural wonderland for a National Park. The decision ensured that the breath-taking Maligne Canyon, glacial-fed Maligne Lake, Mount Edith

Cavell, which marks the Great Divide, the Columbia Icefields, known as the Mother of Rivers, and numerous lakes . . . will belong, forever, to the people of Canada.

Why not some bragging?

A district resident admitted that Bragg Creek, less than an hour's drive west and south of Calgary, has much to brag about. But there is another, more reasonable explanation for the choice of name. The selection was a tribute to Warren Bragg, a Nova Scotia-born pioneer who built a cabin close to the point at which the creek discharges into the Elbow.

David Thompson, the greatly respected explorer and surveyor, may have seen the Bragg Creek wonderland in 1787 when he met Piegan Indians somewhere near the Elbow River and wintered with them. But the first representatives of the immigrant race to show a calculated interest in the region were the Montana whiskey traders and later the missionaries.

Frontiersman Fred Kanouse had a trader's post on the Elbow in 1871 but was probably too busy dispensing firewater and exchanging gunfire with angry Indians to take serious stock of the rare landscape. However, in 1873 — two years before the Mounted Police came to establish at Fort Macleod and three years before they built Fort Calgary — Father Constantine Scollen arrived. He was the first English-speaking Catholic missionary to reside in the area that is now Alberta and was, for a time, the only missionary in the southern part of the province. Father Scollen went farther up the Elbow River to a riverside log cabin which was promptly dedicated as a mission and called Our Lady of Peace.

With its heavy cover of trees and violent undulations, the foothill land was not immediately attractive to homesteaders and farmers but Calgarians were quick to discover the natural values in the creek and river region. Some built summer homes there; some built permanent homes and demanded a good road between the two places. And then, as further testimony to the park-like qualities, the government of Alberta established the Bragg Creek Provincial Park and saw it gain instant popularity.

Although Bragg Creek hamlet does not fall in any way within Calgary jurisdiction, the district is one of the city's finest assets. Local people and others going there are advised that to gain full appreciation of the area, they should travel by the Priddis road westward. Following this route, travellers will experience the mounting intensity of the foothills, the rapidly growing intimacy of the mountains, the sudden forest character of the trees, and the sure realization that this was created for recreation and park purposes.

Big Country

"This is big country," said the man at the gasoline pump at Hanna. "You can see from here to the middle of next week and you shouldn't be surprised at anything."

It is tourist zone number three, embracing what is commonly called east central Alberta. Drumheller and Hanna are its biggest towns, and it is a land given to extremes. Near Drumheller, the visitor will see wheat land ranking with the best in the world. Numerous international championship samples of grain have come from the area, while not far away there is land still clinging to its sagebrush and buffaloberries.

With irrigation at Strathmore, citizens can grow almost anything — including apples — while in nearby districts, soil remains dry enough to suit the primitive cactus plants. Cacti, with their complex of needles, offer a warning to humans to keep their hands to themselves. They are considered to be lowly forms until they break out in June bloom, and then, for a few brief days, their beauty is sufficient to bring flower lovers from distant parts.

As for scenery, the zone holds everything from conventional beauty as seen on the upper Red Deer River to the naked badland hoodoos. It is this latter area that is known to generate eerie feelings, especially when dusk is falling over the valley.

Nor will residents let visitors forget that this is outstanding Canada goose country. Just as Vegreville greets incoming travellers with a mounted model of the world's biggest Ukrainian Easter egg and Drumheller displays a dinosaur model, so Hanna, at its eastern entrance, proudly displays a handsome, oversized model of a Canada goose. The region lacks enough water to give it importance as goose nesting ground, but the northern-hatched geese winging to favored wintering parts in the south fancy that eastern Alberta flyway. Year after year, the migrating flocks of majestic birds set down to rest and feed and run the risk of being within the range of the hunter's gun. . . .

The Old Fur Trader's Highway

During the peak years of the fur trade when all goods were transported by canoe, the North Saskatchewan River was the country's Number One Highway, a water highway, of course.

The voyageurs of earlier times, were probably too busy paddling at the usual rate of forty strokes per minute to admire the beauty of summer skies smiling down on wild flowers and poplar bluffs. The loaded canoes carrying eight or more voyageurs, created some added scenery and certainly did much to enliven the river's story.

. . . A scene where the river bends as it winds through the parklands might well cause one to pause instinctively and scan the river for fur brigades. Failing to see one, it would be tempting to listen for the words and notes of an old French chanson being sung by the voyageurs.

For the North West Company men, the paddling would end at Montreal, and for the servants of the Hudson's Bay Company, at York Factory on Hudson Bay. The former would break their journey at Grand Portage or Fort William on Lake Superior and exchange cargoes with canoemen from Montreal. In this way, the western crews would reach Fort Augustus or some point on the Athabasca before winter set in.

The bend in the North Saskatchewan River is only a few miles from the spot where the Frog Lake Massacre occurred on April 2, 1885, signalling the onset of the North West Rebellion. The trouble began with discontent on the part of Gabriel Dumont and Louis Riel's Métis people on the South Saskatchewan south of Prince Albert, but Big Bear's Crees got into the act at Frog Lake and killed nine whites on that tragic day. Local Indians who chose to advance to Fort Pitt or join Riel may have placed their canoes in the river at this point.

Natural beauty and local history seem to insist upon mingling. A person can make a random selection of any point in Alberta — or any point in the West — and is likely to discover that the area harbors more beauty and more romance than its residents had ever stopped to appreciate.

The Badlands

No one who sees the Red Deer River Badlands can ever forget the weird and spectacular landscape that cuts deeply into the rockbound records of prehistory. In the words of one photographer who visited the scene recently, "the formations serve as an illustrated textbook of time."

Alberta's written history is brief, but the story that is revealed here by the timeless forces of erosion relate some of Nature's secrets from a hundred million years ago. Then the district of Drumheller was a marshy delta washed by an inland sea and inhabited by strange dinosaur forms making their way through tropical everglade forests.

There are still many Canadians who are familiar with Florida, Hawaii and Italy, but have not seen Dinosaur Provincial Park. In 1980, it was one of the few North American areas to be admitted to the UNESCO-sponsored list of World Heritage Sites. Other Canadian sites accorded this internatonal recognition include Kluane National Park in the Yukon, Nahanni National Park in the Northwest Territories and L'Anse aux Meadows in Newfoundland, where a Norse village of the 11th century has been identified.

In placing the name of the Red Deer River site before UNESCO, the federal and provincial governments declared that the area "represents the most important fragment of the dinosaurian world known to mankind."

Provincial law now prohibits unauthorized digging or the removal of dinosaur bones or other rare materials, but there is nothing to prevent visitors from inspecting, studying and enjoying the rare panorama. It is also possible to view the area where Charles Sternberg recovered many of the dinosaur skeletons now seen in Canadian and other museums.

Most visitors to the provincial park at Steveville complain that they did not bring enough film for their cameras. They may not wish to spend a dark night amid the strange and spooky shapes carved by the hand of time, but as a daytime adventure they declare that there is nothing quite like the Red Deer River Badlands.

The Charm of Winter

People who discover beauty and charm in all seasons are truly fortunate.

Canadians have experienced little difficulty in finding attraction in the seasons of greenery and growth, but have been downright slow in recognizing similar attraction in the long spells of snow and icy temperatures. For too long, they felt sorry for themselves.

Early settlers were led to believe that western winters were unhealthy as well as unpleasant and dangerous. Most residents found comfort in the thought that they would remain in the country just "long enough to make some money and be able to retire where the winters were less severe." Vancouver Island and California, it seemed, were for prairie people who could afford to leave.

It took a while but public attitude changed. Slowly, it was accepted that Alberta's winters can be seasons of dazzling beauty; winter can allow for relaxation in activities that are peculiar to the season: curling, hockey, skating, skiing and snowshoeing.

Western winters may not be as cold as they were in homestead years, but the greater change has been in public thinking. A new appreciation for a returning world of snow-white adventure has been aided by increased insulation in home construction, better heating systems in homes and cars, and warmer, lightweight clothing.

One Albertan, after catching the spirit of good winter living, remarked: "Instead of going to California for the period of cold winter, I invested a small fraction of the cost of a California holiday in the best winter togs I could find and then went out and defied the weather and had a great time curling and skating and skiing. I'm shocked to think that I had to live so long before discovering the real charm of the Alberta winter."

"An Oasis in the Great American Desert"

Contrary to an early writer's opinion, cypress trees do not grow on the Cypress Hills. The trees in question were lodgepole pines and the error was not serious. One point was beyond dispute: the vegetation and character of these hills to which both Saskatchewan and Alberta have claim, were enough to make them objects of rare beauty. Rising above the altitude of Banff, they completely contradict the vegetative limitations of the prairie lands on all sides.

Captain John Palliser, who visited the hills in 1859, saw them as "an oasis" in the "Great American Desert." The Hills have always been distinctive in precipitation and flora and fauna. Residents get more snow and more rain than neighbors on lower levels. The Hills even escaped ice age glaciation thousands of years ago.

Since the beginning of ranching in the Canadian Northwest, the Cypress Hills were seen as favored cattle country with higher than average carrying capacity. The Hill grass was not superior to the shorter grass of the plains but there was more of it.

Today's cattlemen may think they have a primary claim upon the Hills, but there are others who can present strong cases. Cameramen love the Hills. . . . Bird lovers and biologists of every stripe find reasons to go there for study. Students of prairie history find important clues to events like the Cypress Hills Massacre of 1873, the birth of ranching, and the arrival of the Mounted Police. Two provincial parks — one on each side of the Saskatchewan-Alberta border — with beautiful Elkwater Lake nestling on the Alberta side, testify to the unique holiday and recreational resources to be found there.

Up from Coal

If Edmonton had its beginning in the fur trade and Calgary got its start with the arrival of the North West Mounted Police, then Lethbridge owed its origin to coal from the riverbank mine of Nicholas Sharon. The mine opened in 1872 at what was then called Coal Banks, on the west side of the Oldman River. It was two years after Blackfoot and Cree tribesmen engaged in their last big and bloody battle in the coulees within today's city limits, and two years before the coming of the Mounted Police. The mine was the first of its kind in Alberta.

The enterprising Sharon would personally load his coal wagons and haul them by oxteams to make sales at Fort Whoop-Up, or as far away as Fort Benton, Montana. His operations led, in 1882, to the formation of the Northwestern Coal and Navigation Company, with William Lethbridge of England as president and Elliott T. Galt as manager.

The place that had been known as Coal Banks and then Coalhurst was officially named Lethbridge on October 15, 1885. By this time, the high quality of the prairie grass in the region was being recognized and ranching was becoming popular. As an added lure for cattlemen, there were the chinook winds that brought winter relief with more than average frequency.

Lethbridge residents have never been short of wind, and the subject has often been treated with mirth. A farmer made the point that it was "a good district for windmills," and another, without trace of a smile, observed that while most farmers around Calgary received enough wind for one windmill per farm, "every Lethbridge farmer got enough for at least two."

But Lethbridge was in the area of relatively low rainfall, and when crops suffered, the city suffered too. The Dominion Experimental Station, established almost at the city limits, did much to ensure better dry farming methods and then to promote irrigation. Thanks to irrigation water, the city and much of the surrounding country boast big trees, and fine shelterbelts and parks, to say nothing of better crops.

It is to the city's great credit that Lethbridge, more than most cities of its size, was conscious of the importance of agriculture to the area.

Gateway to the North

Like Winnipeg, the big and bustling City of Edmonton had its roots in the fur trade. Although incorporation as a town came eight years later than Calgary, the first fort to bear the name was built in 1795, making modern Edmonton the oldest of Alberta cities.

Edmontonians, ever more conscious of their history, enjoy looking back. They recall with disappointment that the big Fort Edmonton, occupying ground beside the Legislative Building, was demolished in 1915. But city leaders were determined to reconstruct the landmark post on another site, sparing no cost and making it authentic in every possible detail. Included, of course, was the "Big House" or "Rowland's Folly," which, when initially completed in 1832, stood as the biggest structure of its kind between Fort Garry and the Pacific Ocean.

But by 1892 when the town was incorporated, Edmonton had outgrown the fur trade and was sensing new destiny. Nearby soil was demonstrating its unusual fertility and settlers began flocking to it. Edmonton was discovering that good soil is a city asset as much as a rural asset, and farm progress was reflected in city prosperity.

Then came the Klondike Gold Rush with thousands of would-be miners converging upon the Yukon. Edmonton merchants persuaded many prospectors to outfit in their town and take the overland route to the goldfields. It was poor advice because the Edmonton route was hazardous. But the memory of the gay days of '98 remained and

Edmonton adopted the Klondike Days theme to promote its unique summer festival.

Still, there were bigger things ahead for the city. There was the opening of the North and discovery of the huge part that Edmonton could and would play in servicing it. Edmonton became the unmistakable gateway, by land or air.

Then came the discovery of oil at Leduc in 1947. It marked a new day and the city boomed. New buildings pierced the clouds; the Edmonton Eskimos became an outstanding football team; the city played host to the Commonwealth Games and added to its international distinction; and, altogether, Edmonton became a city of enviable affluence while keeping the vigor of its youthful years.

The Cinderella City

Nothing occurring at Fort McMurray, it seems, is ever ordinary or commonplace. Fabulous is the word for the oil that clings to the Athabasca sands and romantic is the word for the local history. Even most of the people whose names are associated with the area's development possessed rare individuality.

Peter Pond, accused of one or two murders and described as the "wild man of the fur trade" was the first member of the white race to stand on the ground where Fort McMurray was to be built. It was 1778 and Pond had paddled up the Churchill River and down the Clearwater, looking for fresh fur country. North of today's Fort McMurray and west of the Athabasca River, he built "Pond's House," the first structure of its kind in the present area of Alberta. Here, too, he grew the first garden within today's province.

Alexander Mackenzie, trader and explorer who was later knighted, followed Pond and marvelled at the oily sands. It took time, however, for the great magnitude of the oil resources trapped in the sands to be understood, but every successive estimate seemed to be bigger than the previous one until oil experts were suggesting a total of 600 billion barrels, a figure comparable to that of the total proven reserves in the Middle Eastern fields.

But the Fort McMurray oil was not of much value unless it could be separated from the sand and marketed. Federal and provincial governments built pilot plants and programs of research were initiated. Success did not come quickly but eventually the oil industry moved to make huge capital investments in equipment, plants and pipelines, and bused hundreds of staff to distant work sites to produce needed oil. The town of Fort McMurray mushroomed during this period, and in 1980, became Alberta's newest city. It also earned the distinction as the fastest growing city in Canada.

Much of the acitivity in Fort McMurray ceased in the spring of 1982 following the collapse of the Alsands project. But the oil is still there and Fort McMurray will likely see great days once again.

The Sweep of Scenery

Anyone who stands at the grave site of Twelve-Foot Davis and surveys the converging valleys of the Peace and Smoky Rivers can never forget the scene.

The high hilltop overlooking Peace River Town has been described as Canada's most exclusive burying place. The bones of the man who became a legend of the Peace are there alone.

Twelve-Foot Davis was not twelve feet tall. In fact, he was relatively short, but when he joined the Gold Rush to the Fraser River in the 1860s, he got a hunch that two of the prominent claims exceeded regulation size by twelve feet. He was right, and after filing on the narrow strip, he took about $20,000 worth of gold from it. Thereafter, he was known as Twelve-Foot Davis.

From the Fraser, he adventured eastward over a height of land and descended the Peace River to Dunvegan and Peace River Crossing, panning for more gold, trading for furs and winning friends in his humble and kindly way. His honest dealings attracted trade and his open house hospitality attracted travellers of all races.

When he died at Slave Lake in 1900, he was buried there. But his friend Jim Cornwall recalled the Davis love for the river scene from the eminence back of Peace River Town, and the spot at which the little man had expressed a hope of being buried. Cornwall arranged to have the remains moved to the favored place. There a distinctive gravestone was fashioned, bearing the oft-quoted epitaph with some of the qualities of a sermon:

H. F. Davis,
Born Vermont, 1820,
Died at Slave Lake, 1893 (sic)
Pathfinder, Pioneer, Miner and Trader,
He was every man's friend and never locked
his cabin door.

Appendix
Books by Grant MacEwan

The Science and Practice of Canadian Animal Husbandry, with A. H. Ewen. Toronto: Thomas Nelson and Sons, 1936.

General Agriculture, with A. H. Ewen. Toronto: Thomas Nelson and Sons, 1939.

Breeds of Farm Livestock in Canada. Toronto: Thomas Nelson and Sons, 1941.

Feeding Farm Animals. Toronto: Thomas Nelson and Sons, 1945.

Sodbusters. Toronto: Thomas Nelson and Sons, 1948.

Agriculture on Parade. Toronto: Thomas Nelson and Sons, 1950.

Between the Red and the Rockies. Toronto: University of Toronto Press, 1952. Reprinted by Western Producer Prairie Books, 1979.

Eye Opener Bob. Edmonton: Institute of Applied Art, 1957. Reprinted by Western Producer Prairie Books, 1974.

Fifty Mighty Men. Saskatoon: Western Producer Prairie Books, 1958.

Calgary Cavalcade. Edmonton: Institute of Applied Art, 1959. Reprinted with revisions by Western Producer Prairie Books, 1975.

John Ware's Cow Country. Edmonton: Institute of Applied Art, 1960. Reprinted by Western Producer Prairie Books, 1973.

Blazing the Old Cattle Trail. Saskatoon: Western Producer Prairie Books, 1962.

Hoofprints and Hitchingposts. Saskatoon: Western Producer Prairie Books, 1964.

Poking into Politics. Edmonton: Institute of Applied Art, 1966.

Entrusted to My Care. Saskatoon: Western Producer Prairie Books, 1966.

A Short History of Western Canada (originally titled *West to the Sea*), with Maxwell Foran. Toronto: McGraw-Hill Ryerson Limited, 1968.

Harvest of Bread. Saskatoon: Western Producer Prairie Books, 1969.

Tatanga Mani: Walking Buffalo of the Stonies. Edmonton: Hurtig Publishers Ltd., 1969.

Power for Prairie Plows. Saskatoon: Western Producer Prairie Books, 1971.

Portraits from the Plains. Toronto: McGraw-Hill Ryerson Limited, 1971.

Sitting Bull: The Years in Canada. Edmonton: Hurtig Publishers Ltd., 1972.

This Is Calgary, with photographer Toby Rankin. Calgary: Calgary Real Estate Board Co-operative, 1973.

Battle for the Bay. Saskatoon: Western Producer Prairie Books, 1975.

And Mighty Women Too. Saskatoon: Western Producer Prairie Books, 1975.

Memory Meadows. Saskatoon: Western Producer Prairie Books, 1976.

Cornerstone Colony. Saskatoon: Western Producer Prairie Books, 1977.

The Rhyming Horseman of the Qu'Appelle. Saskatoon: Western Producer Prairie Books, 1978.

Pat Burns, Cattle King. Saskatoon: Western Producer Prairie Books, 1979.

Grant MacEwan's Illustrated History of Western Canadian Agriculture. Saskatoon: Western Producer Prairie Books, 1980.

Métis Makers of History. Saskatoon: Western Producer Prairie Books, 1981.

Alberta Landscapes, in collaboration with Rusty Macdonald. Saskatoon: Western Producer Prairie Books, 1982.

Notes

Introduction

1. *Saskatoon Star-Phoenix,* November 22, 1952; *Calgary Herald,* January 3, 1953; *Victoria Daily Colonist,* February 15, 1953; *Saskatchewan History,* May, 1953; *Winnipeg Free Press,* September 19, 1953.
2. *Prairie Perspectives,* David P. Gagan, ed., Department of History, University of Calgary (Holt, Rinehart and Winston of Canada Limited, 1970).
3. Historian and author of *The Birth of Western Canada* (Toronto: University of Toronto Press, 1960). First published by Longmans, Green Co. Ltd., 1936.
4. George F. G. Stanley, historian, is an example of such a writer himself, having been born in Calgary and later pioneering in writing western Canadian history.
5. *Prairie Perspective 2,* selected papers of the Western Canadian Studies Conference, 1970-71, prepared by the Department of History, University of Calgary (Holt, Rinehart and Winston of Canada Limited, Toronto and Montreal, 1975.)
6. R. H. Macdonald, *Grant MacEwan: No Ordinary Man* (Saskatoon: Western Producer Prairie Books, 1979).
7. Dr. Ward in his CBC review (Critically Speaking, November 30, 1952) said, "While we do not appear to have on the prairies the makings of a heroic literature, some of Mr. MacEwan's stories are nevertheless impressive."
8. An article in the *Canadian Library Journal* (February, 1976) by Norma Gutteridge credits *The Western Producer* with being first on the prairies to begin a "sustained" book publishing enterprise with the publication of *Fifty Mighty Men* in 1958. As will be seen above, Richards' Institute of Applied Arts brought out its first book nine years before Prairie Books and thirteen years before *Fifty Mighty Men.*

Chuck-Wagon Romance

1. In the spring of 1951 a young Alberta farmerette, interviewed on one of the CBC farm broadcasts for Ontario and Quebec, was asked if she "always wore that ten-gallon hat." "Oh, yes," she replied quickly, "whenever I come East."
2. What is said to be the biggest roundup of all time was Roundup No. 15 in Eastern Wyoming in 1884, in which 400,000 cattle were gathered.

Bull Faces the Commission

1 Macleod, James Farquherson. Letter to his wife, Mary Isabella (Drever), October 12, 1877.
2. Turner, *The North-West Mounted Police, 1873-1893*, I, 363.
3. *Sessional Papers of Canada*, 1878, No. 4, Appendix E, 47.
4. *Sessional Papers of Canada*, 1878, No. 4, Appendix E, 48.
5. Macleod, James Farquherson. Letter to American Commissioner in *Sessional Papers of Canada*, 1878, No. 4, Appendix E, 49.
6. George Shepherd, "Wood Mountain Post," *Canadian Cattleman*, December, 1945, 123.

Caroline "Mother" Fulham

1. *Calgary Tribune*, April 9, 1890.
2. *Calgary Tribune*, December 2, 1891.
3. *Calgary Herald*, October 12, 1901.
4. *Calgary Herald*, September 12, 1904.

The Growing Grassland Empire

1. Sale Agreement, Burns' Papers, Glenbow-Alberta Archives.
2. Clifford, Raymond, opinion expressed in conversation, High River, Nov. 2, 1977.
3. *Calgary Herald*, Feb. 5, 1902.
4. Burns, Patrick, Burns' Papers, Nov. 1, 1927, Glenbow-Alberta Archives.
5. George Lane and Company, Ltd., Burns' Papers, Nov. 10, 1927, Glenbow-Alberta Archives.

The "Ugly Duckling"

1. Sir George Simpson, Evidence before the Select Committee of the House of Commons in London, "Looking into the Affairs of the Hudson's Bay Company," *Parliamentary Papers*, 1857, Feb. 26.
2. John Palliser, *Palliser Report*, presented to the Houses of Parliament, May 19, 1863.
3. Bishop Alexandre Taché, quoted by John Macoun in *Manitoba and the Great North-West* (Guelph: World Publishing Co., 1882), p. 454.

William Kennedy

1. William Kennedy, *A Short Narrative of the Second Voyage of the Prince Albert in Search of Sir John Franklin.* (London: W. H. Dalton, 1853), p. XXIII.

2. Sir John Franklin, *Narrative of a Journey to the Shores of the Polar Sea* (London: John Murray, 1823), p. 48.
3. *Manitoba Free Press,* February 10, 1890.
4. William Kennedy, *A Short Narrative of the Second Voyage . . .,* p. VI.
5. Joseph René Bellot, *Memoirs of Lieutenant Joseph René Bellot* (London: Hurst and Blackett, 1855), p. 184.
6. Ibid., p. 103.
7. William Kennedy, *A Short Narrative of the Second Voyage . . .,* p. 89.
8. Joseph René Bellot, *Memoirs,* Vol. II, p. 1.
9. *Manitoba Free Press,* January 27, 1890.
10. *Nor'-Wester,* February 28, 1860.
11. Ibid., June 14, 1860.

Index

Agriculture, the industry, 156-59
Ahenakew, Rev. Edward, 32
The Albertan (Calgary), 25

Badlands, The Red Deer River, 174
Barkerville, B.C., 65
Bedford, S. A., 10
Belgian horses. *See* Horses
Big Country, east central Alberta,
   173
Blackfoot Indians, 97
Books by MacEwan, 180
Bragg Creek, Alberta, 172
Brandon Agricultural Society, 6-11
Brandon Exhibition, 6-11
Brandon, Manitoba, ix, 3, 4, 49
British Columbia, gold, 63-67
Brown, John G. "Kootenai," 70
Burns, Pat, 150

Calgary, 69, 123-125
Canadian Broadcasting Company, x,
   xi
Canadian Historical Review, xi
Canadian Seed Growers' Assn., 79
Chater, Manitoba, 1, 4
Churchill, Port of, 119
Clark, F. J., 10
Clydesdale horses. *See* Horses
Cochrane, Archbishop, 69
Confederation and Rupert's Land, 73
Council of Assiniboia, 68, 71
Crowfoot, Chief, 95-104
Cypress Hills, 175

Dalgliesh, Robert, 117
Dauphin, Manitoba, 4

Davidson, W. M., 26
Dinosaur Provincial Park, 174
Dinsdale, Hon. Walter, 61

Edwards, Bob, 19-27
Ewen, A. H., ix
Eye Opener (Calgary), 20-27

Foran, Maxwell, ix, xvi
Fort Edmonton, 69
Fort Garry, 69
Fort McMurray, 178
Fulham, Caroline "Mother," 126
Fort Macleod, 15, 17

Gillese, John P., xii
Glazier, Kenneth, xii
Globe and Mail, xi
Gold Rush, 69
Grant, John, 6, 7

Halpen, Arthur, 25
Harrison, Stanley, 142
Henday, Anthony, 68
Hill's Bar, discovery strike, 63
Hill, Jim, 76
Horses, Belgian, 90; Clydesdale, 86;
   Shire, 87; Suffolk Punch, 88
Hudson's Bay Company Territory, 69
Hudson Bay Route, xvi, 115
Hudson's Bay Co., trading post, 44
Humesville Church, 9
Hurtig, Mel, xiv
Hurtig Publishers Ltd., xiv

Institute of Applied Art, xiv

Jasper National Park, 171

Kennedy, Capt. William, 162
Kennedy, Eleanor Cripps, 167
Klassen, Henry C., xii

Lacombe, Fr. Albert, 71
Lethbridge, 176

Macdonell, Miles, 44, 140
MacEwan, Grant vii-xvi, 53-57
Macleod Hotel, 15
Manitoba, ix
Maski-pitoon, Chief, 28-33
McCourt, Edward, xii
McDougall, Rev. John, 17, 29, 32, 71
McEwen, Jessie, xi
McLean, George, 81
McLean, John, 72
McLeod, Commissioner James, 105
Melfort, 133
Métis, 69
Mitchell, W. O., xii
Montreal *Star*, xi
Moosomin, horse racing, 49
Morton, Arthur S., x, xv, 46, 159

Nisbet, Rev. James, 69
Norris, T. C., 4
North West Company, 136
North West Passage, 162-170
Nova Scotia, ix

Old Bill, horse, 132
Overlanders, The, 64

Peace River, 179
Peguis Press, xiv
Percheron, horses, 87
Portage la Prairie, 7, 72
Prairie Perspective, 2, xii
Prince Albert, 69
Pyramid Lake, Jasper National Park, 171

Rasporich, Anthony W., xii
Rebellion of 1885, 101

Red Fife wheat, 76
"Republic of Caledonia," 68, 71
Resources for Tomorrow Conference, 61
Richards, William C., xiv
Riley, Senator Dan, 18
Ross, Sinclair, xii
Rundle, Rev. Robert, 70
Rupert's Land, 68

Saskatchewan River, 173
Selkirk, Lord, 135-141
Selkirk Settlement, x, 43, 135-141
Selkirk, steamboat, 76
Shelley, E. A., 22
Shire horses. *See* Horses
Sioux Indians, 98, 105-113
Sitting Bull, Chief, 105
Spence, Thomas, 71
Stanley, George F. G., xii
Steele Brothers, 77
Suffolk Punch. *See* Horses

Taylor, Harry "Kamoose," 15
Temperance and Moral Reform League, 24
Territorial Exhibition, Regina, 10
Thibault, Fr. Jean-Baptiste, 70
Thomas Nelson and Sons, x
Toronto *Star*, xi
Tractors, 91
Treaty Number Seven, 99
Trotter, Beecham, 7
Tupper, Sir Charles, 8

University of Manitoba, xvi
University of Saskatchewan, 53

Vimy Ridge, poem, 146

Walking Buffalo, Chief, 81
Walsh, Maj. James M., 105
Ward, Norman, xi
Ware, John, 34-42
Waterton Lakes National Park, 70
Webb, W. P., 12

Western Canadian Studies Conference, xii
Western Producer, The, xiv
Western Producer Prairie Books, xiv
Wheat, first western export of, 77
Whoop-Up, Fort, 70

William's Creek, 63, 64
Winnipeg, horse racing, 48
Winter in Alberta, 175

Young, David, 78

Grant MacEwan

Grant MacEwan's notable career has embraced many fields — academic, agricultural, public service, and political — but he is best known as one of western Canada's foremost historical writers. *The Best of Grant MacEwan* commemorates the occasion of his eightieth birthday in the year of the publication of his thirty-first book.

Born in Manitoba in 1902, Dr. MacEwan spent most of his early years on a farm near Melfort, Saskatchewan. He earned a B.S.A. from the Ontario College of Agriculture and did postgraduate work in Iowa. His career has included serving as the dean of agriculture at the University of Manitoba. Grant MacEwan has been named a Member of the Order of Canada and has served as the mayor of Calgary and the lieutenant governor of Alberta.

R. H. Macdonald

R. H. ("Rusty") Macdonald began a journalistic career of thirty-six years as a reporter for the *Regina Leader Post.* He joined the staff of *The Western Producer* as a feature writer in 1949; he later became executive editor, a position which he held until 1977.

R. H. Macdonald is uniquely suited for the task of editing the excerpts in this collection. He draws upon a long relationship with Grant MacEwan and is the author of MacEwan's biography, *No Ordinary Man.* Their association and collaboration continues to the present with the 1982 release of *The Best of Grant MacEwan* and *Alberta Landscapes,* text by Grant MacEwan and photographs by R. H. Macdonald.